8.50

Piers Plowman

AND SCRIPTURAL TRADITION

PRINCETON STUDIES IN ENGLISH

No. 31

𝔓iers 𝔓lowman

AND SCRIPTURAL
TRADITION

BY D. W. ROBERTSON, JR., AND
BERNARD F. HUPPÉ

1969
OCTAGON BOOKS
New York

For

M. L. H.

and

B. H. R.

Now have I therto this condicioun
That, of alle floures in the mede,
Thanne love I most these floures white and rede,
Swyche as men calle dayesyes in oure toun.

Preface

THE purpose of this book is to present a coherent account
of the thought structure of the B-text of *Piers Plowman* in
the light of medieval interpretations of Scripture. Although
no such systematic study of the poem as we offer has hith-
erto been made, our indebtedness to the work of those who
have studied the poem before us has been great. The gen-
eral conclusions reached by Chambers, Coghill, Dunning,
Gerould, and Wells, all of whom have demonstrated in
one way or another the essential unity of the B-text, have
furnished an indispensable steppingstone to our own inves-
tigations. However, in this book our point of departure and
our aim have been different from those of our predecessors,
so that we have neither summarized their results in general
nor indicated points of contact with them in detail. Our
work is in no sense a substitute for theirs; they remain
necessary aids to any student of the poem. The reader will
discover, for example, a few striking similarities between
our materials and those employed by Father Dunning, but
because of differences in both method and subject, our
general results are usually different. We felt in this instance
that nothing would be gained by any attempt to indicate
differences in interpretation or similarities which are the
result of coincidence, especially since Father Dunning's
book on the A-text is readily accessible. Economy rather
than ingratitude has directed our decision to refer only
when absolutely necessary to modern criticism of the poem.
This decision is made easier by the existence of M. W.
Bloomfield's survey of *Piers Plowman* scholarship in *Spec-
ulum* (1939).

The basic materials for our study are exegetical. Since no
definitive history of medieval exegesis has been written, we
were obliged to develop our own perspective with regard

ix

to the exegetical tradition as we wrote. Studies already in existence demonstrate the importance of this tradition, but the works of Glunz, Spicq, and Smalley show a considerable lack of agreement. And the situation has been confused further by the studies of De Bruyne and Curtius on medieval aesthetics. In this confusion of voices we determined at the outset to rely on a method of trial and error. Although this method led eventually to certain conclusions about Biblical exegesis and its significance, we feel that this study is not the place for them. Experience since this book was written has convinced us that we might well have relied more heavily on the work of St. Augustine. If we were to write Chapter I again, we should devote considerable attention to the *De doctrina Christiana*. This fact, however, in no way alters our conclusions. Although St. Augustine is undoubtedly the fountainhead of the medieval exegetical tradition, quotations or paraphrases from the later writers whose work we have used serve to show the continuity of the doctrinal tradition which is evident in *Piers Plowman*. No study of this kind would have been possible without the groundwork of such distinguished scholars as Dom Wilmart, Pierre Glorieux, and the authors of the indispensable *La renaissance du XIIᵉ siècle*.

Our book is the result of unusually close collaboration. The basic ideas and attitudes underlying our approach were worked out in a series of preliminary conversations. Both the research work and the writing were undertaken jointly, so that the conclusions expressed are always the product of actual discussions. In fact, many of the sentences in this book are partly the work of one author and partly that of the other. We are equally responsible, both for whatever may be valuable and whatever may be reprehensible in our study. The results presented here belong neither to one of us nor to the other; they arose from the interaction of two rather different approaches.

PREFACE

We are indebted to our colleagues for assistance of various kinds. Professor G. E. Bentley's enthusiasm for the promotion of humanistic research has not only given us constant moral encouragement, but has been influential in obtaining very substantial financial assistance for us from the Princeton University Research Committee. We cannot express too strongly our gratitude for the generosity of this committee. Professor John Weld not only furnished us very useful bibliographical information, but frequently allowed himself to be used as a judge of specific interpretations. Professor George R. Coffman, Father J. B. Dwyer, S.J., and Professor G. H. Gerould read the book in manuscript. We owe much to their friendly vigilance and patience, but whatever errors the book contains are our own.

May 25, 1950

D.W.R., JR.
B.F.H.

Contents

But nathelees, this meditacioun
I putte it ay under correccioun
Of clerkes, for I am nat textueel;
I take but the sentence, trusteth weel.
Therfore I make a protestacioun
That I wol stonde to correccioun.

1. The Method

In medieval schools students were taught to read books on three distinct levels. The procedure was definite and systematic. First, a work was considered in terms of its grammatical structure and syntax. When this preliminary was thoroughly mastered, the students were led to consider the obvious meaning of what they had read. If it were narrative, for example, the second step would be to learn the outline of the narrative. Finally, students were taught the higher meaning, the doctrinal content, or, as we might call it, the theme of what they had read. These three levels were called *littera, sensus,* and *sententia,* respectively. The first two levels were preliminaries to the third, for the importance of any work was thought to lie in its higher meaning, or as Chaucer would have said, in its *sentence.*[1] If medieval readers considered the works they read in this way, it is only natural that medieval writers should have deliberately composed their works with a definite *sentence* in mind. In other words, the medieval writer or reader would never have been content, as the modern naturalist professes to be, with a "slice of life." The underlying meaning, the theme, had to be always clear. It should be understood that this meaning was not a fortuitously applied "moral." On the contrary, it was frequently integrated skillfully with the matter of the work itself so that it formed the dominant unifying element. The relative importance of matter and *sentence* is indicated by Chaucer's Nun's Priest, who compares the matter of his tale to the chaff, its *sentence* to the fruit. As an allegory, *Piers Plowman* is directly concerned with a higher mean-

[1] See G. Paré, A. Brunet, and P. Tremblay, *La renaissance du xiie siècle: Les écoles et l'enseignement* (Paris and Ottawa, 1933), pp. 116-17. The four senses of Scriptural commentary were developments of the *sentence.*

1

ing in the medieval sense, and it is with this meaning that we shall be concerned in this study.

The existence of a large body of Scriptural quotations in the text of the poem furnishes a key to the ultimate source of its allegorical meaning. As we shall show, these quotations are not haphazard, decorative, or macaronic, but are connected intimately with the *sentence* of the poem. The truth of this observation is not clear until it is understood that the Bible did not exist alone in the Middle Ages. It was surrounded by a nexus of traditional interpretation which was the source of the homiletic and liturgical offices by means of which the ordinary Christian learned the Catholic doctrine. Biblical exegesis was at the same time the culmination of all scholastic exercises. Even theology was at first but an aid to a true understanding of the sacred text.[2] It is to this nexus of interpretation that the poet directs us when he tells the reader to consult the "glose." Like vernacular literature, Scripture was read on three levels[3] with the further elaboration that the highest level, or *sentence*, might be developed in three ways. The distinction between the level of the sense and that of the *sentence* was again sharply defined. As Spicq puts it:

Le sens littéral ou historique se distingue du sens spirituel ou allégorique comme l'humanité visible du Christ de sa divinité invisible, ou plus prosaïquement comme l'écorce de l'amande. . . . L'emploi des vocables est significatif de l'estime réciproque que l'on a pour l'un et l'autre sens. L'exégèse littérale est qualifiée de "carnaliter, secundum sensus corporeos, secundum superficiem, etc. . . . ," l'in-

---

[2] *Ibid.*, pp. 257-58. Cf. Beryl Smalley, *The Study of the Bible in the Middle Ages* (Cambridge, 1941), pp. xiv-xv. For a systematic survey of Biblical exegesis, see C. Spicq, *L'exégèse latine au moyen age* (Paris, 1944).

For the reader who wishes to follow the Biblical references in an English text, it should be noted that references are to the Vulgate throughout this study. Since neither Ecclesiasticus (Ecclus.) nor Sapientia (Sap.) appears in the King James Version and since the numbering of the Psalms differs in the two Bibles, the Douay Bible should be consulted for references to these three books.

[3] See Paré, *et al.*, *op. cit.*, p. 228; Spicq, *op. cit.*, pp. 99-100.

2

terprétation spirituelle est "secundum mysterium, secundum symbolum, spiritualiter, secundum intelligibilem sensum" ou "intelligence mystique, intérieure" et "spirituelle"; en un mot, les deux exégèses s'opposent, selon la dichotomie paulinienne, comme la lettre à l'esprit.[4]

Rind and core, chaff and fruit, the letter and the spirit in Paul, are expressions indicating the supreme importance of *sentence* in the study of the Bible. The three levels by means of which this *sentence* might be elaborated, although they varied somewhat among authorities, were tropological, allegorical, and anagogical. The tropological meaning was that which applied to the individual so that it was frequently moral in application. The allegorical sense was used originally to interpret the Old Testament in the light of the New, or to interpret it as it applies to the Church. The anagogical sense is concerned with the heavenly mysteries. These three levels may be regarded as the classical division.[5] The Scriptural quotations in *Piers Plowman* should be examined in the light of the exegetical tradition which developed on the basis of this technique. Moreover, we shall attempt to show that throughout the poem, even in passages unsupported by direct quotation from the Bible, the author had the *sentence* of Scripture constantly in mind. This *sentence* as it appears in traditional exegesis forms a completely objective test of the meaning of the allegory of the poem.

The examination of traditional ideas in medieval exegesis is made difficult by the fact that only a small percentage of the commentaries which exist in MS have been printed.[6] Moreover, very little is known of the commentaries of the fourteenth century.[7] It is true, however, that

---

[4] *Op. cit.*, p. 19.

[5] See Spicq's discussion and the references he gives, *op. cit.*, pp. 21-25.

[6] Some conception of this situation may be gained from an examination of the lists of MSS given by Spicq, pp. 318-30; 343-48.

[7] Cf. Miss Smalley's remarks, *op. cit.*, p. xiv. However, Spicq (*op. cit.*,

the traditions of exegesis were very strong, so that the essential meanings established by the Fathers were not greatly altered in the course of time. Although it is impossible under these circumstances to determine what commentaries the author of *Piers Plowman* used, it is not difficult to find his interpretations in printed commentaries which may be regarded as standard. The most obvious approach would have been to use a glossed Bible of the type found among *incunabula*, but the comments in such works are frequently too brief to be clear to anyone not versed in Biblical exegesis, sometimes being little more than references to more extended commentaries; moreover, such Bibles are less readily available than more recently printed commentaries. With these considerations in mind, we have relied heavily on the Fathers, particularly on Augustine, Gregory, Jerome, and Bede. We have used the conveniently extensive comments of Rabanus Maurus and of Bruno Astensis frequently. Commonplaces of tradition are readily available in the *Glossa ordinaria*, although these again are frequently mere references; and a wealth of material from various sources is available in Peter Lombard's comments on the Psalms and on the Pauline Epistles. We have made occasional reference to other homiletic and exegetical materials printed in the *Patrologia latina*, notably to the works of Hugh of St. Victor, St. Bernard, and Rupert. We have used commentaries by members of the fraternal orders sparingly, for reasons which shall appear.[8] For theological materials we have depended chiefly on the *Sententiae* of Peter Lombard and on the quodlibets of Godefroid de Fontaines. Here again we have tried to

---

p. 331) affirms that the commentaries of the fourteenth century do not differ essentially from those of the thirteenth century.

[8] The magnificent Quaracchi edition of St. Bonaventura, however, with its full indices and careful notes, has helped us over many a difficult passage. The selection of commentators was largely empirical, but information concerning their importance may be found in Spicq, *op. cit., passim.*

4

confine ourselves to the secular as opposed to the fraternal tradition.

The medieval student of theology was thoroughly trained in the interpretation of Scripture so that he would command several traditional interpretations of any important Scriptural passage. In his study, he would not confine himself to any single commentator, but would deliberately familiarize himself with the tradition of patristic comment and with such subsequent comments as he had available or considered important. Indeed any commentary he might have consulted, from the summarizing *Glossa ordinaria* to the fullest commentary, such as Bonaventura on Luke, would have enforced the necessity for richness and flexibility of selection. Almost any page of a typical commentary like Peter Lombard on the Psalms, where differing authoritative interpretations are set down side by side as permissible variants, would have made clear the existence and importance of alternative interpretations. Moreover, the poet might have had available not only concordances to the Vulgate, but what amount to alphabetical concordances of key words from Scripture arranged either according to the senses of Scripture or according to variants in patristic interpretations. The variations are accompanied by citations or quotations from the Biblical text. In general, these *répertoires exégétiques,* as Spicq calls them, served as a guide to the Biblical *sentence* of important objects or conceptions. For example, in the twelfth century *Allegoriae in sacram scripturam* the word *dormitio* is given seven meanings: the quietness of contemplation, spiritual torpor, death, sickness, blindness, falling into sin, sexual embrace.[9] Clearly, the number of possible meanings for the concept sleep is large and various.

[9] *PL,* 112, 913. The work is erroneously attributed there to Rabanus Maurus. See Spicq, *op. cit.,* p. 63. There is an extensive discussion of the *répertoires* in Chapter 3.

A poet using one of them in an allegory would make his selection clear either through the context of his own work or by the citation or suggestion of a determining text in Scripture. In *Piers Plowman*, for instance, the notion of sleep is used in the sense of spiritual torpor at the beginning of Passus I, and in the sense of the quietness of contemplation at the beginning of Passus XVI. These meanings are obvious in relation to the context of the poem. In composing his allegory, therefore, the poet was forced to select from a variety of possibilities. In many instances, he may not have remembered the exact source of a given interpretation. In our explanations we are not dealing with sources. We are simply attempting to discover which among several possible traditional interpretations the author had in mind. If a given series of our explanatory notes represents a variety of sources, we do not imply that these were the poet's sources, but simply that they represent the traditions which illuminate the text. In most instances, it would have been possible to show further authoritative substantiation for the interpretations adduced, but in view of the traditional character of interpretations in standard commentaries, we considered this sort of added machinery to be superfluous except for a few instances at the beginning of our comment where we thought it necessary to demonstrate the uniformity and persistence of certain traditions.

The selection of explanatory materials has been in part determined by the character of the poem itself and by its position in a definite theological and ecclesiastical tradition. As we shall demonstrate, Piers Plowman represents in part what Konrad Burdach described as the "Urbild und Vorbild des Apostels Petrus und seiner päpstlichen Nachfolger."[10] We should say, however, that he represents

---

[10] *Vom Mittelalter zur Reformation*, III, 2 (Berlin, 1926-1932), p. 189. Cf. pp. 294-314. We consider the remainder of Burdach's definition, only part of which is quoted here, to be misleading.

God's ministry on earth in the *status praelatorum;* that is, the patriarchs, the prophets, Christ, the disciples, and the subsequent representatives of the apostolic tradition, who are, in the secular tradition, the popes, the bishops, and the parish priests. Piers is the ideal, actualized in Christ, of what the men in this status should be. An important theme in the poem involves the fact that the function of those in the *status praelatorum* has been usurped by certain members of the *status religiosorum* with the result that God's hierarchy has been upset, to the detriment of the Church as a whole. Specifically, the function of Piers has been usurped by the friars, who maintained what the poet thought of as invalid pretenses to the apostolic succession. The criticism of the friars in *Piers Plowman* is not, however, simply a matter of conventional abuse based on observation; it is rather a clear and definite continuation of the struggle between the seculars and the friars having as its focal point a debate on the states of perfection. This debate reached a climax in the thirteenth century when William of Saint-Amour made a spectacular attack on the position of the fraternal orders. It is significant that the central point in William's argument corresponds exactly with the position taken by the author of the poem:

Il établit que ceux-là seuls ont la droit de prêcher qui en ont reçu la mission; il oppose à la hiérarchie traditionnelle, sans les nommer, les Ordres nouveaux qui n'ont point charge d'âme et veut établir que le Souverain Pontife lui-même n'a pas entendu leur donner dans l'Eglise une mission générale qui serait au détriment de celle confiée déjà aux évêques et aux prêtres séculiers.[11]

[11] Maurice Perrod, *Étude sur la vie et sur les œuvres de Guillaume de Saint-Amour* (Lons-le-Saunier, 1902), p. 157. Cf. p. 159. On the beginnings of the subsequent quarrel over perfection, see P. Glorieux, " 'Contra Geraldinos.' L'enchainement des polémiques," *Rech. Théol. anc. med.,* VII (1935), 129-55; K. Schleyer, "Disputes scolastiques sur les états de perfection," *ibid.,* X (1938), 279-93. The opening remarks of Schleyer's discussion, p. 279, are instructive: "Parmi les grands problèmes agités par les penseurs scolastiques, de la moité du XIIIᵉ au début du XIVᵉ siècle, se range la question du *status perfectionis.* Les partis en présence étaient d'un côté

Apart from the thesis that the friars have unjustly usurped the apostolic tradition, there are striking parallels in detail between William's argument and the poem. In the Prologue the friars stand accused of false preaching, of false "clothing" or outward status, of abusing confession. The poet warns that unless the friars are brought in line with Holy Church, the greatest mischief will ensue (ll. 58-67). In Passus III, a friar calls on Lady Meed and indicates that he is more interested in the temporal reward she offers than in any attempts to reform her. Indeed, he professes himself willing to serve her evil purposes in corrupting knights and clerks (ll. 35-63). In Passus VIII, two Minorites meet Will and indicate their fraternal pride in announcing that Dowel has always and will always live with them. They illustrate, moreover, the easy repentance which the friars offered (ll. 8-56). In Passus XIII, a Dominican, proud to be a "master," takes a place at the head of the table and demonstrates himself to be an arrant hypocrite.[12] He is attacked in the poem on the basis of a text which William of Saint-Amour used to great advantage in his own attack on the friars, *periculum est in falsis fratribus* (ll. 33-97). Finally in Passus XX, the friars are shown to be followers of Antichrist, as William of Saint-Amour implied, and their entry into Holy Church is shown historically from a secular point of view. In illustrating the result of their seizure of control, the poet goes even further than William of Saint-Amour by having Conscience turn aside from the church in pursuit of Piers. These detailed

---

les maîtres séculiers, de l'autre les ordes mendiants. Tous deux prétendaient posséder dans leur état la plus haute perfection, c'est-à-dire le rang le plus élevé dans l'ordonnance hiérarchique de l'Eglise. Il est évident qu'il ne s'agissait pas ici d'une revendication purement théorique. L'opposition entre le clergé séculier et les ordres mendiants s'étendait bien au delà des universités."

[12] On the title "master" and the desire of the friars to dominate, see the letter of the University of Paris in Denifle and Chatelain, *Chartularium*, I, 252-58.

accusations may be found in William of Saint-Amour's writings. The poet's added conclusion would have been out of place in the *De periculis*, since it warned of dangers not yet fully realized. The poet described what he considered to be the results of a failure to heed that warning.[13]
· Historically, William's doctrines were condemned in a council held before the Pope. Assembled to refute him was an imposing task force of authorities, including Humbert de Romans, Albertus Magnus, St. Thomas Aquinas, and St. Bonaventura. William was not allowed to defend his position, perhaps because of the fame of his eloquence. In spite of the condemnation and the cleverness of the opposition, he did not recant. Indeed, his position was maintained in direct succession by Gérard d'Abbeville and by Godefroid de Fontaines and by Jean de Pouilli at Paris.[14] In England, the central traditions of secular theology were defended vigorously against the friars throughout the thirteenth and fourteenth centuries:

The quarrel in Oxford was in truth but a symptom of the great feud between the friars and the seculars which divided the whole church of England—indeed the whole church of Europe—throughout the fourteenth century. In England as in France the universities were but the organs of the secular clergy at large. . . . Occasional bickerings between the secular masters and the friars continued, however, to be among the normal incidents of university life.[15]

Among the most prominent of the secular apologists was

[13] The details of William of Saint-Amour's attack may be found conveniently described in the works of Perrod, Glorieux, and Schleyer mentioned in the notes above, and in the excerpts from the *De periculis* in Bierbaum, *Bettelorden und Weltgeistlichkeit*, Franziskanische Studien, Beiheft II (Munchen, 1920). Specific references to the more striking correspondences are given in our notes.
[14] The quarrel continued at Paris well into the fifteenth century. See F. M. Powicke and A. B. Emden, eds., *Rashdall's Medieval Universities* (Oxford, 1936), I, 396-97. See "Jean de Pouilli," *Dictionnaire de théologie catholique*.
[15] *Ibid.*, II, 74, 76.

9

Archbishop Richard Fitz-Ralph, who died defending his cause at Avignon in 1360.[16] A typical and easily accessible fourteenth century attack on the friars is the *Contra querelas fratrum* of Uhtred de Boldon.[17] It is not to be expected that William's successors who, it must be emphasized, represented the central traditions of scholastic theology,[18] should have regarded the men who condemned William and their doctrines with the veneration accorded them by certain moderns. In vernacular literature, the importance of the secular tradition is well attested in the popularity of such works as the *Roman de la Rose*, where Jean de Meun not only openly defends William but attacks the friars violently in the character of False-Semblaunt. The accounts of the friars in the *Roman de la Rose* and in *Piers Plowman* have much in common. For these reasons we have avoided commentaries by friars, except when they repeat exegetical commonplaces without controversial purpose. These considerations also explain why we have not made frequent allusion to the theological works of St. Bonaventura, of Occam, of Scotus, of Albertus Magnus, and, most important, of St. Thomas Aquinas.

The anti-fraternal attitude in the poem does not limit the scope of *Piers Plowman* any more than the Dominican

[16] *Ibid.*, II, 75. Cf. Aubrey Gwynn, S. J., *The English Austin Friars in the Time of Wyclif* (Oxford, 1940), pp. 79-89. He says concerning the B-text of *Piers Plowman* that the complaints against the friars are "in the familiar tradition of Guillaume de Saint-Amour, Jean de Pouilli, and Richard Fitz-Ralph."

[17] Ed. Mildred Marcett, *Uhtred de Boldon, Friar William Jordan, and "Piers Plowman"* (New York, 1938), pp. 25-37.

[18] Pierre Glorieux, "Pour une édition de Gérard d'Abbeville," *Rech. Théol. anc. med.*, IX (1937), p. 56, has this to say of William's immediate successor: "Gérard d'Abbeville est, plus et mieux que tous les autres, le type du théologien du maître séculier du XIIIe siècle. Il encarne en quelque sorte 'l'Ecole'; non point l'école thomiste à laquelle ce nom passera par la suite; mais la scolastique officielle, l'enseignement traditionnel qui trouvera en lue son expression le plus exacte." As a result of the special interests of most modern scholars, almost no attention has been paid to the traditions of the "scolastique officielle" after the lifetime of St. Thomas.

attitude of St. Thomas, for example, limits the scope of the *Summa theologica*. The attitude is an important attribute of the tradition in which *Piers* was written; it is by no means the whole of the poem. In the poem are expressed most of the guiding ideas of the central tradition of medieval Christianity since the poet's object is not only to show the evils of the church but to place these evils against a background of positive ideals and aspirations. Although these ideals will appear in the course of our discussion, that discussion will be easier to comprehend if the reader has in mind the conventional frame of reference against which they were placed.

The most fundamental doctrine of medieval Christianity is that the end of all Biblical study is the promotion of *caritas*, the love of God and of one's neighbor. As perfect charity is the end of Christian behavior, so it was felt to be the ultimate *sentence* of the Bible. St. Augustine explains this principle clearly in the *De doctrina*:

Omnium igitur quae dicta sunt, ex quo de rebus tractamus, haec summa est, ut intelligatur Legis et omnium divinarum Scripturarum plenitudo et finis esse dilectio rei qua fruendum est, et rei quae nobiscum ea re frui potest. . . . Quisquis igitur Scripturas divinas vel quamlibet earum partem intellexisse sibi videtur, ita ut eo intellectu non aedificet istam geminam charitatem Dei et proximi, nondum intellexit. Quisquis vero talem inde sententiam duxerit, ut huic aedificandae charitati sit utilis, nec tamen hoc dixerit quod ille quem legit eo loco sensisse probabitur, non perniciose fallitur, nec omnino mentitur.[19]

What was not in accord with charity was automatically erroneous. Charity is thus an informing principle of medieval thought, providing the inspiration for and controlling the bent of all written attempts to set forth truth. For truth is charity, and like charity must be approached

---

[19] I, xxxv, xxxvi; *PL*, 34, 34. See also Peter Lombard, *Sententiae*, II, xxxviii, PL, 192, 743: "Omnia praecepta divina referuntur ad charitatem." Cf. Paré, etc., *op. cit.*, 214-15.

through faith and hope, as St. Paul reveals. Clearly the opposite of charity is *cupiditas*, the love of one's self or the world. There are thus two loves, each representing a direction in which the human will may turn. As Rabanus Maurus points out, the Holy Scripture inculcates charity and condemns cupidity:

Non enim praecipit Scriptura nisi charitatem, nec culpat nisi cupiditatem; et eo modo informat mores hominum. Charitatem voco motum animi ad fruendum Deo propter ipsum, et se atque proximo propter Deum, Cupiditatem autem motum animi ad fruendum se et proximo, et quolibet corpore non propter Deum.[20]

Passages in the Bible which do not literally promote charity must be interpreted figuratively:

Ergo in locutionibus figuratis regula sit hujusmodi, ut tam diu versetur diligenti consideratione quod legitur, donec ad regnum charitatis interpretatio perducatur. Si autem hoc jam proprie sonat, nulla putetur figurata locutio. Si praeceptiva locutio est, aut flagitium, aut facinas vetans, aut utilitatem aut beneficientiam jubens, non est figurata. Si autem flagitium aut facinus videtur jubere, aut utilitatem et beneficentiam vetare, figurata est.[21]

Since charity is the New Law which Christ brought to mankind, the commentators felt that this Law should be revealed in both the Old Testament and the New. Charity is the end of the human will; it is the basis of perfection in any status. Symbolically, from the Father and the Son springs the Holy Spirit, or charity, so that man, the image of God, is thereby inspired to charity.[22] Thus the Christian has faith and hope that he may achieve charity. Conscience and intellect direct the will to strive for charity.[23] But the

[20] *De cler. inst.* III, xiii, *PL*, 107, 389. These words are quoted from St. Augustine, *De doctrina Christiana*, by Rabanus.

[21] *Ibid.*, c. 390.

[22] Cf. Peter Lombard, *Sententiae*, I, x, *PL*, 192, 549: "Spiritus sanctus amor est, sive charitas, sive dilectio Patris et Filii. Unde Aug., in lib. 15 de Trin., c. 17, ait: Spiritus sanctus nec Patris est solius, nec Filii est solius, sed amborum; et ideo communem qua invicem se diligunt Pater et Filius, nobis insinuat charitatem."

[23] Cf. *ibid.*, III, xxv, *PL*, 192, 811: "Cor accipit pro intellectu, et con-

will, directed by conscience and intellect, cannot turn toward charity unaided; an act of divine Grace is necessary.[24] Furthermore, the will must be directed within the Church which Christ established, where perfection may be sought in three states: *conjugatorum,* or active, *viduarum* or contemplative, *virginum sive martyrorum* or prelatical. Perfection may be reached through charity in any one of these.[25]

Obversely, cupidity is the end of human failing, descending from the love of the world and a love of the flesh to a union with the Devil in his struggle against charity, that is the sin against the Holy Spirit.[26] Against the love of God stands the love of one's self, Augustine's *amor sui.* In the ignorance of conscience and the weakness of intellect, the misguided will turns inward on its own desires so that it is filled with cupidity. Thus there are two ends to human life: charity and cupidity. These two ends are most

---

scientiam pro spe. Qualis, inquit, charitas est finis praecepti procedens de corde puro, id est de puro intellectu, ut nihil nisi Deus diligatur; et conscientia, id est, de spe bona et fide non ficta, id est non simulata. Non ergo charitas fidem et spem, sed fides et spes charitatem praecedere videntur." The authority is Augustine.

[24] *Ibid.,* II, XXXIX, *PL,* 192, 746: "Dici enim quod homo subjectus peccato facit quod non vult, quia naturaliter vult bonum. Sed voluntas haec semper caret effectu, nisi gratia Dei adjuvet et liberet."

[25] See Hugh of St. Victor, *Miscellanea,* VI, XXV, *PL,* 177, 825: "Triplex est descriptio: Alii ad conjugium, alii ad continentiam, alii describuntur ad virginitatem. In his tribus est tota descriptio Christi: qui non est in aliqua istarum non est Christi, sed potius ad censum diaboli pertinet." On the possibility of perfection within any status see Godefroid de Fontaines (Louvain, 1932), 140-41.

[26] See Peter Lombard, *Sententiae,* II, XLIII, *PL,* 192, 756: "Si quis vero sancti Spiritus dignitatem, majestatem et potestatem abneget sempiternam, et putet non in Spiritu Dei ejici daemonia, sed in Beelzebub, non potest ibi esse exhortatio veniae, ubi sacrilegii plenitudo est. . . . Peccatum enim in Patrem id intelligitur, quod fit per infirmitatem, quia Patri Scriptura frequenter attribuit potentiam; peccatum in Filium, quod fit per ignorantiam, quia sapientia Filio attribuitur; tertium expositum est. Qui ergo peccat per infirmitatem vel per ignorantiam, facile veniam adipiscitur, sed non ille qui peccat in Spiritum sanctum. Cum autem una sit potentia, sapientia, bonitas trium, quare Patri potentia, Filio sapientia, Spiritui sancto bonitas saepius assignetur, superius dictum est."

13

generally symbolized in the figure of the two cities, Jerusalem and Babylon, which grow out of charity and cupidity respectively.[27] Human living is ideally a pilgrimage from Babylon to Jerusalem. The two cities stand as ends of human living, and specifically each has its levels of significance. Rabanus Maurus describes the four conventional meanings of Jerusalem as follows: historically, the city itself; allegorically, the church of Christ; anagogically, the Heavenly City; tropologically, the soul of man praising God.[28] Babylon too is historically a city. In the *Allegoriae in sacram scripturam* its meaning on the three levels of the *sentence* appear: allegorically, the church of the Gentiles; anagogically, Hell; tropologically, the corrupted spirit.[29] The idea of human life as a pilgrimage is beautifully illustrated in one of Gregory's homilies on Ezechiel, where he discusses the meaning of the Prophet's admonition to his people that they leave Babylon. The Prophet must be understood for his *sentence*, declares Gregory. Whoever falls from right doing to wrong doing comes to the confusion of Babylon from the peace of Jerusalem:

Quod vero ad transmigrationem populi admonendam propheta mittitur, non solum ea transmigratio debet intelligi quae ejus populi erat in corpore, sed etiam quae facta fuerat in mente. A Jerusalem quippe ad Babyloniam venerat. Et quid Jerusalem nisi visio pacis, quid Babylonia nisi confusio vocatur? Quisquis vero a rectis operibus in perversis actibus cadit, quoniam a bono studio ad vitia defluit, quasi ab Jerusalem ad Babyloniae civitatem venit. Culmen enim bonae contemplationis deseruit, atque in transmigratione confusionis jacet. Quod illis solet saepe evenire qui cum bona agunt, in his de sua virtute gloriantur.[30]

[27] St. Augustine, *Civitas Dei*, XIV, XXIX.
[28] *In Gal.*, PL, 112, 331.
[29] PL, 112, 872. Of course other meanings of Babylon are given here, but they are simply variations of the above: civitas reproborum, peccatum, impii, caro nostra, hic mundus.
[30] PL, 76, 894. The two cities have their most famous exposition in Augustine's *Civitas Dei*.

Central in this symbolic edifice is the will of man turned toward Jerusalem or toward Babylon, but the will alone cannot turn toward Jerusalem without Christ's Redemption. The lesson of the Redemption is imparted to the will through the succession which Christ founded to lead His bride, the church. The human will must be directed in its pilgrimage by Peter, in our poem the plowman who sows in the human heart the seed of Scripture, the word of God. The church is in itself insufficient to the guidance of the true wayfaring Christian. It must be a church informed and guided by the successors of Peter in the *status praelatorum*. As the church is the bride of Christ, it must also be the bride of Piers Plowman. If it is not, the will can never find the straight road to Jerusalem.

In dealing with these ideas and such others as appear in the poem, our method has always been inductive. Our first approach to a section of the poem was always to consult a variety of interpretations of the passages from the Vulgate quoted in the poem. Here a difficulty presented itself. The Biblical quotations were often as important for the parallel passages within the Scriptures that they were intended to invoke as they were for themselves. In locating any citation we were forced to take into account not only the passage in question but related passages as well.[31] Sometimes there was no problem in limiting the meaning of a citation and its nexus of parallels, since a general agreement existed

[31] The remarks of Spicq concerning the technique of Scriptural commentary with regard to the citation of parallels are pertinent, *op. cit.*, p. 223: "Les médiévaux ont appris à lire dans la Bible. Celle-ci, conformement à son étymologie grecque, est réelement le livre par excellence, à peu pres le seul dont on dispose aisément; ils en ont une connaissance familière, vivante et religieuse. Ils en savent par cœur de longs et nombreux passages, et leur vocabulaire comme leur style et leurs images sont comme naturellement empruntés à ceux des Livres saints qui se sont en quelque sorte incorporés à la substance de leur esprit. C'est dire que les exégètes sont comme des concordances vivantes; une maxime biblique éveillera donc automatiquement le souvenir de toutes les autres sentences exprimant les mêmes idées ou contenant les mêmes mots."

15

as to a unique interpretation. More frequently, however, we were obliged to select from among alternative interpretations the one most closely related to the passage in question and through which the passage might best be understood. In this process of selection and interpretation the fact of our collaboration was especially useful, since it permitted an extensive consideration of alternative possibilities in the course of debate, resolved—sometimes only after several days—when the evidence made one alternative indisputable. Many parts of the poem containing no Biblical citations were readily interpretable with reference to the context of the poem itself. When a portion of the poem contained no Biblical text and could not be understood entirely from its context, we attempted to ascertain its Biblical milieu through the use of a concordance or of a *répertoire exégétique* such as the *Allegoriae in sacram scripturam*. Most passages of this kind revealed a Biblical inspiration, often to the point of verbal similarity. Having limited the Biblical reference, we proceeded as before to consider the commentaries. We have made no extensive use of homiletic literature, although it might have been pertinent, on the grounds that like *Piers Plowman* itself, homilies are derivatives from the exegetical tradition.[32] Our study is not exhaustive. It is merely a beginning which indicates a direction for fruitful study of the poem.

[32] Cf. Spicq, *op. cit.*, Chapter X, on the secondary character of homiletic interpretation.

2. Holy Church

THE PROLOGUE

IN *Piers Plowman* the basic contrast between Jerusalem and Babylon is suggested at once by the dreamer's opening vision of the Tower of Truth, the Dungeon of Hell, and, in between, the Field of Folk. It is significant that the Folk are not assembled in an orderly pilgrimage toward the Tower: they are occupied with the world,

> Worchyng and wandryng   as the worlde asketh. (19)

This situation represents the underlying problem in the poem. The folk of the world are preoccupied with worldly affairs, "wandryng" in confusion. But not all of them seem hopeless. The dreamer's attention is at once called to the hard working plowmen:

> Some putten hem to the plow   pleyed ful selde,
> In settyng and in sowyng   swonken ful harde,
> And wonnen that wastours   with glotonye destruyeth.
> (20-22)

Unfortunately, the plowmen are accompanied by false plowmen, by persons who dress as plowmen through pride:

> And some putten hem to pruyde   apparailed hem there-
> after
> In contenaunce of clothyng   comen disgised. (23-24)

That the plowmen are not intended to represent simple peasants is suggested not only by the position of preeminence accorded them but also by the fact that they have proud imitators. Conventional Scriptural exposition gives the plowman a unique symbolic significance. In Luke 9.62,

17

Christ warns that no one who puts his hand to the plow should look back: *Ait ad illum Jesus: Nemo mittens manum suam ad aratrum et respiciens retro aptus est regno Dei.* In a comment on this passage attributed to St. Jerome, plowing is made synonymous with preaching:

Manum super aratrum, id est, opus super Evangelium; *retro*, id est, in mundo; vomeres, id est, charitas; quatuor boves, id est, quatuor evangelistae.[1]

Bede on Luke 17.7 explains the servant plowing and nourishing as a doctor of the Church, "ecclesiae doctor."[2] The symbol of plowing for the exercise of the prelatical life was sufficiently commonplace to appear in the *De universo* of Rabanus Maurus:

Aratrum enim mystice significat opus praedicationis evangelicae, in quo cultus agri Dominici exercetur, ita ut vomere verbi divini exstirpentur vitia simul, et eradicentur noxia desideria, sicque praeparetur terra cordium humanorum ad accipienda semina virtutum.[3]

It reappears in a comment on Ecclus. 38.26 in the standard handbook of exegesis for the later Middle Ages, the *Glossa ordinaria*:

Qui tenet aratrum. Praedicatores sanctos significat, qui omni tempore docendo, exhortando, auditores suos instruunt ut interioris

---

[1] *PL*, 30, 591. The *quatuor boves* appear later in *Piers Plowman*, XIX, 256ff. Both Dominican and Franciscan commentators agree in this interpretation. Albertus adds to the notion of preaching that of spiritual perfection, *Opera Omnia* (Paris, 1890-1899), XXII, 699-700: "Attende quod Dominus per metaphoram arantis viam docet perfectionis. Iste enim et temporalium voluit habere solatium, et tamen sequi Dominum in via perfectionis, et verbi Dei praedicationis: putans eamdem viam perfectis et imperfectis esse propositam." A similar explanation is given by St. Bonaventura, *Opera* (Quaracchi, 1892-1902), VII, 251: "*Nemo mittens manum suam ad aratrum* etc., id est ad divinae perfectionis et praedicationis exercitium, quod recte per *aratrum* designatur propter culturam et fructum."

[2] *PL*, 92, 540. Bede illustrates the method of parallel passages by quoting Luke 9.62 on plowing and John 21.17 on nourishing.

[3] *PL*, 111, 610-11. The *semina virtutum* appear later in *Piers Plowman*, XIX, 269. See Alcuin's symbolic characterization of Gregory the Great as a "ploughman" in his *De sanctis Eboracensis Ecclesiae*, ed. Wattenbach and Duemmler (Berlin, 1873), p. 84.

hominis virtutem eliciant, et animan humanam ad imaginem Dei reformen.[4]

The image appears in Peter Lombard's comment on 1 Cor. 9.10:

Quoniam qui arat, id est praedicator qui corda aperit ad fidem, *debet arare* in *spe* stipendiorum temporalium, non propter hanc spem.[5] If we assume that the plowmen of the poem are the true followers of the prelatical life, then the food that they produce must be the spiritual food of the church,[6] and the "glotonye" with which it is wasted is symbolic of the misuse of this food resulting from too much concern for what "the worlde asketh." The false plowmen are those who assume the vesture of the prelatical life through pride, the chief of the vices. Allegorically, the dreamer sees the folk of the world in a confusion of temporal concern; they waste the spiritual food of the plowmen, and their plight is made more critical by the fact that there are false plowmen who can do nothing but mislead them.

Following the plowmen, the dreamer sees folk who lead a life of contemplation:

> In prayers and in penance   putten hem manye,
> Al for loue of owre lorde   lyueden ful streyte,
> In hope forto haue   heuenriche blisse;
> As ancres and heremites   that holden hem in here selles,
> And coueiten nought in contre   to kairen aboute,
> For no likerous liflode   her lykam to plese. (25-30)

Since these folk are not curators, but live "for loue of owre

---

[4] *PL*, 113, 1221. Cf. *ibid.*, on Luke 17.7, *PL*, 114, 318, quoted below, Chapter 4, note 2.

[5] *PL*, 191, 1609. The persistence of the image as a Biblical cliché is illustrated by the following remark from Walton's *Life of Donne* called to our attention by Mr. J. Arnold, "And sure, if he had consulted with flesh and blood, he had not for these reasons put his hand to that holy plough the ministry."

[6] The image of spiritual food is commonplace. See the elaboration of it in John 6. It may also be found conveniently in discussions of the miracle of the loaves. The comment attributed to St. Jerome on Luke 9.13, *loc. cit.*, explains "*Vos date illis manducare* (v. 13), id est, praedicate gentibus."

lorde," they are not directly responsible for the welfare of the people as a whole. They are followed by folk directly concerned with worldly affairs, the merchants:

| And somme chosen chaffare | they cheuen the bettere |
| As it semeth to owre syȝt | that suche men thryueth. |

$$(31\text{-}32)$$

Such people profit better "to owre syȝt," that is temporally. The sequence plowmen-anchorites-merchants is not fortuitous; its rests on a traditional classification of the types of men in the church: (1) those who follow the prelatical life, (2) those who follow the contemplative life, and (3) those who follow the active life. A statement of this convention which is not only typical but which also bears directly on the image of the Folk in the Field may be found in Quodlibet v of Godefroid de Fontaines:

Tres sunt status in ecclesia sub quibus omnes alii continentur, scilicet: status saecularium laicorum, et status clericorum et religiosorum, et status praelatorum. Hoc patet per illud quod dicitur Matthaei, vigesimo quarto: erunt duo in agro, duae molentes in mola, duo in lecto. Glossa: duo in agro sunt duae differentiae praedicatorum in ecclesia quasi in agro laborantium; duo in lecto sunt duae differentiae continentium sive contemplativorum qui eligunt quietem, quae lecti nomine significatur, nec in saecularibus sunt nec in ecclesiasticis negotiis occupati; duae in mola, duae differentiae coniugatorum sive sequentium orbem rerum mobilium. Non sunt autem alia genera hominum in ecclesia quam ista tria.[7]

At the opening of the poem, the dreamer sees the folk of the church in terms of their three conventional states: prelatical, contemplative, and active. He finds them in a kind

---

[7] Q. xvi (Louvain, 1914), 72. See Rabanus Maurus, *De Universo*, PL, 111, 79: "Duo in lecto, illi significantur qui remoti a turbis in otio quodam vitae vacare videntur. Duae molentes in mola, qui negotiis temporalium rerum circumferuntur. Duo in agro, qui in ministerio Ecclesiae tanquam in agro Dominico operantur: ex quibus, adveniente saeculi adversitate, id est nocte, quidam permanent in fide, et assumuntur ad vitam, quidam decedunt, et relinquuntur ad poenam." The last part of the quotation is particularly applicable to Piers and the mocking priest in the Pardon Episode, below, p. 94.

of Babylonian confusion, wasting the spiritual food of the plowmen; and he notices particularly that among those who should be directing the rest toward the Tower of Truth, there are sinful pretenders.

At the time *Piers Plowman* was written, as we have seen, the three states, and especially the character of the highest state, had become a central issue in the controversy over perfection between the regulars and seculars precipitated in the thirteenth century by William of St.-Amour.[8] It was agreed that whereas there are no limits to the degree of perfection attainable in any given state, the contemplative life requires a greater degree of perfection than the active life; and the seculars maintained that the life of the bishop requires a still greater degree of perfection, if not earthly perfection itself. Moreover, the followers of William of St.-Amour held that the status of the parish priest is higher than that of the regular.[9] The Friars maintained their own claim to the apostolic tradition, and delighted in pointing out the imperfections of the priests and bishops. The nature and function of the prelatical life and of the apostolic tradition had become topics of fundamental interest in the fourteenth century. Moreover, in view of the corruption of all orders of the clergy, the author of *Piers Plowman* may well have felt misgivings about the personal imperfections of all those claiming the highest status, and about the effects of these shortcomings on society. In his poem, he is concerned with the causes of decay, but he also reasserts the basic ideals of the three states, emphasizing especially the crucial importance of the highest state.

[8] See Chapter 1 above.
[9] See Wm. of St. Amour, *Tractatus de periculis*, ed. Bierbaum *Bettelorden und Weltgeistlichkeit*, "Franziskanische Studien," Beiheft 11 (Münster, 1920), 9: "Ab ecclesia recte eliguntur episcopi, qui apostolis successerunt; et parochialis presbyteri, qui discipulis 72 successerunt, et eorum loca tenent, dist. 21. can. *In novo testamento*. Unde Luc. 10 in principio dicit glossa Sicut in 12 apostolis forma est episcoporum, sic in 72 discipulis forma est presbyterorum. Nec plures sunt in ecclesia gradus ad regendum constituti." Cf. the long discussion by Godefroid, *op. cit.*, 73-76.

When he has indicated the three divisions of the folk with respect to status, the poet suggests that there is frequently a disparity between status and personal perfection.[10] There are those who use the goods of the world properly for the worship of God,[11] who praise the Lord without desire for temporal reward:

> And somme murthes to make   as mynstralles conneth,
> And geten gold with here glee   synneles, I leue.[12]

But there are those in all three states, who make a mere pretense of worship; actually, they are primarily interested in earthly reward. They allow their wills to rule their wits,[13] so that they depart altogether from the way of Truth:

> Ac iapers and ianglers   Iudas chylderen,
> Feynen hem fantasies   and foles hem maketh,
> And han here witte at wille   to worche ʒif their sholde.
> That Poule precheth of hem   I nel nought preue it here;
> *Qui turpiloquium loquitur*   is Luciferes hyne. (35-39)

[10] The existence of such a disparity had been recognized. Thus Aegidius Romanus, *De ecclesiastica potestate*, ed. R. Scholz (Weimar, 1929), 7, wrote: "Dicamus, quod duplex est perfeccio, duplex sanitas sive duplex spiritualitas: una est personalis, alia secundum statum, ut status clericorum est perfeccior statu laicorum et praelatorum quam subditorum. Sed si loquamur de perfeccione personali, multi sunt laici qui sunt sancciores et spiritualiores quam multi clerici." The author of *Piers Plowman* was interested not so much in a comparison of the various states, as in the fact that the individuals belonging to each state were failing to live up to the degree of perfection appropriate to the state concerned.

[11] Cf. Passus I, 15ff.

[12] It should be borne in mind that it is the desire for *temporalia* which is evil, not the *temporalia* themselves. Cf. Godefroid (Louvain, 1924), 106: "Et hoc dicit Augustinus, tertio De Doctrina Christiana, capitulo duodecimo: in omnibus rebus quibus utimur, non usus ipsarum rerum, sed libido utendi in culpa est, fieri non potest ut sine aliquo vitio cupiditas vel voracitas pretiocissimo cibo sapiens utatur, insipiens vero foedissima gulae flamma in vilissimum ardescat; nam in omnibus huiuscemodi rebus non ex earum rerum natura quibus utimur, sed ex causa utendi et modo appetendi probandum est vel improbandum quod fecimus."

[13] Compare the phrase "and han here witte at wille" with the poem "Will and Wit," ed. C. Brown, *English Lyrics of the XIIIth Century* (Oxford, 1932), no. 39, p. 65.

22

The figure of "making mirth" was probably suggested by Scriptural phrases like that introducing Ps. 99: *Iubilate Deo, omnis terra.* In commenting on the Psalm, Peter Lombard stresses the notion that *jubilate* means *voce et corde.* He contrasts true praise with false earthly jubilation.[14] The good "mynstralles" are reminiscent of those in Apoc. 14.2-3: *et vocem, quam audivi, sicut citharoedorum citharizantium in citharis suis. Et cantabunt quasi canticum novum.* And the *Glossa ordinaria* explains *citharizantium* "Quod ex officio habebant, opere implebant."[15] To worship God properly, one must not only profess the faith, but act accordingly. For the false minstrels, the poet refers us to St. Paul. Although the phrase *qui turpiloquium loquitur* does not appear in the Epistles,[16] the idea may have been suggested by several passages there. For example, *stultiloquium* is condemned in Ephes. 5.4. More to the point, *vaniloquium* is associated with departure from the Truth in 1 Tim. 1.5-7:

Finis autem praecepti est caritas de corde puro et conscientia bona et fide non ficta; a quibus quidam aberrantes conversi sunt in vaniloquium volentes esse legis doctores, non intelligentes neque quae loquuntur neque de quibus adfirmant.

In Titus 1.10-11 certain *vaniloqui* offer false doctrine for temporal reward:

Sunt enim multi etiam inoboedientes, vaniloqui et seductores, maxime qui de circumcisione sunt; quos oportet redargui, qui universas domos subvertunt docentes quae non oportet turpis lucri gratia.

[14] *PL*, 191, 897-98: "Jubilatio autem vera fit voce et corde. Quasi dicat: Si jubilat vox exterius, cor intelligat interius. Sonus enim cordis est intellectus. . . . Hic autem jubilus sit a bonis in confessione; a malis vero in confusione, cum de terrenis adeo gaudent. . . . Justi vero gaudent videntes mundo corde, quis Deus, quanta et quo ordine, et quam mirifice fecit."

[15] *PL*, 114, 735.

[16] It is possible that *turpiloquium* may be a pun on *turpis lucri.* Cf. the passage from Titus quoted below. The word, however, appears elsewhere. See, for example, the tree of the vices below, p. 192, or *Glossa ordinaria*, *PL*, 113, 459.

23

The false minstrels are not mere jesters or entertainers. They are those who profess the faith but do not work accordingly, who have abandoned Truth for the world. What is worse, they "feynen hem fantasies" or false doctrine so that other pilgrims are led astray. Like Lucifer himself, they divert the folk in their Babylonian captivity. In the contrast between the true minstrels and the janglers the poet emphasizes the basic contrast we have already seen between external status and performance within the status. The janglers symbolize all those in whatever status who fail to live up to their profession of holy worship. The poet proceeds to deal with them in detail.

In the development of the details concerning those who are false to their status, the poet uses thematic images established in his description of the plowmen and the minstrels. These are images concerning food, clothing, money, and false speech, the last of which we have just explained. The food and clothing images, reflected in the "glotonye" of the wasters and in the "countenaunce of clothyng" of the false plowmen, were probably suggested by one of Christ's admonitions to his disciples regarding the proper attitude toward *temporalia*. The poet seems to have had in mind especially Luke 12.22:

Dixitque ad discipulos suos: Ideo, dico vobis, nolite solliciti esse animae vestrae quid manducetis neque corpori quid induamini.[17]

Desire for food and clothing, representative of *temporalia* in general, was the chief hindrance to perfection in any status. The Folk of the Field are corrupted by gluttony,

---

[17] Cf. Luke 12.29: *Et vos nolite quaerere quid manducetis aut quid bibatis et nolite in sublime tolli*; Matt. 6.24-25: *Nemo potest duobus dominis servire: aut enim unum odio habebit et alterum diliget aut unum sustinebit at alterum contemnet. Non potestis Deo servire et mammonae; ideo, dico vobis, ne solliciti sitis animae vestrae quid manducetis, neque corpori vestro quid induamini; ibid.*, v. 31: *Nolite ergo solliciti esse dicentes: Quid manducabimus aut quid bibemus aut quo operiemur?* To the poet, one of these passages probably suggested the others automatically. See Chapter 1, note 31. The image of food, as we have described it, should be taken to include drink.

concern for material rather than spiritual food and drink; by pride in clothing, the hollow pretense to status to whose ideals they do not adhere; by desire for money, representative of the world's treasure rather than the treasure of Truth; and they glose their shortcomings in the mockery of false speech. They have forgotten the admonition, *Non potestis Deo servire et mammonae.* The poet has traced in the distinctions among the three states, and under the images of food, clothing, money, and speech he has indicated the evils to which these states are subject.

The subject of evangelical poverty was one of the major issues in the controversy between the friars and the seculars, and the subject of wealth and its uses by the clergy was of the greatest importance in the mind of the author of *Piers Plowman.* The good minstrels in the prelatical status, that is, the good plowmen, win their gold without sin from those whom they serve in the manner recommended by Christ in Luke 10.4-7:

Nolite portare sacculum neque peram neque calceamenta et neminem per viam salutaveritis. In quamcumque domum intraveritis primum dicite: Pax huic domui; et, si ibi fuerit filius pacis, requiescet super illum pax vestra; sin autem, ad vos revertetur. In eadem autem domo manete edentes at bibentes quae apud illos sunt; dignus est enim operarius mercede sua.[18]

But not all follow the advice of Matt. 10.9: *Nolite possidere aurum neque pecuniam in zonis vestris.* The poet illustrates the evils resulting from failure to follow this advice in those who are directly connected with the church, in ascending order, from the irregular beggars who claim ecclesiastical protection, to the head of the church, the Pope. The thematic images are used to tie together the illustrations. The "bidders and beggeres," disregarding the precept of Luke 10.4 quoted above, went about "with her belies and her bagges of bred ful ycrammed"; they

[18] Cf. Passus II, 118ff.

"fayteden" in false speech for their food, going to bed in "glotonye" and remaining spiritually asleep.[19] Pilgrims and palmers went about lying. Hermits who "loth were to swynke," clothed themselves "in copis" for their own ease. The Friars preached falsely for their own profit and to "clothen hem at lyking." They are especially dangerous, since their activity disrupts the church as a whole:

Many of this maistres freris   mowe clothen hem at lykyng,
For here money and marchandise   marchen togideres.
For sith charite hath be chapman   chief to shryue lordes,
Many ferlis han fallen   in a fewe ʒeris.
But holychirche and hij   holde better togideres,
The moste myschief on molde   is mountyng wel faste.[20]

(62-67)

The pardoner preached disguised as a priest, deceiving the people with false speech. He "blered here eyes" for gold, that he and his like might be sustained in gluttony. He connived with the parish priest, a spiritual jangler singing "for symonye." Bishops and other members of the beneficed clergy had "cure vnder criste and crounyng in tokne" that they might do the work of the plowman "and the pore fede," but instead they occupied lay offices for their own profit. Those who have the chief responsi-

[19] See below, note 42.
[20] The poet's description of the Friars recalls vividly the accusations of Wm. of St.-Amour: e.g., Bierbaum, *op. cit.*, p. 6, "Praedicit apostolus, 2 Timoth. 3.2 dicens, quod *erunt* in ecclesia quidam *homines se ipsos amantes*, per quos instabunt dicta pericula. Illi autem dicuntur amare se ipsos, qui licet velint alios corrigere, tamen nolunt ab aliis hominibus corrigi in factis suis, quamvis aliquando perversis. Unde tales se plus quam veritatem, et id circo plus quam Deum, qui est *veritas*, J. 14.6; ut enim dicit Gregorius in Pastorali: Qui perversa vult agere, et ad ea ceteros vult tacere, ipse testis sibi est, quod se plus veritate vult diligi, quam contra se non vult defendi. Item plus diligit se quam Deum, qui plus quaerit honorem suum, quam honorem Dei; unde Augustinus De vita christiana: Illi Deum diligunt, qui non aliud, quam unde nomen Dei glorificetur, exercent. Illi ergo maxime qui in statu perfectionis sunt et tamen honorem suum temporalem etiam cum multorum offendiculo appetunt et quaerunt, plus diligunt se, quam Deum." The "moste myschief on molde" probably refers to Antichrist, also associated with the Friars by Wm. of St.-Amour, *op. cit.*, 19-20.

bility for the keys of Peter, the Cardinals and the Pope, are not specifically attacked by the poet; but he leaves no doubt of his misgivings concerning them.[21]

From the clergy, representative of the prelatical and contemplative states, the poet turns to consider those in the active state symbolized earlier by the merchants. Since laymen do not fall so readily into a neat hierarchy as the clergy, he uses a more general picture of a temporal realm: the ruler, his council, and the ruled. The king was supported by his knights, but his power rose ultimately from the "miȝt of the communes." However, his council did not consist of a representative body of his subjects; it was made up of clerks appointed by Kind Wit or *scientia*.[22] The king, his barons, and the clergy, neglecting their responsibilities, decided that the commons must take care of themselves, so that the commons, also resorting to *scientia*, found it necessary to establish "plowmen." Together, the king and his commons, guided by *scientia*, formulated law and loyalty for the protection of private property, "eche man to knowe his owne" (120-21). That this is not a proper goal is evident from 1 Cor. 10.24: *Nemo quod suum est quaerat*.[23] The guiding principle of perfection in any status is charity; in a sense, *amor sui* is its opposite. St. Augustine

---

[21] The association of the cardinal virtues with "hinges" to the gates of Heaven in ll. 103-6 was conventional. Cf. the descriptions in O. Lottin, "La théorie des vertus cardinales de 1230 a 1250," *Melanges Mandonnet*, II, 233-59. Cf. Rabanus, *De universo*, *PL*, 111, 265. In this passage the power of the Keys is associated with the greatest of the theological virtues, Charity, and with the four cardinal virtues: Prudence, Justice, Temperance, and Fortitude. Theoretically, the power of the Keys was transferred in the sacrament of ordination. But the discrepancy between the status of the person ordained and his actual character frequently gave rise to difficulties. The poet here stresses the necessity that personal character should be consistent with status. Cf. note 12, above.

[22] The poet shows an admiration for the traditional feudal council. This passage should be considered in the light of the bitter struggles during the later Middle Ages over the character of the king's council. On *scientia*, see below.

[23] Cf. v. 33; *ibid.*, 13.5; 2 Cor. 12.14; Ph. 2.4.

wrote: "In quo autem est charitas, fratres? Qui non sua quaerit in hoc vita."[24] Or, again, "Prima hominis perditio fuit amor sui."[25] Positive law which does not reflect natural or Divine Law necessarily leads to a Babylonian confusion. This is one thesis of Augustine's *Civitas Dei*.

As the ideal of perfection provides a necessary background to an understanding of the departure from Truth of the prelatical and contemplative states, so the ideal of the good ruler provides a necessary background to an understanding of the departure from Truth in this temporal realm. One of the most authoritative pictures of the ideal ruler is that furnished by St. Augustine:

Sed felices eos dicimus, si juste imperant, si inter linguas sublimiter honorantium et obsequia nimis humiliter salutantium non extolluntur, sed se homines esse meminerunt; si suam potestatem ad Dei cultum maxime dilatandum majestati ejus famulam faciunt; si Deum timent, diligunt, colunt; si plus amant illud regnum, ubi non timent habere consortes; si tardius vindicant, facile ignoscunt; si eamdem vindictam pro necessitate regendae tuendaeque reipublicae, non pro saturandis inimicitiarum odiis exserunt; si eamdem veniam non ad impunitatem iniquitas, sed ad spem correctionis indulgent; si, quod aspere conguntur plerumque discernere, misericordiae lenitate et beneficiorum largitate compensant; si luxuria tanto eis est castigatior, quanto posset esse liberior; si malunt cupiditatibus pravis, quam quibuslibet gentibus imperare.[26]

The ideal king must guard himself against flattery and self-aggrandizement, recognizing that his power comes from God. In his administration of justice, he must act not willfully, but for the good of the realm. He must temper justice with mercy. Traditionally, the king, who was *vicarius Dei in terris*, ruled in accordance with Divine Law. The perception of Divine Law requires something higher than *scientia*; as Peter Lombard explains, it requires the higher reason, whose end is *sapientia*:

[24] *Ennaratio in Ps.* CXXI, PL, 37, 1629.
[25] Sermo XCVI, PL, 38, 585.
[26] *Civitas Dei*, V, 24.

Rationis autem pars *superior* aeternis rationibus conspiciendis vel consulendis adhaerescit, portio *inferior* ad temporalia gubernanda deflectitur. Et illa rationis intentio, qua contemplamur aeterna, *sapientiae* deputatur; illa vero, quae bene utimur rebus temporalibus, *scientiae* deputatur.[27]

Without *sapientia*, Godefroid asserts, the ruler is little more than a beast:

Unde dicit [Aristotle, *Pol.* II 1287a] ibi quod qui iubet intellectum, id est leges secundum rectam rationem institutas principari, videtur iubere principari Deum et ipsas iustas leges; qui autem iubet principari hominem, apponit et bestiam.[28]

The king in *Piers Plowman*, together with knights, clergy, and commons, has concern only for *temporalia*. His kingdom is guided on all levels by *scientia*. Significantly, he is flattered by a lunatic, a man without reason.

This flattery is not left unchallenged. An angel from Heaven, who speaks the word of God, warns the king of the need for *pietas* in his rule: "Nudum uis a te vestiri vult pietate." The pious king rules for the good of his realm, not for himself. Before the king may receive the heavenly rewards which the lunatic has wished for him, he must assume the responsibilities of his office; he must clothe himself in *pietas* as the prelates must clothe themselves without guile in the clothes of the spiritual plowman. But the words of the angel are corrupted through the false speech of a "goliardeys a glotoun of wordes." He employs the device of partial quotation:

Dum rex a regere   dicatur nomen habere,
Nomen habet sine re   nisi studet iura tenere. (141-42)

This etymological verse repeats the standard derivation of *rex* from *regendo* as in Isidore of Seville. But the goliard stops at a point which omits an important part of Isidore's discussion. Like the angel, Isidore does not deny the need

---

[27] *Sententiae*, II, XXIV, V; in Bonaventura, *Opera*, II, 551.
[28] Godefroid (Louvain, 1932), 77.

for justice in the king, but he insists that he have piety as well:

Reges a regendo vocati; sicut enim *sacerdos a sanctificando,* ita est *rex a regendo*: non autem regit qui non corregit. Recte igitur faciendo regis nomen tenetur, peccando amittitur. Unde et apud veteres, tale erat proverbium. Rex eris si recta facies, si non facies, non eris. Regiae virtutes praecipue duae, justitia et pietas; plus autem in regibus laudatur pietas; nam justitia per se severa est.[29]

What the goliard says is not wrong; what is wrong is his omission: "nam justitia per se severa est." Or, as James says in his Epistle: (2.12-13):

Sic loquimini et sic facite sicut per legem libertatis incipientes iudicari. Iudicium enim sine misericordia illi qui non facit misericordiam; superexaltat autem misericordia iudicium.

In his comment on this passage, Bede remarks "Lex libertatis lex charitatis est."[30] Justice without mercy is a violation of the higher principle of charity.

The oppression inherent in a realm not directly under the guidance of reason and the fundamental virtue, charity, is felt by the commons:

> And thanne gan alle the comune   crye in vers of latin,
> To the kynges conseille   construe ho-so wolde—
> 'Praecepta Regis   sunt nobis vincula legis.' (143-45)

The force of "vincula legis" is made perfectly clear in the fable:

> For a cat of a courte   cam whan hym lyked,
> And ouerlepe hem lyʒtlich   and lauʒte hem at his wille
>   (149-50)

The commons imply that the commands of the king have supplanted the law to which he himself was subject in political theory: "Temperet igitur potentiam suam per legem quae fraenum est potentia quod secundum leges

---

[29] *Etymologiae*, IX, iii. Cf. Bernard F. Huppé, "The Authorship of the A and B texts of *Piers Plowman*," *Speculum*, XXII (1947), 587.

[30] *PL*, 93, 20. The subsequent discussion, cols. 20-22, is illuminating.

vivat."[31] The timidity of the commons evident in their ambiguous Latin complaint is emphasized by the fable itself: although the mice and rats agree to the desirability of belling the cat, of clothing him in a "collar," they are all equally unwilling to attempt the dangerous task of imposing it. Such pusillanimity on the part of the commons was thought to be conducive to tyranny:

In tali autem casu, scilicet cum princeps solo suo consilio privato contentus tale onus imponit nec vult quod aliis causa vel necessitas propter quam imponitur innotescat, deberent subditi resistere, si possent, quousque esset per praedictos prudentes sufficienter discussum; alioquin paulatim regnum in tyrannidem converteretur et subditi liberi redigerentur ad condicionem servorum subditorum. Et est timendum ne propter multorum pusillanimitatem et aliorum infidelitatem hodie communiter ita fiat. Propter quod vis invenitur rectus et iustus principatus; sed fere omnes principes conantur principari ut tyranni, omnia ad suum proprium honorem vel commodum referendo, etiam cum detrimento subditorum.[32]

A mouse defends the weak attitude of the commons as a proper mode of conduct. He repeats in changed terms the argument of the goliard for a strong rule, lest

> . . . many mannus malt   we mys wolde destruye,
> And also ȝe route of ratones   rende mennes clothes.
> (197-98)

Superficially, this is an argument for peace, but like the goliard's it is sophistical. The peace for which the mouse appeals is slothful peace, willingness to compromise with evil through fear of the world. It is the peace which Christ denied when he said (Matt. 10.34), *Non veni pacem mittere, sed gladium.* The *Allegoriae in sacram scripturam* defines it as the peace of carnal consent: inordinate, false,

---

[31] Bracton, *De legibus*, III, ix, 3. Godefroid (Louvain, 1932), 76, wrote: "Sed quantumcumque aliquis princeps esset bonus . . . et regnum suum debet ordinare principaliter non ad bonum suum privatum sed ad bonum totius communitatis, ideo talis debet regere secundum leges recte institutas et non secundum suam propriam prudentiam." Cf. Huppé, *op. cit.*, 587-88.

[32] Godefroid (Louvain, 1932), 78.

wrongful, and wicked. It makes man obey the Devil rather than God:

Non veni, etc. id est, nolo fovere in carne molliciem, sed a carne separationem. Est pax *inordinata,* est *simulata,* est *inquinata,* est et *scelerata.* Prima, superborum, qui contempto superiore obediunt inferiori; contempto videlicet Deo, obediunt diabolo; contempto coelo, obediunt mundo; contempto spiritue, obediunt carni. Secunda duplicium, . . ore suo benedicebant, et corde suo maledicebant. Tertia, immundorum, qui turpiter prostituti requiescunt, refecti in fecibus suis. Quarta . . . et universitati Ecclesiae auctoritatem contradicunt.[33]

The mouse's appeal is based entirely on a concern for *temporalia,* food and clothing. He is willing to forget the principles of natural and Divine Law so that the ruler may do "as hym-self wolde to do as hym liketh." The king may be placated with "venesoun." As for the mice and rats, they should forget the principle of charity, each devoting himself to *amor sui:*

> For-thi vche a wise wiȝte I warne   wite wel his owne.
>
> (207)

Over this realm where safeguarding private property is the chief concern of king, council, and commons, there hover the sergeants of the law, richly dressed "in houues of selke," who plead for money "and nouȝt for loue of owre lorde." The corruption in high places, the failure to live up to the requirements of the active state among the powerful and rich, has its counterpart in the failure of the laboring classes to recognize their responsibilities:

> Of alkin libbyng laboreres   lopen forth somme,
> As dykers and deluers   that doth here dedes ille,
> And dryuen forth the longe day   with 'dieu vous saue,
>   Dame Emme!' (222-24)

The members of the prelatical, contemplative, and active

---

[33] *PL,* 112, 1016. Rabanus calls the mouse "pusillum animal," *De universo, PL,* 111, 226.

states, to whatever class they might belong, were alike in their disregard for Christ's warning:

Nolite sollicite esse animae vestrae quid manducetis,
neque corpori quid induamini.

They spent their days in false and idle speech, in corruption of the word of God and of the law of charity. They pursued corporal food and clothing, "worchyng and wandryng as the worlde asketh," not as God would. Their disregard for Christ's admonition is symbolized at the close of the Prologue in the shrill cries of enticement to partake of the food of the body:

> . . . hote pies, hote!
> Gode gris and gees   gowe dyne, gowe! . . .
> White wyn of Oseye   and red wyn of Gascoigne,
> Of the Ryne and of the Rochel   the roste to defye.

Sufficient evidence has now been adduced to make possible an analysis of the character of the dreamer himself. He approves the speech of the mouse who recommends submission to injustice (l. 182). He has also been identified, not unreasonably, with the flattering lunatic. This epithet suggests the lunatic of Matt. 17.14ff. who is described by Bede as one given over to the world, who fluctuates impatiently from vice to vice.[34] This dubiousness of character is further suggested in the opening description:

> I shope me in shroudes   as I a shepe were,
> In habite as an heremite   vnholy of workes,
> Went wyde in this world   wondres to here. (2-4)

Like those who "putten hem to pruyde" and "comen disgised," the dreamer is clothed as if he were a "shepe"; that is, he resembles the false prophets in sheep's clothing of the Gospel (Matt. 7.15):

[34] *PL,* 92.82: "Juxta tropologiam lunaticus, qui in coepto non persistit, significat eos qui nunc in ignem libidinis, nunc in aquam cupiditatis feruntur." Cf. Hugh of St. Victor, *Allegoriae in novum testamentum, PL,* 175, 796.

Attendite a falsis prophetis, qui ueniunt ad uos in uestimentis ouium: intrinsecus autem sunt lupi rapaces; a fructibus eorum cognoscentis eos.

He is actually dressed like a hermit, outwardly holy, but in works he is unholy; he is like one of the "grete lobyes and longe that loth were to swynke."[35] This description does not mean that the dreamer is to be taken as a rascal. When the name Will is first introduced later in the poem it is accompanied by a play on its meaning as the faculty of will. This play on the name of the dreamer and his character as it is developed in the poem together suggest that the dreamer is representative of the faculty will rather than of any individual person.

The function of the dreamer in the poem is to seek Piers Plowman so that he may learn and be instructed in the ways of perfection. As the object of such instruction the faculty of will is peculiarly appropriate, since it was considered to be the source of moral action:

Cum ergo quaeritur: utrum aliquis actus sic vel sic factus plus accedat ad perfectionem virtutis vel malitiam vitii aut plus recedat a perfectione virtutis vel malitia vitiosa; si consideretur id quod est ex parte voluntatis, tunc quanto voluntas in eligendo et operando aliquid est maior vel ferventior sive promptior, tanto opus quod secundum speciem vel circumstantias est bonum vel malum.[36]

But the will can be good only in so far as it is guided by reason:

Actus voluntatis mensuratur et habet rationem boni et perfecti in habitudine ad actum intellectus; actus enim voluntatis bonus est secundum quod concordat rationi rectae; malus autem secundum quod declinat ab ea, non autem e contrario.[37]

The wisdom which is a function of the higher reason

---

[35] For an extended description of false hermits, see C-text, Passus X, 188f.

[36] Godefroid (Louvain, 1924), 126.

[37] *Idem* (Louvain, 1914), 205. We are aware of the fact that there was a voluntaristic position contrary to the above which was especially popular among English Franciscans; however, we have found no evidence of voluntarism in *Piers Plowman*.

alone is capable of apprehending the laws of God and of applying them to human action. The dreamer, at the beginning of the poem, represents the will unguided by reason. Hence his optimism about the king's rule and his approval of the mouse's defense of it. He is in a state of sin from which he may recover only through the action of Divine grace as administered by the priesthood of the church. But Will naturally desires the good, and it is this principle which makes him, in spite of his lapses, a seeker after truth. The human will, which is easily misguided, not only offers the poet an excellent means of disclosing the corruption in the church, but serves at the same time as a universal representing every Christian and the problems he must confront. Through Will's errors, the reader may learn the pitfalls which lie in the path of any Christian in a corrupt church. And through his perception of the true way, the reader may learn the direction in which his salvation also lies. Fundamentally, Will is a device by means of which the poet may reveal what he considers to be the need of the church for guidance by Piers Plowman.

PASSUS I

In Passus I Holy Church appears to Will and proceeds to instruct him in the fundamentals of faith. Her lesson is based upon Will's vision in the Prologue, and it develops the thesis which is to be illustrated in the ensuing vision. As we have shown, the dreamer, representative of the untutored will, has approved some of the evils which he has seen in his vision, the slothful peace and the wrongful fear of the mouse who counsels against any attempt at basic reform. Since he is in need of instruction, Holy Church, dressed in linen, descends from the Tower of Truth to teach him. Her descent from the three-fold tower on the toft, truly made, has significance beyond the mere conduct of the action.[38] In Biblical commentary, we find an intimate relationship established between a tower on a mountain and the church. In fact, certain comments indicate clearly the traditional character of the picture which is graphically presented in *Piers Plowman*: notably those on Luke 9.29-33, Ps. 14.1, Apoc. 21.2-11. In the first of these, Luke 9.29-33, Christ is transfigured and stands with Moses and Elias on a mountain in the view of his disciples. Peter thereafter wishes to build three separate tabernacles in commemoration. In this desire Peter is mistaken, since a threefold unity is betokened. This threefold unity of Christ and the prophets, as Bede explains it, represents Holy Church:

Sed et usque nunc imperitia notatur, quisque legi, prophetis, et Evangelio tria tabernacula facere cupit, cum haec nequaquam valeant ab invicem separari, unum habentia tabernaculum, hoc est Ecclesiam Dei.[39]

Ps. 14.1 refers to a tower on a mountain:

> *Domine, quis habitabit in tabernaculo tuo,*
> *aut quis requiescet in monte sancto tuo?*

For Peter Lombard, following Augustine, the tabernacle is not only the *visio pacis*, the heavenly Jerusalem, but also *ecclesia*.[40] In the Apoc. 21.2-11, the Church as the Bride of Christ descends from Heaven as a voice exclaims, "Behold the tabernacle of God!":

Et ciuitatem sanctam Hierusalem nouam uidi descendentem de caelo a Deo, paratam sicut sponsam ornatam uiro suo. Et audiui uocem magnam de throno dicentem; Ecce tabernaculum Dei cum

---

[38] The wordplay in "trielich ymaked" should not be overlooked. For a discussion of this and further examples of wordplay in *Piers Plowman* see Bernard F. Huppé, *"Petrus id est Christus*: Word Play in *Piers Plowman*, the B-Text," *ELH*, XVII (1950), pp. 163-190. A discussion of Will appears on pp. 188-190.

[39] *PL*, 92, 455. Father John B. Dwyer, S.J., has called our attention to the identification of a woman representing Holy Church with a tower in the Apocryphal *Pastor Hermas*, Vision III.

[40] *PL*, 191, 167.

hominibus . . . Ueni ostendam tibi sponsam, uxorem Agni. Et sustulit me in spiritu in montem magnum et altum, et ostendit mihi ciuitatem sanctam Hierusalem descendentem de caelo a Deo, habentem claritatem Dei.

According to the homiletic exposition of the Apocalypse attributed to Augustine, the mountain is Christ; heavenly Jerusalem is the church, the bride of the Lamb:

Montem Christum dicit. . . . Haec Jerusalem est Ecclesia, civitas in monte constituta, sponsa Agni.[41]

Here would appear to be some of the ultimate sources for Langland's striking picture of Holy Church, dressed in linen, descending from the mountain of Truth.

Similarly, Holy Church's question, "sone, slepestow?" is intended to suggest allegorically Will's state of sinful ignorance in his approval of the corruption of the Folk of the Field.[42] The daughter of Truth, Holy Church comes

[41] *PL*, 35, 2450. See also Bede, *PL*, 93, 194-95; St. Martin Legionensis, *PL*, 209, 403-6. The linen clothing worn by Holy Church signifies the *justificatio sanctorum*, cf. Bruno Astensis, *PL*, 165, 708.

[42] The notion of sleep as representing spiritual blindness is an exegetical commonplace. For example, Rabanus Maurus on Eph. 5.14; *PL*, 112, 451: "*Propter quod dicit, surge, qui dormis et exsurge a mortuis et illuminabit tibi Cristus.* (Ambr.) Dormitionem hanc, stuporem mentis significat, quae alienatur a vera via; alienatio vera haec species mortis est, ex qua resurgere commonetur, ut resipiscens agnoscat veritatem, quae est Christus." Sleep in the *Glossa ordinaria*, *PL*, 113, 963, is said to represent the forgetting of the treasure of God (Truth) through concern with the treasures of the world (These two contrasted treasures are to be mentioned later by Holy Church); Ps. 75.6 "*Dormierunt* (Cass.) a bonis aeternis refrigescentes, carni acquieverunt, pro futura non videntes. Somnum suum, qui discat a quiete bonorum: quia iste fallax est; videntes per somnium se habere thesauros, cum evigilant nihil inveniunt." Augustine on this same passage enforces this contrast between the two treasures, *PL*, 36, 1963: *Dormierunt somnium suum, et nihil invenerunt omnes viri divitiorum in manibus suis.* Amaverunt praesentia et dormierunt in ipsis praesentibus; et sic illis facta sunt ipsa praesentia deliciosa: quomodo qui videt per somnium invenisse se thesauros, tamdiu dives est, quamdiu non evigilat. Somnium illum divitem fecit; evigilatio pauperem facit. . . . Tales sunt et isti: venerunt in hanc vitam, et per cupiditates temporales quasi obdormierunt hic; et exceperunt illos divitiae et vanae pompae volaticae, et transierunt: non intellexerunt quantum inde boni posset fieri."
In their spiritual sleep Will and the Folk of the Field resemble the foolish

to correct Will's misapprehension about the world. He has not understood the significance of their occupation with the world,

> Worchyng and wandryng   as the worlde asketh.
>
> (Prol. 19.)

Holy Church makes clear in Passus 1 the falsity of most of the folk:

> The moste partie of this poeple   that passeth on this erthe,
> Haue thei worschip in this worlde   thei wilne no better;
> Of other heuene than here   holde thei no tale. (7-9)

Like Will, they are in spiritual slumber. They live in a dream, blind to the treasure of heaven because their eyes are dazzled by the false treasure of this world:

> Amaverunt praesentia, et dormierunt in ipsis praesentibus. . . . venerunt in hanc vitam, et per cupiditates temporales quasi obdormierunt hic.[43]

The problem which naturally arises is that of how the folk must handle *temporalia* so that they may become pilgrims on the way to Truth (*via ad Hierusalem*). Holy Church directs her attention to precisely this problem of the use of temporal goods, which, she says, are handled properly when they are used for the worship of God:

> And therefore he hyȝte the erthe   to helpe ȝow vchone
> Of wollen, of lynnen   of lyflode at nede,
> In mesurable manere   to make ȝow at ese. (17-19)

Here she seems to recur directly to Luke 12.22 and 29,

---

virgins who are contrasted with the wise virgins who "swonken ful harde"; thus Pseudo-Jerome, *PL*, 30, 577: Matt. 25.1-14 "*Quinque prudentes,* eo quod propter regnum Dei laboraverunt: *Quinque fatuae,* ostendit qui pro retributione humanae laudis gesserunt. *Dormitare,* est ante mortem languescere, dormire vero, in morte quiescere est. *Media nocte,* id est, in errore, sive in securitate negligentes. Nescio vos, id est, nescio opera vestra bona." Luke 9.32 can also be cited as a source for this symbolic use of sleep; Luke 9 contains, as we have seen, the image of Holy Church's descent from the mountain. In the poem, Will's spiritual sleep is usually indicated by a sleep *within* the sleep necessary to his vision.

[43] Augustine on Ps. 75.6, quoted in the preceding note.

texts, as has been shown, of basic importance in the development of the Prologue:

Nolite solliciti esse animae vestrae quid manducetis, neque corpori quid induamini. . . . Nolite quaerere quid manducetis, aut quid bibatis et nolite in sublime tolli.

The *Glossa ordiniaria* on this passage furnishes the idea of moderation, "mesurable manner":

Perfectius esset pauperibus omnia dare, et de mammona iniquitatis amicos facere; sed quia plerumque devotio fidei infirmitate revocatur, non prohibet providentiam, per quam in sudore vultus panis praeparatur, sed vetat sollicitudinem quae mentem perturbat et ab aeternis revocat. . . . Non ait: Nolite quaerere vel solliciti esse de cibo vel vestimento, sed expressius *quid manducetis aut quid bibatis.* In quo videntur argui hi qui, spreto victu vel vestitu communi, lautiora vel austeriora prae his cum quibus vivunt, alimenta vel indumenta requirunt. *Nolite in sublime.* Prohibita sollicitudine victus vel vestitus, quae sunt ad necessitatem, prohibet etiam superbiam quae solet de istis superabundantibus consequi: ideo haec ne requiratis, quia talis sollicitudo facit infidelibus similes.[44]

Man's true purpose on earth is to worship God. He fulfills this purpose when he uses God's temporal gifts in moderation so as to fit himself the better to serve God. The temporal gifts necessary are the simple, basic ones which God has ordained:

And God comaunded of his curteisye   in comune three
     thinges;
Arne none nedful but tho   and nempne hem I thinke,
And rekne hem bi resoun   reherce thow hem after.
That one is vesture   from chele the to saue,
And mete atte mele   for myseise of thi-selue,
And drynke whan thow dryest   ac do nouȝt out of re-
     soun;

---

[44] *PL*, 114, 296-97: Cf. Godefroid de Fontaines (Louvain, 1924), 110: "Mediocritas igitur in istis rebus temporalibus maxime est eligenda. Et hoc quidem est rationabile, quia quamvis, ut dictum est, perfectio essentialiter non consistat in ipsis divitiis vel in habere vel non habere illas, sed in actu mentis perfecto secundum virtutem, tamen paucorum est posse esse perfectos et uti perfectione in abundantia. Similiter etiam et in penuria."

That thow worth the werse   whan thow worche shuldest.

(20-6)

Referring to the *Glossa ordinaria* on Matt. 6.32, we find, significantly for the lines in question, the basis for God's commanding the three necessary things:

Provisa sunt haec [food, drink, clothing] a Deo, qui novit nobis haec invia sua esse necessaria. . . . Sic filios de bonitate et providentia patris securos reddit, absque cura scilicet.[45]

The verses in Matthew (25-33) are closely related to those in Luke 12 (above), warning against concern with food, drink, clothing to the neglect of the spirit. In what she says Holy Church emphasizes the truth that the use of *temporalia* must be directed toward the worship of God. Holy Church now warns against drunkenness. Her intention is to be understood in terms of her lesson in the proper use of *temporalia*. Drunkenness symbolizes lack of moderation, blindness to spiritual treasure; it is connected with spiritual sleep to which Holy Church refers in beginning her speech to Will. Peter Lombard, for example, comments on 1 Thess. 5.6-7:

Sed vigilemus et sobrii simus, id est vigilet mens nostra attendens haec caduca, et sobrie eis utamur, non quasi bonis nostris, sed ad sustentationem datis. . . . *Et qui ebrii sunt,* his temporibus immoderate utendo . . . . *sed sobrii simus,* moderate his utentes, et ad pugnam contra hostes parati.[46]

[45] *PL,* 114, 106.

[46] *PL,* 192, 307. The connection between spiritual sleep and drunkenness is also to be found in Eph. 5.14 (cf. note 42), where the reference to spiritual sleep is shortly followed by an admonition against drunkenness which prevents man from worshiping God (5.19): *Et nolite inebriari uino, in quo est luxuria; sed implemini Spiritu, Loquentes uobismet ipsis in psalmis et hymnis, et canticis spiritualibus, cantantes et psallentes in cordibus Domino, gratias agentes.* The worship of God is the end of the use of all temporal good; drunkenness is in direct violation of this primary law. Luke 12.45 also contains a warning against drunkenness, a warning which follows closely the admonition to moderation (12.22), basic in Holy Church's teaching on the use of *temporalia*. The story of Lot (27ff.) seems to be used illustratively; like Eph. 5 it connects drunkenness with *luxuria*.

Holy Church then sums up (35-42) her teaching on Measure, "Mesure is medcyne."

Will has not entirely understood Holy Church's teaching on the proper handling of *temporalia* to the end that God may be worshiped. He wishes to know concerning the vision of the Field of Folk, "What of the money in the world? To whom does this belong?" (43-5) The question is that by which the spiritually blind Pharisees attempted to ensnare Jesus. Holy Church replies to Will in the words of the Lord to the Pharisees, "Give unto Caesar the things that are Caesar's." Christ's reply is explained by Bede as indicating that *temporalia* are under the command of the secular powers, but that God demands the gifts of the spirit; the soul must be filled with light, and the goods of this earth must be so handled that they do not cloud the light of the soul.[47] On the basis of this important distinction between the true and false handling of worldly goods, Holy Church proceeds to an explanation of the treasure of the Field. She establishes the contrast between treasure which is handled in accordance with Reason (54-6) and the treasure of the world which is desired for itself and which leads man into destruction (65-70).[48] Under the figure of

[47] *PL*, 92, 85.

[48] There are several Scriptural passages which might have supplied the figure of the treasure, but it is significant that the image of treasure is central in Luke 12, a chapter to which Holy Church has recurred in establishing the principle of "mesurable manner" in the handling of *temporalia*. The first use of the image of treasure in Luke 12 occurs at verse 21: *Sic est qui sibi thesaurizat, et non est in Deum dives*. The distinction between the two treasures, made by Holy Church, is established in the *Glossa ordinaria* on the basis of this text, *PL*, 114, 296: "In Deum dives est qui transitoria contemnens pauperibus distribuit, cujus expectatio Dominus est, cujus substantia, id est conscientiae possessio qua sustentatur et pascitur, est apud Deum, non in sacculis terrae." Bede in glossing the same verse associates the concern for earthly treasure with a spiritual darkness resembling the image of sleep used by Holy Church in the beginning of her speech to Will (*PL*, 92, 492): "Si is qui sibi thesaurizat, et non est in Deum dives, stultus est et in nocte rapiendus, ergo qui vult esse in Deum dives, non sibi thesaurizat, sed pauperibus possessa distribuat. Sic enim sapiens et filius lucis esse merebitur." (Cf. Eph. 5.14; Ps. 75.6; Matt. 25.1-14 and commentary quoted in footnote

41

treasure Holy Church has described a method of handling worldly goods which will lead to salvation. Will misses the point and asks her to teach him no further about treasure but only about salvation (83-84). This request leads Holy Church to explain to him the spiritual meaning of treasure. There is a treasure of truth, and it is about this treasure that Holy Church speaks in a "sermon" based on the theme *deus caritas*.[49] God is the treasure of truth and

---

42.) Luke 12.33 is the next verse having to do with treasure: *Vendite quae possidetis et date elimoisinam. Facite uobis sacculos qui non ueterescunt, thesaurum non deficientem in caelis: quo fur non adpropriat, neque tinea corrumpit.* The *Glossa ordinaria* makes clear, on the basis of this verse, the distinction between the ephemeral treasure of temporal wealth and the eternal treasure arising from charity (*PL*, 114, 297-98): "Temporalia, vel ex sua fragilitate deficiunt, vel si quid solidum superest, ut lapides pretiosi, a furibus possunt tolli. Sed data pro Christo aeternum fructum conferrunt in coelis." The next verse (12.34) continues the discussion of treasure: *Ubi enim thesaurus uester est, ibi et cor uestrum erit.* Here the *Glossa* mentions the money which has puzzled Will, and identifies the heavenly treasure with Christ (Truth): "Universaliter, et de pecunia et de omnibus voluptatibus. Gulosi thesaurus est venter, ubi habet cor, sic et de aliis. Nam si in terra, cor est deorsum; si in coelestibus, est in Christo fixum. Necesse est enim, ut quo praecesserit dilectionis thesaurus, illic et cogitationis sequatur affectus." It will be remembered that Holy Church's conversation with Will begins on the theme of spiritual sleep. Significantly in terms of structure the discussion of treasure in Luke 12 ends with a reference to those who, like the virgins of Matt. 25.1-14 await the bridegroom. These *vigilantes* are likened in the *Glossa* to those who avoid the darkness of spiritual sleep (*PL*, 114, 298): "Vers. 37.—*Vigilantes.* Vigilat qui oculos apertos in vero lumine tenet, ut tenebras negligentiae evitet; qui etiam quod credidit operatur, qui sollicitus est in cura gregis sibi commissi. Quid vero vigilantibus debeatur subdit." Cf. Matt. 6.19ff.

[49] The theme *deus caritas* is from 1 John 4.8, 16, which serves to connect the sermon with what has preceded, since the first epistle of John develops the contrast between spiritual light, which is manifest in Faith, and spiritual darkness, which is manifest in "japing," i.e. false belief (cf. 1 John 1.6-8, 2.4-6, 2.9-11). There is a further implicit textual connection in that this theme is also developed in Luke 12; in fact, as we have seen (note 47), Holy Church's identification of the heavenly treasure of truth with God is made in the *Glossa* on Luke 12.34. Further, the theme from the epistle (*deus caritas*) serves to make the fundamental connection between Truth and Charity, the dynamic principle of Christian living. This connection is made by Saint Augustine in his commentary on 1 John 4.8, *PL*, 35, 2031: "*Nos ex Deo sumus. Videamus quare: videte si propter aliud quam propter charitatem. Nos ex Deo sumus. Qui novit Deum, audit nos: qui non est ex Deo, non nos audit. Ex hoc cognoscimus spiritum veritatis et erroris. . . . Vi-*

42

God is love (85-87). It follows that man must be like God to have the treasure of truth: he is like God if he is "true of his tongue" (faith), "works thereafter" (charity), and thus "desires good." (88-93).[50] True speech is basic to the treasure of Truth as its opposite, false speech, or jangling, is a sign of involvement in worldly treasure, a fact which Holy Church has already pointed out (64-70; cf. Prologue, 33ff.).

Holy Church develops the fundamental contrast between the followers of False and the followers of Truth by means of examples. True kings and knights are like Christ in ruling by Reason: They take "transgressors"

---

deamus quid monet, et audiamus eum potius in spiritu veritatis monentem; non antichristos, non amatores mundi, non mundum: si ex Deo nati sumus, *Dilestissimi . . . . diligamus invicem.* Quare? *quia homo monet? Quia dilectio* [Vulgate, *caritas*] *ex Deo est.* Multum commendavit dilectionem, quia dixit *ex Deo est*: plus dicturus est, intente audiamus. Modo dixit, *Dilectio ex Deo est*: *et omnis qui diligit, ex Deo natus est, et cognovit Deum. Qui non diligit, non novit Deum.* Quare? *Quia Deus dilectio est.* Quid amplius dici potuit, fratres? Si nihil de laude dilectionis diceretur per omnes istas paginas hujus Epistolae, si nihil omnino per caeteras paginas Scripturarum, et hoc solum unum audiremus de voce Spiritus Dei, *Quia Deus dilectio est;* nihil amplius quaerere deberemus." It is Charity which gives spiritual light, the treasure of truth.

[50] Faith (truth of tongue), and Charity (working thereafter and desiring good) make man like to "god agrounde and aloft" according to 1 John 4.16 and 17: *Et nos cognouimus et credidimus caritati quam habet Deus in nobis. Deus caritas est: et qui manet in caritate, in Deo manet, et Deus in eo. In hoc perfecta est caritas Dei nobiscum, ut fiduciam habeamus in die iudicii: quia sicut ille est, et nos sumus in hoc mundo.* In Augustine's exposition of verse 17, *PL*, 35, 2047, we find the basis for the line, "god bi the gospel agrounde and aloft" (90). Augustine is concerned with defining the similarity between God and man; man is not God but like to God (God by the gospel agrounde, *in mundo*, and alofte, *in die iudicii*). In the next line "and like to owre lorde bi seynte Lukes wordes" reference is made to Luke 6.35: *Uerum tamen diligite inimicos uestros, benefacite et mutuum date nihil inde sperantes, et erit merces uestra multa, et eritis filii Altissimi, quia ipse benignus est super ingratos et malos.* In the exercise of charity man becomes, like Christ, a son of God. The connection between *filii altissimi* and the first epistle of John is not fortuitous. Bede in commenting on Luke 6.35 makes reference to 1 John 4.12, *PL*, 92, 407. Augustine in the exposition to which allusion has just been made brings in Matt. 5.44-6, these verses being almost identical with Luke 6.33 and 35.

(96), that is, those who are defined by James (2.8-9) as violators of the basic law of charity:

Si tamen legem perficitis regalem secundum scripturas: Diliges proximum tuum sicut te ipsum, bene facitis; si autem personas accipitis, peccatum operamini redarguti a lege quasi transgressores.[51]

She cites the example of David and his knights and that of the greatest exemplar, Christ, who drove from Heaven Lucifer and his legions.[52] Lucifer is the opposite of those who live by charity and follow reason. He is the father of falsehood. Those who work after his teaching will be rewarded by eternal damnation as those who work according to the precepts of charity will be rewarded in heaven (126-31). After calling attention to her dependence on textual commentary ("bi siʒte of thise textis," 132), Holy Church

[51] This discussion of *transgressores* in James leads immediately to a statement of the relationship in ruling between mercy and justice (2.13-14), a subject of central importance in the political portion of the Prologue. See Bede, *PL*, 93, 21-2. Since Holy Church's theme is charity (*deus caritas*), it is not difficult to grasp the connection between the quoted text from James and her argument.

[52] In the description of Lucifer's fall, a Biblical reference needs explanation: *Ponam pedem in aquilone, et similis ero altissimo* (118). Skeat refers to this verse as an "inexact quotation from Isaiah 14.13, 14." But Alanus de Insulis quotes the line almost as in our text, *PL*, 210, 705. "In Psalmo: Ponam sedem meam ad aquilonem, et similis ero Altissimo." Except for what may be a scribal error, *pedem* for *sedem*, the two versions are identical. Alanus does not refer to Isaiah but to the Psalms. The problem is solved when we turn to Augustine's commentary on Ps. 1, *PL*, 36, 69, where the quotation as it appears in Alanus is found. The apparent use of Augustine's commentary rather than the Vulgate Text, by both Alanus and Langland is not without significance. It is a small indication of the manner in which the medieval thinker considered his Biblical text, surrounded with traditional significance. Here the discovery of the text in Augustine's commentary on Ps. 1.4 reveals its appropriateness to Holy Church's general discussion. The verse is: *"Non sic impii, non sic: sed tanquam pulvis quem projicit ventus a facie terrae."* Augustine comments: "Terra hic accipienda est ipsa stabilitas in Deo . . . . Similitudo autem hinc ducta est; quia ut haec terra visibilis exteriorem hominem nutrit et continet, ita illa terra invisibilis interiorem hominem. . . . Ab hac terra projecit superbia eum qui dixit: *Ponam sedem meam ad Aquilonem, et ero similis Altissimo.*" The verse is concerned, in terms of Augustine's commentary, with the proper and improper use of *temporalia*, with the end and purpose of the *visibilia* which nourish and clothe the body. This concept is, of course, central to Holy Church's discussion.

points out how opposite are the rewards for the followers of Truth and the followers of False; this contrast, in turn, suggests the recurrence for emphasis to the main theme of treasure:

Whan alle tresores arne ytried   treuthe is the beste,
Lereth it this lewde men   for lettred men it knowen,
That treuthe is tresore   the triest on erthe. (133-35)

She has now demonstrated to Will the two treasures: that of Truth betokened in the works of charity and having as its end the *patria* of heaven; that of False, betokened in japing and transgression of the law of charity, and having as its end eternal damnation in Hell.

Will indicates that he does not entirely understand Holy Church. He asks to know how the treasure of truth may be obtained. Holy Church reproves him for his dullness and proceeds to an exposition of the psychology of grace. In her previous discussion, Holy Church has shown that the treasure of truth is one with *caritas*. She now shows that the treasure of the heart which leads one to love God is a natural faculty which pertains to charity.[53]

[53] This faculty, speculative rather than practical, is described by Godefroid (Louvain, 1931), p. 315: "ita et respectu finis supernaturalis consequendi quantum ad intellectum, infunditur homini a Deo quidam habitus in quo virtualiter adduntur homini quaedam principia supernaturalia quae divino lumine capiuntur, et haec sunt credibilia de quibus est fides; et quantum ad voluntatem quaedam dispositio vel affectio sive unio spiritualis quae consistit in quadam conformitate ad ipsum finem, et hoc pertinet ad caritatem." In Q. VI of the same quodlibet Godefroid considers the problem of whether it is possible for the natural reason to grasp the speculative principle that one should love God better than oneself. He says, in part, p. 319, "et sic secundum dictamen naturalis rationis habet etiam homo sine gratia iudicare quod Deus est super omnia diligendus, alioquin gratia et caritas destruerent et non perficerent naturam sive naturalem inclinationem." Elementary principles of action as distinguished from metaphysical principles are guided, Godefroid says, p. 84, by synderesis: "Unde omnis notitia quae conscientia dicitur efficaciam habet a primis principiis agibilium quae ad synderesim dicuntur pertinere, quae dicitur esse quidam habitus intellectus naturalis qui est intellectus primorum principiorum in agibilibus." We do not feel that this last concept applies here.

'It is kynde knowyng,' quod he   'that kenneth in thine
                                            herte
For to louye thi lorde   leuer than thi-selue;
No dedly synne to do   dey thouȝ thow sholdest:
This I trowe be treuthe;   who can teche the better,
Loke thow suffre hym to sey   and sithen lere it after.
For thus witnesseth his worde   worche thow there-after;
For trewthe telleth that loue   is triacle of heuene;
May no synne be on him sene   that vseth that spise
And alle his werkes he wrouȝte   with loue as him liste;
And lered it Moises for the leuest thing   and moste like
                                              to heuene,
And also the plente of pees   moste precious of vertues.'

                                                  (140-50)

The first Epistle of John, the book from which Holy Church takes her theme *deus caritas*, contains the doctrine of the "triacle" of heaven by means of which man may learn truth (2.27):

Et vos, unctionem quam accepistis ab eo, maneat in vobis. Et non necesse habetis ut aliquis doceat vos; sed sicut unctio eius docet vos de omnibus; et verum est, et non est mendacium, et, sicut docuit vos, manete in eo.

Bede makes clear the connection between the unction and charity within the human heart which teaches man to observe the laws of God:

Potest unctio de qua loquitur, ipsa Dei charitas intelligi, quae diffunditur in cordibus nostris per Spiritum sanctum, qui datus est nobis (Rom. 5), *quae citissime ad observanda Dei mandata cor quod implet inflammat.*[54]

The "kynde knowyng" pertains to love, and love is God, *Deus caritas*. To illustrate this unity Holy Church introduces Christ in the figure of the plant of peace which originated in heaven but grew also on earth, a figure which is

---

[54] *PL*, 93, 96. The continuation of Bede's comment make clear the reason for Will's failure to grasp Holy Church's teaching. His gift of charity remains unexercised, so that all teaching is in vain: "Quia nisi idem Spiritus cordi adsit audientis, otiosus est sermo doctoris. Nemo ergo docenti homini tribuat quod ex ore docentis intelligat, quia nisi intus sit qui doceat, doctoris lingua exterius in vaccuum laborat." Cf. *Glossa ordinaria, PL,* 114, 698.

elaborated in Passus XVI. Christ's life and mission are briefly sketched. He came upon earth and arose from the dead. He is God, the Redeemer, and also the mediator ("mene") between God and man. Finally, He is *Veritas*, the Judge of men's deeds (150-72). It follows that the only true treasure in earth comes from obeying the precepts of charity, which teach the love of Christ.

Holy Church now recurs to the subject which has afforded the occasion for her lecture to Will, his vision of the Field of Folk and of the use of treasure there. Thus she apostrophizes the rich. They have treasure only if they expend their temporal goods in almsgiving, the symbolic act of charity. Similarly the spiritual pastors ("curators") into whose hands is given the teaching of spiritual truth must conduct themselves according to the precepts of charity; only thus do they possess treasure and provide treasure for their flocks (173-97). This exposition is based on Luke 6.38, which is quoted twice (176, 199). She refers also to Matt. 7.12,13 in the figure of love as the "graith gate" (202ff.):

Omnia ergo, quaecumque uultis ut faciant uobis homines, et uos facite illis; haec est enim lex et prophetae. Intrate per angustam portam, quia lata porta et spatiosa uia est, quae ducit ad perditionem, et multi sunt qui intrant per eam.

The connection between the "golden rule," a fundamental precept of charity, and the narrow gate to Heaven is suggested in the Gospel by the juxtaposition of the verses. The identification of the two is made in the poem.[55]

[55] Thus Holy Church brings her teaching on charity to bear upon the fundamental problem which beset Will at the beginning of the Passus. Since these same chapters in Luke and Matthew have previously served Holy Church in her exposition, the "texts" to which she refers give structural unity to her lesson. It is a unity which escapes the reader who approaches the poem with the idea that the Scriptural references represent mere elaboration or citation of authority.

A further example of this structural unity is the understood transition between the false clergy who have chastity and not charity and the "graith gate" (*angustam portam*) of Matt. 7.13. Matt. 7.15 is concerned with false

The Prologue presents a picture of confusion and disorder, to be understood only by those who know true doctrine. Most of the people of the field are, like Will, in a state of spiritual slumber. It is to rescue him from ignorance that Holy Church descends from the mountain. Utilizing the basic images of speech, clothing, money, food and drink, Holy Church gives Will his preliminary lesson in Truth. *Temporalia* are given by God, not to promote *amor sui*, but for the worship of God. To use them in this way, the will must be guided by the principle of moderation, bestowed by reason. The best treasure is not earthly treasure but the treasure of Truth, which is God. God is love, and to be like him we must practice charity. Those who are charitable possess the treasure of Truth. As the Prologue pictures the world and sets its most fundamental problem, Passus 1 establishes the basic principle governing the use of *temporalia*, charity. Once the Scriptural basis for her argument is understood, Holy Church's exposition becomes clear, proceeding step by step on the basis of the texts. From the point of view of the poem as a whole, Holy Church has set forth certain fundamental theological principles which may be taken as premises for exposition in the rest of the poem. It is here that the poet has the anagogical church, the church celestial, reveal the principles of charity which is the foundation of Jerusalem. She stands as an ideal toward which the allegorical church, the church militant should strive. Tropologically her principles serve to distinguish the true from the false in every status. Although the obligations of rich man and priest differ, both must have charity.

---

prophets, the wolves in sheep's clothing. The transition in the poem is apparently suggested by the same transition in the gospel. For the false curators of 193ff. see 2 Cor. 6.6,7. Again the actual citation and linking in the poem of Luke 6.38 and James 2.20 is illustrated in Bede's citation of Luke 6.38 in his commentary on James 2.13, *PL*, 93,20. Furthermore, the discussion of faith without charity in Jas. 2.14-20 follows the discussion of the *transgressores* already utilized by Holy Church (96) in her sermon on the theme, *deus caritas*.

3. Lady Meed

PASSUS II

IN THE Prologue and in Passus I, Will saw the vision of earth in the perspective of the two final values, Jerusalem and Babylon. He was instructed concerning the treasure of truth and the nature of charity which directs man toward it. At the beginning of Passus II, he wishes to know false, since it is only through the knowledge of evil that fallen man can know good. Holy Church complies with Will's request and tells him to look on his left, where he will see False, Favel, and their companions. Her command to look to the left is clear enough, since the left implies evil.[1] But in looking to the left, Will fails to see False; rather he sees another woman, this one dressed not in linen but in scarlet robes, her hands gleaming with precious stones. Astonished, Will asks who she is. Holy Church replies that she is "Meed," who has deprived her of the loyalty due her and has corrupted lords. Meed is the daughter of False, as Holy Church is the daughter of God. Holy Church quotes the Athanasian Creed, verse 7, and Matt. 7.17 in connection with her genealogy. The first verse is concerned with the divinity of Christ and the Holy Spirit and is used to suggest her anagogical significance as the Eternal Church. The second quotation is tropological, indicating that the true members of the church militant and hence the potential members of the Eternal Church reveal their properly directed wills through good

---

[1] See the *Allegoriae in sacram scripturam, PL,* 112, 1055. A few equivalents are *vita praesens, opus pravum, reprobri homines.*

works.[2] Lady Meed's scarlet robes and the gems strike Will with wonder, just as St. John was struck with wonder, *miratus . . . admiratione magna,* at the sight of the resplendent whore of the Apocalypse, the *filia Babylonis* of Ps. 136. Significantly, the *filia Babylonis* was traditionally associated with the left hand and contrasted sharply with the Church, Jerusalem:

Dextera mea. (id.) Quidquid facis pro aeternis, dextera operatur; si et alio intenderis, sinistra se immiscuit; et in ea delectatus quasi in dextera perdis aeterna . . . . *Filia* (Aug.) Per successionem facta est filia Babylonis civitas malorum, sicut Ecclesia: Jerusalem scilicet, civitas bonorum per successionem filia Sion.[3]

John's vision of the Whore of Babylon is, in the light of the commentaries, clearly related in other ways to the description of Lady Meed and to her function in *Piers Plowman*. First, like Will, John is guided in his vision by Holy Church.[4] Second, there is a striking similarity between the clothing of Lady Meed and that of the Whore (Apoc. 17.4,6):

Et mulier erat circumdata purpura et coccino, et inaurata auro, et lapide pretioso et margaritis. . . . Et miratus sum cum uidissem illam admiratione magna.

Lady Meed is described as follows (8-18):

> And was war of a womman   wortheli yclothed,
> Purfiled with pelure   the finest vpon erthe . . . .

---

[2] St. Bruno, *PL*, 142, 562, explains the verse from the Creed as follows "Quia sicut Pater aeternus est vel omnipotens seu invisibilis, similiter est et Filius et Spiritus sanctus." The traditional explanation of the good tree is given by Bede, *PL*, 92, 38: "Per arborem intelligimus seu bonam seu malam voluntatem. Fructus autem opera, quae nec bonae voluntatis, mala, nec malae esse possunt voluntatis bona, quae fit etiam bona, dum convertitur ad summum et incommutabile bonum, et impletur bono, ut faciat fructum bonum."

[3] *Glossa ordinaria, PL*, 113, 1057. Cf. St. Augustine, Enn. in Ps. 64, *PL*, 36, 773: "Jerusalem ad dexteram erit; Babylon ad sinistram."

[4] The seven angels of the Apocalypse were taken to represent the Church. See the exposition of the Apoc. attributed to St. Augustine, *PL*, 35, 2438. Cf. Bede, *PL*, 93, 177: "*Angelos septem.* Id est, Ecclesiam septiformi gratiam plenam."

Fetislich hir fyngres   were fretted with golde wyre,
And there-on red rubyes . . . .
Hire robe was ful riche   of red scarlet engreyned,
With ribanes of red golde   and of riche stones;
Hire arraye me rauysshed   suche ricchesse saw I neuere;
I had wondre what she was   and whas wyf she were.

Third, the Whore's clothing signifies for the commentators the allurements of falsehood, particularly such allurements as deceive rulers.[5] As Holy Church says, Lady Meed has calumniated Loyalty and lied about her to lords. Her father is False, who has a hypocritical tongue (25-26). Finally, Lady Meed's subsequent attempt to deceive the King (Passus III and IV) is not only suggested by the commentaries concerning the Whore of Babylon, but also in the Scriptural text itself, where the angel describes her as one with whom the kings of the earth have fornicated (Apoc. 17.2), *cum qua fornicati sunt reges terrae*. If Lady Meed is understood in the light of her Scriptural prototype, it becomes clear that she is the direct opposite of Holy Church and that it is her influence which best accounts for the condition of the Field of Folk in the Prologue.[6] Her clothing, symbolic of temporal concern, continues and reinforces the image of clothing established in the opening description.[7] The image of food and drink

[5] E.g., *Glossa ordinaria, PL*, 114, 740: "*Circumdata purpura*. Id est regali veste dicent se reges ut decipiant. *Auro*. Quia videbuntur divina sapientia illuminati." Cf. Bede, *PL*, 93, 183: "In purpura fucus simulati regiminis, in coccino cruentus habitus impietatis demonstratur. *Et inaurata*, etc. Id est omnibus illecebris simulatae veritatis."

[6] On the historical level, Lady Meed was probably meant to suggest Alice Perrers, the mistress of Edward III. We find that such historical suggestions in the poem, however, are illustrative rather than structurally fundamental. Later in the poem, the poet considers both Holy Church and Lady Meed internally, showing what they mean as psychological processes in the mind of the ordinary Christian. In other words, the broad, general contrast in this passus is preliminary to a more minute analysis in other terms.

[7] The contrast between the resplendent temporal clothing of Lady Meed and the simple, unadorned linen with which Holy Church is clothed is also to be found in the Apocalypse. In 16.15, preceding the description of the whore, reference is made to the pure clothing of the just: *Beatus qui uigilat*

is also found in the statement that the Whore makes the
people of the earth drunk (17.2): *et inebriati sunt qui
inhabitant terram de uine prostitutionis eius.* Those who
inhabit the earth, or who love *temporalia,* are made drunk
by Lady Meed in a manner which Holy Church has al-
ready described (1, 27ff.). St. Martin of Lyons describes
these people who are blind and do not fear of the Lord:

Sicut ebrius nihil timet, sic terrenis inhaerentes in tantum excaeca-
buntur amore terrae, ut nec Deum diligent, nec poenas inferi ti-
meant.[8]

The author of *Piers Plowman* was not the first to contrast
the two cities, Jerusalem and Babylon, or the love of God
as opposed to that of *temporalia,* in the figures of two
women. The contrast is explicit in a commentary attributed
to St. Augustine:

*Mulier quam vidisti, est civitas magna, quae habet regnum super
reges terrae*: id est, omnes mali et impii. Sic et de Ecclesia dictum
est: *Veni, ostendam tibi mulierem Agni: et ostendit mihi civitatem
descendentem de coelo.*[9]

But it is clearly implicit in the Apocalypse itself.

Before taking leave of Will, Holy Church refers
directly to the two loves. Those who love her are rewarded
in heaven; those who love Meed lose a "lappe of *caritatis.*"
As St. Augustine had put it,

Duas istas civitates faciunt duo amores: Jerusalem facit amor Dei;
Babyloniam facit amor saeculi. Interroget ergo quisque quid amet,
et inveniet unde sit civis: et si se invenerit civem Babyloniae, ex-
stirpet cupiditatem plantet charitatem.[10]

---

et custodit uestimenta sua, ne nudus ambulet, et videant turpitudinem eius.
According to St. Martin of Lyons, *PL*, 209, 383, these vestments are spirit-
ual, "id est innocentium in baptismo acceptam, et charitatem, et caeteras
virtutes." This passage in turn recalls a more fully developed earlier passage,
Apoc. 3.3-5, which is related in meaning to 1 Thess. 5, where the three
images of clothing, soberness, and wakefulness are brought together.
[8] *PL*, 209, 385. [9] *PL*, 35, 2443.
[10] In Ps. LXIV, *PL*, 36, 773.

She clarifies the distinction by a reference to Ps. 14, which begins, *Domine, quis habitabit in tabernaculo tuo*. Peter Lombard calls this psalm an instructional response

plenae definitionis, quos clare ostenditur qui vere sint de praesenti Ecclesia, et in futura beatificandi. Et est intentio Prophetae comprimere eos qui se jactant esse de Ecclesia, cum non sint.[11]

The psalm is well suited to the poet's purpose, since it presents a specific guide for distinguishing those who falsely claim status within the Church. In the commentary attributed to Bede, the psalm is characterized with relation to Babylon and Jerusalem:

Verba populi in captivitate Babyloniae optantis reditum ad patriam, enumerantisque quibus meritis quis ad hanc pervenire queat.[12]

The psalm is further suited to the poet's purpose since it begins with a reference to the tabernacle which became the Tower on the Toft.[13] It contains, in verse 6, a suggestion for Lady Meed's name:

Qui jurat proxime suo, et non decipit; qui pecuniam suam non dedit ad usuram, et munera super innocentum non accepit.

The three requisite virtues mentioned in this verse, Peter Lombard explains, are not among the seven virtues necessary to those who would dwell in the tabernacle; rather they are fundamental preliminaries to any virtue:

Haec tria non sunt magna, sed qui nec ista multa minus potest loqui veritatem in corde, et non agere dolum in lingua, et non facere malum proximo.[14]

To refuse Meed is not in itself a great positive virtue, but to accept Meed is a very fundamental vice which bars the receiver from the church. In an alternative interpretation of the psalm which applies it to the life of Christ, Lombard

---

[11] *PL*, 191, 167.   [12] *PL*, 93, 556.

[13] Peter Lombard, *PL*, 191, 167, glosses *in tabernaculo tuo* "in praesenti Ecclesia," and *in monte sancto tuo* "in aeterna beatitudine ubi est visio pacis [i.e. Jerusalem] et supereminentia charitatis."

[14] *PL*, 191, 169.

shows that Christ accepted reward, but not against the innocent:

Accepit Christus munera quidam, ut a magis, et quotidie pias oblationes a fidelibus in Ecclesia, sed non contra innocentes, imo animam pro eis dedit.[15]

Christ's act of redemption is the direct opposite of the misuse of reward. Lady Meed represents wrongful reward. She is the daughter of False and is associated with Liar, who instigates the proposed marriage between Meed and False-Fickle-Tongue. The lying characters may have been suggested by verse 3 of the psalm:

Qui loquitur veritatem in corde suo; qui non egit dolum in lingua sua.

Liar and False-Fickle-Tongue are the opposites of those who speak truth, the dwellers in the tabernacle. They constitute an elaboration of the "false speech" image in the Prologue, just as Lady Meed is an elaboration of the clothing and food images. Meed's marriage to False-Fickle-Tongue makes explicit the misuse of temporal reward for the injury of the innocent. In terms of the poem those who consent to this marriage have been "enchanted" by Favel (lying flattery); through Liar's leading they have succumbed to the temptations of earthly reward (40-42).[16] They are those who claim to be of the Church but are not. They are disloyal to Holy Church, to Jerusalem; they are, in short, the Babylonian captives. Will should have no difficulty in evaluating the members of the Field of Folk on the basis of their attitude toward the marriage of Meed; but he himself is not to judge them. In regarding the sinful and their number, he should

[15] *Ibid.*, 170.
[16] Cf. Augustine in Ps. 85.6, *PL*, 36, 963: "venerunt in hanc vitam, et per cupiditates temporales quasi obdormierunt hic; et exceperunt illes divitiae et vanae pompae volaticae, et transierunt: non intellexerunt quantum inde boni posset fieri."

not despair of their salvation or lose hope in God's mercy.[17]

> To-morwe worth ymade   the maydenes bruydale,
> And there miȝte thow wite, if thow wolt   which thei ben
>   alle
> That longeth to that lordeship   the lasse and the more.
> Knowe hem there if thow canst   and kepe thi tonge,
> And lakke hem nouȝt, but lat hem worth   til lewte be
>   iustice,
> And haue powere to punyschen hem   thanne put forth thi
>   resoun. (43-48)

In accordance with Holy Church's teaching, the preparations for the marriage illustrate the principle that devotion to worldly treasure leads to corruption of society. Will cannot "reckon the rout," the number and variety, of those "that ran about Meed." It is Favel, the enchanter of the Folk, who takes the lead in arranging the marriage. The enfeoffment of Meed and False-Fickle-Tongue with the seven vices suggests the fundamental place of concern for *temporalia* in the life of sin. The reward is eternal damnation. Wrong, who represents extortion, forceful oppression, the violent taking of reward to the injury of the innocent, is the first to witness the charter. He is followed by a number of particular representatives, such as reeves, millers, and so on. The deed is attested by Simony and Civil. Finally, Theology objects to the marriage on the

---

[17] Cf. Peter Lombard's discussion of the sin against the Holy Spirit, *Sententiae*, II, XLIII, *PL*, 192, 755: "Ista impoenitentia vel cor impoenitens, quandiu quisque in hac carne vivit, non potest judicari. De nullo enim desperandum est, quamdiu ad poenitentiam patientia Dei adducit: paganus est hodie; judaeus infidelis est hodie; haereticus est hodie; schismaticus est hodie; quid si cras amplectatur catholicam fidem, et sequatur catholicam veritatem? Quis si isti quos in quocumque genere erroris notas, et tanquam desperatissimos damnas, antequam finiant istam vitam agant poenitentiam et inveniant veram requiam et vitam in futuro? *Nolite ergo ante tempus judicare quemquam* (1 Cor. 4). Ex his ostenditur pro singulis peccatoribus in hac vita esse orandum; nec de aliquo esse diffidendum, quia converti potest dum in hac vita est; quia non potest sciri de aliquo utrum peccaverit ad mortem vel in Spiritum sanctum, nisi cum ab hac vita descesserit, nisi forte alicui per Spiritum sanctum mirabiliter revelatum fuerit."

grounds that Meed is a daughter of Amends and thus should not be given to False.[18]

There is no contradiction between Holy Church's claim that Meed is a bastard, the daughter of False, and Theology's statement that Meed is a "moilere," that is, a legitimate child, the daughter of Amends. Holy Church is warning Will, prior to his vision of False, against Lady Meed as the symbol of the misuse of *temporalia*. Theology, a figure in the vision itself, is the first to complain—on abstract grounds appropriate to him—that the marriage of Lady Meed is a flaunting defiance of the true, God-given principle of reward. Theology refers specifically to Luke 10.7: *Dignus est operarius* (122). The Gloss explains that those who labor in the work of God may expect temporal as well as heavenly reward:

Dignus est enim. Nota quod· uni operi praedicatorum duae mercedes debentur: una in via, quae nos in labore sustentat; alia in patria, quae nos in resurectione remunerat.[19]

Simony and Civil have falsely distorted this principle and do not reward the shepherds but the wolves in sheep's clothing. It is against this misuse that Theology protests, and in his protest illustrates Holy Church's generalized initial warning lesson to Will.

Theology may point out evil; it may not actively prevent or destroy evil. Civil agrees to Theology's demands (141) since the civil law is not itself evil; it is evil when it becomes the exclusive concern of ecclesiastics seeking worldly reward, not the true "hire" for religious work. Simony refuses to heed Theology unless money is forth-

[18] If it is objected that there is no clear distinction between the father of Meed and her proposed husband, it should be remembered that, on the other side, Holy Church is both the daughter of God and the bride of God in His aspect Christ; moreover, Holy Church is the mother of the good Christian and the bride of the good Christian. These relationships are allegorically intended so that their specific character may be varied to suit a given context.

[19] *PL*, 114, 284.

coming; that is indicative of Simony's nature—Simony is evil: whatever it does it must do for money. It is through the nature of Simony that False is able to restore his control, challenged by Theology. False gives money to Guile, who spreads it and wins the assent of the people, including False Witness. Meed remains "amaistried" by False (153). The procession represents again the temporal corruption of the world. Its members are those who violate the preliminary virtues to which Holy Church refers in parting from Will. They bear false witness, demand usury, and accept reward to the injury of the innocent.

The truth about the followers of False has been shown, but the world goes on its way. Ecclesiastical officials and false beggars alike are dependent on wrongful reward. They follow False and Meed in an attempt to win the assent of civil authority to their evil ways. Since the purpose of this vision is to show Will the ways in which False may be overcome, Soothness reaches the King's court before False. Soothness declares to Conscience the guile of the following of Meed. Conscience informs the King. The King, moved by Conscience, declares that he will have False and his followers punished. They flee in dread, leaving Lady Meed alone to be attached by the King's officers. Significantly, Liar ultimately finds refuge with the friars:

Freres with faire speche   fetten hym thennes,
And for knowyng of comeres   coped hym as a frere.
Ac he hath leue to lepe out   as oft as hym liketh,
And is welcome whan he wil   and woneth wyth hem oft.
(229-32)

In sharp contrast to Will's first vision of Meed in splendid array, preparing for her triumph when the world will assemble to witness her marriage, she stands alone, "trembling for dread, weeping and wringing." Theology, in telling the truth, and Civil authority in heeding the truth, are able to isolate Meed, to bring her to justice.

57

Civil authority has been invoked by Theology because Meed is a temporal concern. The proper handling of *temporalia* is of fundamental importance to the individual Christian and to the Christian community. "What of the money of the world?" Will has asked Holy Church. Here the answer is being given in vision form; just as Holy Church has shown that kings must take transgressors, here she indicates the function of civil authority and its importance.

PASSUS III

At the beginning of Passus III, Meed is brought before the King; but her trial has not yet been prepared. The King must first consult his council and make up his own mind about Meed's character. Meanwhile, a clerk is commanded to take her away and to make her comfortable. In parting, the King promises to determine what man would be most appropriate as Meed's husband. If she will follow his wit and will, he says, he will forgive her. The King reliant on wit and will recalls the King in the Prologue who was governed by the lower rather than by the higher reason, and whose reign was approved by the lunatic Will.[20] Without his higher faculties, necessary to a good king, the King is unable to recognize Meed's true character and to condemn her accordingly. As soon as Meed comes in contact with the court, which, like the court of the king in the prologue, lacks spiritual leadership, she begins to corrupt it. Instead of worshiping God, its members devote themselves to "myrthe and mynstralcye Mede to plese." Their mirth is jangling to please Meed.[21] The corruption of the court from the justices down to the victualers illustrates the process by which the Field of Folk become distracted from the way of Truth.

When the justices have promised Meed that she may

[20] Cf. Chapter 2, p. 33.   [21] Cf. p. 24 above.

marry where she will in spite of Conscience, they are richly rewarded with cups of gold and silver, rings, and other riches. Lady Meed, we recall, is well equipped to distribute such wealth: *Et mulier erat circumdata purpura et coccino et inaurata auro et lapide pretioso et margaritis, habens poculum aureum in manu sua plenum abominatione et immunditia fornicationis eius.* Clerks, seeking temporal advancement, hasten to her. A friar who appears to confess her is not troubled by his recognition of her as the Whore of Babylon.

'Theiʒ lewed men and lered men   had leyne by the bothe,
And falsenesse haued yfolwed the   al this fyfty wyntre,
I shal assoille the my-selue   for a seme of whete,
And also be thi bedeman   and bere wel thi message,
Amonges kniʒtes and clerkis   conscience to torne.'

(38-42)

He offers to forgive her fornication "for a seme of whete," and thereafter to assist her to the detriment of Conscience. After a shameless confession, she agrees to cover his church, build a cloister, whiten the walls, glaze the windows, and decorate so that everyone will recognize her as a sister of his house. In return, he is to forgive lechery among lords and ladies, *fornicatio Babylonis,* which she considers to be "a course of kynde."[22] In depicting Lady Meed's further activities, the poet emphasizes his deep feeling by turning from the world of vision to the world around him. Indeed, in the remainder of this passus there is a level of historical allegory, the purpose of which is undoubtedly to enforce

[22] The fornication referred to here is symbolic of worship of *temporalia.* Lady Meed's argument on the literal level concerning the lightness of the sin of lechery represents an argument which the church systematically combatted. See Wilkins, *Concilia* (1737), I, 577, 636-37, 659, 689; II, 143. On the friars' use of the sacrament for the accumulation of wealth, and on their association with the wealthy, cf. William of Saint-Amour, *De periculis,* XIV, as described by Perrod, *op. cit.,* p. 159. The number fifty in line 41 may be an ironic reference to the falseness of Lady Meed's penance, since the number fifty was traditionally associated with penance. See Peter Bongus, *Mysticae numerorum significationis liber.* Bergomi, 1585), pp. 106ff.

the pertinency of the lesson, and to clarify it so that no one in the audience could miss its significance.[23] He warns lords against inscribing their good works in church windows, since the practice gives rise to pride and "pompe of the worlde": "Crist knoweth thi conscience and thi kynde wille." Alms should be given in accordance with the precept (Matt. 6.3): *Nesciat sinistra quid faciat dextra.* The appropriateness of this text is clear in Bede's comment:

Videtur enim humanae laudis delectatio in sinistra significari, et in dextera intentio implendi praecepta divina. Et quid est eleemosyna in absconso, nisi in ipsa bona conscientia, quae humanis oculis demonstrari non potest, quae et efficitur in voluntate bona, quamvis non sit quod tribuatur in pecunia; nam in his solet sinistra operari, qui eam non intus, sed foris faciunt.[24]

The text implies an active concept of charity, of fulfilling the divine precepts (*implendi praecepta divina*). It is especially applicable to executors, "meires and maceres" of the King's law, which properly should reflect Divine Law. They are responsible for seeing to it that distributors of earthly food, "brewesteres and bakesteres bocheres and cokes," do not oppress the poor, accepting *munera super innocentum.*[25] Lady Meed encourages the enforcers of the law to accept bribes from the victualers in violation of the principles laid down in the Book of Wisdom, described by the poet as a "sarmoun" by Solomon on the theme *Ignis deuorabit tabernacula eorum qui libenter accipiunt munera* (Job 15.34).[26] The poet concludes his apostrophe with a

[23] In *Piers Plowman* we consider the historical allegory to be not central but illustrative. It serves a purpose similar to that of *exempla* in exposition.

[24] *PL*, 92, 31. On *right* and *left*, cf. note 1 above.

[25] This reading implies a colon after *almesse* in 1.75, rather than a period and a paragraph division as in Skeat's text. However, Skeat himself recognized the connection between 1.75 and what follows. See the EETS ed. of the B-text, p. 35, marginal summary.

[26] The *Liber sapientiae*, which begins *Diligite iustitiam, qui iudicatis terram*, was especially directed to those with judicial powers. See Rabanus, *PL*, 109, 673; Bonaventura, *Opera*, VI, 109, 110. The "theme" of the sermon would naturally not be a text from the sermon itself.

warning to rulers to avoid bribes lest they incur the flames of Hell.

Having taken counsel, the King decides to forgive Meed and to marry her to Conscience, who was not among his advisers, but had come "late fro biʒunde." The King's proposal to unite Conscience and Meed indicates his failure to understand her essentially corrupt nature, but it also indicates a willingness on his part to refer the matter to his higher faculties. The poet is illustrating the fact that doubtful questions should not be subject to the will but should be acted on by the conscience. Theology has explained in general terms what Meed ought to be. Guided only by wit and will, when Conscience is "biʒunde," the King is in no position to judge Lady Meed, who is a corruption of Theology's ideal. Conscience, the internal judge of moral action, recognizes her immediately.

When he is asked to marry Meed, Conscience shows a full knowledge of her iniquity. Her treasure leads many astray. Wives and widows become wantons under her influence. She "felled" the King's father, and poisoned popes. A common whore, she is known by monks, minstrels, lepers. She supports assizors, summoners, sheriffs; she bribes jailors and corrupt courts, where she "copeth the comissarie and coteth his clerkes." She corrupts the system of Papal provisions, supports unlettered bishops, maintains priests' concubines. Justices and the law are subservient to her, to the detriment of all the realm. In short, "clergye and coueitise she coupleth togideres," creating wolves in sheep's clothing to prey on those "that coueyten lyue in trewthe." Lady Meed's reply to these charges is a masterly evasion: her equivocations consist (1) in an attack on the fallibility of Conscience, which, directed toward particulars, may err,[27] (2) in an identification of herself with true hire.

[27] Cf. Godefroid (Louvain, 1932). "Utrum conscientia erronea sic liget quod faciens contra eam mortaliter peccet."

First, Conscience has depended on her eleven times in the past (l.180),[28] and she now offers to bribe him again. She uses Conscience's charge that she has been responsible for the downfall of Edward II to introduce an historical illustration of Conscience's fallibility. Conscience, of course, had simply charged her with responsibility for Edward's downfall, not for his death; but she replies that she never killed a king or "conseilled ther-after." Indeed, Lady Meed contends she would have made a better counsellor of Edward III than did his conscience. The conscience of the King had led him to sign the Treaty of Bretigny, which in the course of subsequent events appeared to have been a mistake. In 1369 the wars were resumed, the English had lost whatever advantage they once had, and they had failed even to receive the indemnity promised in the treaty. If she had been the King's counsellor, she would have advocated complete subjugation of the French and the assumption by Edward of the crown of France, which he had renounced under the terms of the treaty.[29] Second, after this side-glance at history, Meed attempts to establish herself as true hire. Conscience had accused Meed of corrupting people of all classes; she replies in some detail, showing that everyone has the right to hire, and that no one can live without meed.

The King seems convinced by Meed's argument, but Conscience explains that there are two kinds of meed, revealing Lady Meed's sophistry. True reward, or "Amendes," is that kind of meed referred to in Ps. 14, quoted earlier by Holy Church.[30] Whereas Holy Church has simply quoted the first line, leaving the rest to the

---

[28] The number eleven signifies the violation of the commandments. Cf. Peter Bongus, *op. cit.*, pp. 16-21, where a number of patristic authorities are quoted to this effect.

[29] Cf. B. F. Huppé, *PMLA*, LIV (1939), 38-42; J. A. W. Bennett, *PMLA*, LVIII (1943), 566ff.

[30] II, 38. See above, p. 53.

understanding of the reader, Conscience quotes and explains that part of the Psalm referring particularly to meed. False reward is explained with reference to Ps. 25.10: *In quorum manibus iniquitates sunt, dextera eorum repleta est muneribus.* As the text indicates, these are those impious ones who lose their souls. The commentaries find them violators of the precepts of charity; moreover, they misuse God's gifts for worldly purposes, "et quidem datum eis ad obtinendam coelestem patriam, illud convertunt ad accipienda munera saeculi, putantes pietatem esse."[31] Conscience refers to hypocritical priests, who sing masses for money, quoting Matt. 6.5: *Amen, amen receperunt mercedem suam.*[32] In true merchandise there is no meed; it is "a permutacioun apertly a penyworth for an othre." (256)

Having disposed of Meed's attempt to identify herself with true reward, Conscience answers her first charge that conscience in its fallibility is a poorer guide to conduct than she. For this purpose, he uses the story of Saul and Agag which demonstrates the fate of a king who deserts his conscience for personal gain. The succession of David to the throne of Saul gives Conscience an example by means of which to predict the state of the world at the millennium. When the higher reason, which Conscience knows through love (282-83), reigns, Lady Meed will no longer rule. The kingdom of Saul may be taken to represent temporal

[31] Bede, *PL*, 93, 611. Cf. Lombard, *PL*, 191, 265: "Et ita impii et viri sanguinum, illi accipiuntur, qui contra duo praecepta charitatis agunt. . . . *Et dextera eorum repleta est muneribus* id est si quid boni agunt, pro muneribus faciunt, pecuniae, vel laudis humanae vel timoris, quo timent divitem offendere; vel injustae misericordiae, dum quis ne reprehendatur, eo quod contra pauperem fecerit opressit justitiam, et protulit contra veritatem sententiam, parcens pauperi in mala causa; vel ita, quasi munus accepit a paupere, quod non arguitur contra pauperem fecisse. Sed beatus est qui excutit manus ab omni munere. Munera enim excaecant oculos, et vim auctoritatis inclinant."

[32] The *Glossa ordinaria*, *PL*, 114, 99, elaborates: "In his non solum vera merces prava intentione evacuatur: sed vitium simulationis et irrisionis contra Deum augetur."

rule at the time of the poem, the rule of Babylon; the coming rule of David, who was frequently identified with Christ in accordance with the allegorical interpretation of the Old Testament, represents the rule of Jerusalem.[33] At the second coming, loyalty will be justice (II, 46-48); there will be no sergeants in silk hoods (Prol., 210-11). Love and conscience will make "lawe a laborere" (Prol., 145; I, 85-104). Swords will be turned into plowshares, so that each man will either "pleye with a plow pykoys or spade, spynne, or sprede donge or spille hym-self with sleuthe" (Prol. 20-21). Priests will apply their diligence to the singing of Psalms rather than to worldly affairs (Prol. 33-39; 87-97). Kings, knights, and their agents will no longer oppress the commons; there will be one court. There will be no war; Jews and Saracens will worship God. It will be an evil day for Meed and Mahomet, for a good name in heaven will be worth far more than earthly treasure, *melius est bonum nomen quam diuicie multe* (Prov. 22.1).[34] This prophetic passage owes much to the early chapters of Isaiah, from which a verse is quoted (2.4). When the prophet has admonished his people and their princes for sin and for devotion to meed (1.23: *principes tui infideles socii furum. Omnes diligunt munera*), he describes a vision of what the poet calls the Tower on the Toft. The prophet then describes the command to all the peoples of the world to ascend to it during the last days (2.2-3):

Et erit in novissimis diebus praeparatus mons domus Domini in vertice montium et elevabitur super colles, et fluent ad eum omnes gentes, et ibunt populi multi et dicent: Venite et ascendamus ad

---

[33] For a more particular historical application of the story in the A-text, see B. F. Huppé, *PMLA*, XL (1939), 60ff.

[34] Cf. Bede, *PL*, 91, 1001: "Nomen bonum dicit, non quod a turbis vulgi imperiti, sed quod fidelium, quamvis paucorum, testimonio laudetur. . . . Nomen ergo bonum est, nomen religionis, quod divitiis mundialibus jure praefertur."

montem Domini et ad domum Dei Iacob, et docebit nos vias suas, et ambulabimus in semitis eius, quia de Sion exibit lex et verbum Domini de Ierusalem.[35]

The verse in Isaiah immediately following is that partially quoted in the poem:

Et iudicabit gentes et arguet populos multos; et conflabunt gladios suos in vomeres et lanceas suas in falces. Non levabit gens contra gentem gladium, nec exercebuntur ultra ad proelium.

The verse is quoted by Conscience to contrast the reign of Truth with the reign of Meed, so that Jerome's comment on the verse is especially pertinent.

Quod quidem et spiritualiter intellegi potest, quando omnis duritia cordis nostri Christi vomere frangitur, et eradicantur spinae vitiorum, ut sementis sermonis Dei crescat in fruges: et postea labores manuum nostrarum manducemus.[36]

More specifically, the verse with its commentary illustrates the applicability of the reign of Love to the fate of the individual Christian. It recalls Holy Church's parting admonition to Will (ii, 44-48):

And there miȝte thow wite, if thow wolt   which thei ben
                                                          alle
That longeth to that lordeship   the lasse and the more.
Knowe hem there if thow canst   and kepe thi tonge,
And lakke hem nouȝt, but lat hem worth   til lewte be
                                                          iustice,
And haue powere to punyschen hem   thanne put forth thi
                                                          resoun.

The purpose of the vision to instruct Will in his search for Piers Plowman must not be forgotten. The symbols in the commentary bring to mind the hard-working plowmen and the basic image of food.[37]

[35] For the identification of the *domus Domini*, see Jerome's commentary, *PL*, 24, 43-44. Many of the details of Conscience's prophecy are to be found in this commentary.

[36] *Ibid.*, 46.

[37] Further, the image of treasure appears in verse 7: *Et repleta est terra argento et auro, et non est finis thesaurorum eius.* Jerome comments, *ibid.*,

Conscience concludes his argument by quoting a verse from Proverbs. Reduced to intellectual impotence, Meed can resort merely to the weakest verbal quibbling. She attempts to cap Conscience's verse with another from the same chapter, apparently favorable to her: *Honorem adquiret qui dat munera.* . . . Conscience exposes the hollow feebleness of the attempt. She has quoted but half the verse; the remainder simply reinforces Conscience's argument:

> . . . *animam autem aufert   accipientium, &c.:*
> And that is the taille of the tixte   of that that ȝe shewed,
> That theiȝe we wynne worschip   and with mede haue
>   victorie,
> The soule that the sonde taketh   bi so moche is bounde.
>   (346-49)

PASSUS IV

AT THE beginning of Passus IV, the King, who is still unguided by *sapientia,* commands Conscience to kiss Meed and to make peace with her. Without his higher reason, he is unable to understand Conscience's argument or to see how sophistical Meed's defense has been. The ideals of the Celestial City are not perceptible to one who is immersed in Babylonian particulars, and Meed's defense has been based on just those particulars which are visible to the King. Conscience refuses to make peace with Meed without the consent of Reason. The King, whose actions in this passus illustrate the procedure in accordance with which the pilgrim may set upon the true way, commands Conscience to fetch Reason, who, he says, shall rule his realm and govern Conscience. The King's difficulty is indicative of a fundamental problem in the life of any man. The world is so evil that it is difficult to perceive the good

---

49, "Unde Dominus praecepit in Evangelio, ne thesaurizemus nobis thesauros in terra, et ne faciamus thesauros, de quibus fur possit eripere, ad extremum inferens: *Non potestis Deo servire et mammonae.*"

in it. The arguments of False masquerading as Truth have a sophistical charm which causes man to mistrust his moral faculties in favor of "practical" arguments. That is why the King apparently demonstrates a distrust of Conscience in his warning to Conscience that Reason will account with him for his advice. Conscience, however, wishes nothing better than to be ruled by Reason, so that he rides directly to him.

Reason agrees to return with Conscience, but first he makes allegorical preparations for his departure reminiscent of those made by the entourage of Lady Meed before they travel to the court. Instead of the summoners, sheriffs, flatterers, and Liar, Reason is accompanied by the proverbial wisdom of Cato, and that hater of legal jangling Tom True-tongue. His horse, Suffer-til-I-see-my-time, is girded with wise speech and bridled with humility. As Reason and Conscience ride toward London, they are followed by Waryn Wisdom and Witty, who represent aspects of the lower reason. These worldly faculties seek Reason's advice, since they have business at the exchequer and at chancery. But Conscience, observing these particulars, warns Reason against them. They dwell with Meed, winning silver where there is wrath and wrangling, but they will not come "there is loue and lewte." In other words, they have no place in the ideal which Conscience had outlined in the preceding passus. They have come to Reason

For to saue hem, for siluer   fro shame and fram harmes.
(30)

Their efforts at bribery are doomed to failure. They cannot escape from the sorrows of the world because they do not know the true way: the fear of the Lord, which is the beginning of wisdom, is not in them. In relation to them Conscience quotes Ps. 13.3 in part:

*Contricio et infelicitas in uiis eorum, et uiam pacis non cognoue-
runt; non est timor dei ante oculos eorum.*[38]

Since they do not know the true way, Conscience bids
Reason "lete hem ride," and he and Reason ride fast "the
riȝte heiȝe gate." When they reach the court, the King
receives Reason well, and seats him between himself and
his son.

As Conscience has predicted, when Reason shall reign
"kynde loue" shall come and make Law a laborer, bring-
ing peace among the people (III, 297-99). Thus Peace now
comes into the parliament to bring his charges against
Wrong. This Peace is a temporal peace, not to be identified
with the incorruptible Peace of the heavenly Jerusalem,
of which it is merely an earthly imitation. But the preserva-
tion of earthly peace is the function of ideal temporal
government, which, according to medieval political theory
should mirror the order of Heaven. In the face of this
threat to his power in the worldly reign, Wrong, like Witty
and Waryn Wisdom, to whom in his blindness he turns
for assistance, is afraid. Wisdom explains that who works
by will often makes enemies, and that Wrong's only salva-
tion lies in Meed. Wisdom and Witty attempt to bribe the
King, but to no avail. They are more successful in corrupt-
ing Peace with a present so that he asks that the King have
mercy on Wrong. But the King refers him to Reason. Rea-
son explains that he will have no mercy on Wrong until
the world is reformed,[39] until Meed no longer has the

[38] See St. Augustine's comment, *PL*, 36, 142: "*Contritio et infelicitas in
viis eorum*: omnes enim malorum hominum viae plenae sunt laboribus et
miseria. . . . *Et viam pacis non cognoverunt*: hanc utique quam Dominus,
ut dixi, commemorat, in jugo leni et sarcina levi. . . . Timuerunt regnum
terrenum amittere, ubi non erat timor; et amiserunt regnum coelorum, quod
timere debuerant: et hoc de omnibus temporalibus commodis intelligendum
est, quorum amissionem cum timent homines, ad aeterna non veniunt."

[39] The reform of the world is expressed in a list of particulars, all of
which either recall earlier details or anticipate later ones. E.g., Pernel's
purfil anticipates the confession of pride, the covetous clerks recall I, 188ff.,

"maistrye." Meanwhile, Reason will act in accordance with the principle "nullum malum impunitum, nullum bonum irremuneratum." To generalize, the king governed by reason is a just king.[40] Finally, Reason admonishes:

Late ʒowre confessoure, sire kynge   construe this vn-
                                                  glosed;
And ʒif ʒe worken it in werke   I wedde myne eres,
That Lawe shal ben a laborere   and lede a-felde donge,
And Loue shal lede thi londe   as the lief lyketh.
                                              (145-48)

In other words, the King should consult his confessor for guidance in interpreting justice. If he acts accordingly, law will bring sin to light and foster contrition so that love will rule the land. For the kingdom and for the individual Christian, confession is a prerequisite to the rule of Charity. The preparation of the field with dung symbolizes an aspect of penance and is intended to suggest the ensuing confession of the folk. In particular, the "agricultural" image suggests the meeting of the folk with Piers Plowman when their hearts have been made ready in this way for his plow.[41]

But the clerk confessors of the King do not heed Reason; they gloss his admonition for the King's profit, not for the comfort of the people or for the good of the King's soul. They are false to their sacred trust just as the friar at the beginning of the Westminster episode was false in his in shriving Lady Meed. Both false uses of confession are preliminary to the efforts of Lady Meed to restore her challenged domination. When the clerk confessors have fin-

---

and the King's council for the common profit should be contrasted with the council in the Prologue, etc.

[40] These are the words of Innocent III, *De contemptu mundi*, xv. The chapter is entitled "De potentia, sapientia and justitia judicis."

[41] Cf. *Glossa ordinaria* on Luke 13.8, *PL*, 114, 303: "*Mittam stercora.* Id est, malorum quae fecit abominationem ad animum reducam, et compunctionis gratiam cum fructibus boni operis quasi de pinguedine stercoris exsuscitem. Peccata enim carnis stercora dicuntur, quae immittuntur ad radicem arboris, quando pravitatis conscientiae tangitur cogitationis memoria, et dum inde poenitet quasi per tactum stercoris redit ad fecunditatem operis."

ished their gloss, the men of law begin to desert Reason for Lady Meed; Waryn Wisdom, who cannot reform, declares his allegiance to her. In short, the restoration of Meed is under way even in the process of the attempt to control her power. The just, however, assent to Reason, and Wit accords with him. Love and Loyalty hold Meed in little esteem. Loyalty sees its time (II, 46-48) and speaks out loudly against her. Meed mourns, but the evil clerics remain faithful to her. The King is finally convinced of the evils of Meed. He charges her strongly. He will have loyalty and law, and he calls for an end to jangling. Conscience, however, raises an objection: unless the commons will assent, it will be difficult to enforce the law. This objection makes clear the necessity for the confessions in the next passus. Finally, Reason declares that he will rule the realm if Conscience is of their council. The King readily agrees. The scene is now prepared for the great appeal to the Field of Folk.

The purpose of Holy Church's lesson to Will in Passus II-IV is twofold: (1) to show specifically how concern for *temporalia* systematically corrupts all orders of society so as to produce an earthly kingdom like that depicted in the Prologue, and (2) to make clear the process by means of which such a kingdom may be improved. This process, illustrated in the person of the King, applies equally well to the individual Christian, regardless of status. The allegory should be read on more than one level, and should not be limited to the representation of any actual sequence of events. In Scriptural terms, an earthly kingdom may become through *cupiditas* like the Kingdom of Babylon, or through *caritas* like the Kingdom of Jerusalem. In terms of scholastic psychology, a kingdom is evil in so far as it is governed by *scientia* directed from below, good in so far as it is governed by *sapientia*. When *sapientia* does not govern, the *scientia* merely follows the will, and the admonitions of conscience are unheeded. But when both *scientia* and will are governed by *sapientia*, the kingdom, or the individual, exists in *caritas*.

Meanwhile, the order and clarity of the structure in this part of the poem should not be overlooked. Nothing appears in these three passus at random. Lady Meed's journey to Westminster with her entourage is balanced by the journey of Reason with his entourage. As Lady Meed confesses to the Friar at the beginning of her attempt to reestablish herself, so the false confessors are introduced at the end of the episode in a final attempt to defend Meed. The fundamental images of the Prologue are not forgotten. This section explains the general state of affairs in the Prologue and at the same time illustrates the basic principles outlined by Holy Church in Passus I. Throughout the three passus, the reader is constantly reminded of the concept of the two contrasting cities. In the Babylonian figure of Lady Meed the poet shows the ultimate source of evil which spreads throughout the church on earth if it is not checked by proper spiritual guides who exemplify and teach the principles of Holy Church.[42]

[42] The clarity of structure is further revealed in the use of Scriptural quotation in Passus III, with its intricate *concordia verborum*. For example, the quotation of Matt. 6.3 suggests the word *mercedem* in verse 2; it also introduces the idea *manus*, supposedly related etymologically to *munus*. (See Isidore, *Etymologiae*, XI, 66: "Manus dicta quod sit totius corpus *munus*; Bede, *PL*, 93, 612: munus a mano est quando pecunia pro aliquo illicito datur.") The next quotation, Job 15.34, speaks of *eorum qui accipiunt munera*. This is followed by three verses of Ps. 14, with the phrase *munera super innocentum*. A verse from Ps. 25 follows: *in quorum manibus iniquitates sunt, dextera eorum repleta est muneribus*. Next we return to Matt. 6.3 directly: *Amen, amen receperunt mercedem suum*. Finally, the quotation of Isa. 2.4 suggests the *munera* of 1.23 and the *thesaurus* of 2.8. Matt. 6.2 also contains the word *synagogis*, echoed in the *tabernacula* of Job 15.34, the *tabernaculo* of Ps. 14, the *domus* of Ps. 25.8, and the *domus* of Isa. 2.2. On the general principles involved here, consult Th.-M. Charland, *Artes praedicandi* (Ottawa, 1936); E. Gilson, "Michel Ménot et la technique du sermon medieval," and "De quelques raisonnements scriptuaires au Moyen Age," in *Les idées et les lettres* (Paris, 1932).

4. Piers Plowman

PASSUS V

In Passus iv, the promises of the King to put down Lady Meed prepared for the sermon of Reason to the people in Passus v. Conscience had warned the King that unless the commons assented it would be difficult to enforce the new law, but Reason had promised to do all in his power to aid him. After the King agrees to be ruled by Reason at the close of Passus iv, we find him appropriately in church at the beginning of Passus v. The dreamer awakes momentarily, and when he dreams again he sees the Field of Folk preparing to hear Reason's sermon. Reason begins with a warning of God's wrath as evidenced in the pestilences and storms afflicting the world, symbols of His more terrible wrath on the Day of Judgment. He addresses generally the wasters of spiritual food and those who come "in contenauce of clothyng" (Prol. 22, 24):

> He bad wastoure go worche   what he best couthe,
> And wynnen his wastyng   with somme manere crafte.
> And preyed Peronelle   her purfyle to lete,
> And kepe it in hir cofre   for catel at hire nede. (24-27)

These folk represent the fundamental evils which beset the Field of Folk in whatever status. He then turns to the members of the three states, warning the people in each to fulfill their obligations. The members of the active state or *status conjugatorum* are warned in terms of disciplining their wives and children. The husband in the active status has as definite obligations to rule those in his charge as does

72

the King in ruling the realm. His obligations are expressed symbolically in terms of the basic images of jangling, clothing, and work (28-33).[1] Parents should instruct their children in the proper handling of *temporalia* (34-41). Reason admonishes those in the prelatical status to teach by example, to live in accordance with the ideal they are supposed to represent (42-45). Those in the contemplative status are warned to live in accordance with their rule (46-48). Turning to the heads of the lay and ecclesiastical orders, he warns the King to cherish the people, who constitute his treasure, and he advises the Pope to govern himself. In general, those in the active status are urged to govern their subordinates, whereas those in the contemplative and prelatical status are told to govern themselves so that they may be fit to govern others. Finally, those who execute the law, either temporal or ecclesiastical, are admonished to covet truth rather than Meed if they wish to be known by God on the Day of Judgment. In short, the folk are reminded at the beginning and at the end of the sermon concerning the Last Day, and are urged to direct their pilgrimage toward Truth.

As a result of Reason's sermon, Repentance causes Will to weep in contrition. The confessions of the various sins follow. That is, *sapientia* has directed the will away from *temporalia* toward charity. Will here should be taken not only as the allegorical character but also as the collective will of the folk. It is significant that the confessions are made in terms of the basic images developed in the Prologue—food, clothing, money, and jangling—and that emphasis is placed on the sins of avarice, gluttony, and sloth. Wrath is also developed in some detail. Although some of the confessions are short and others display an

---

[1] Skeat suggests that the "wyuen pyne" was used to punish scolds (l. 29). We have assumed this to be the correct explanation. It should be observed that charity consists in just correction and guidance rather than in indulgence. This theme is developed more fully later in the poem.

unusual dramatic vigor, they are generally in accordance with traditional pastoral theology. Just as Will represents the will of the folk, Repentance is their collective repentance who guides them in the cleansing of their souls and causes them to pray through him afterward. The prayer of Repentance is essentially a statement of faith followed by a plea for amendment and mercy, combining most of the elements of the Apostolic Creed.[2] It ends with a conventional formula, asking mercy for sins "in worde, thouȝte, or dedes" (513). Aside from the fact that a recitation of the Creed was conventional at confession,[3] the statement of faith here is symbolic of the condition of folk. They have put aside evil and embraced the faith, thus making their preliminary step on the road to Truth. To the spiritual pilgrim the three theological virtues—faith, hope, and charity—were a necessity. It was widely held that although charity is the greatest of these virtues, in actual practice, faith must be obtained first. It may then be followed by hope and finally by charity.[4]

When the folk have acquired faith, Hope appears to them with a horn, *deus, tu conuersus viuificabis nos*, which is a promise of mercy.[5] His message causes the folk to cry

[2] The prayer and the Creed begin in much the same manner and are roughly parallel. The following points may need elucidation. The quotation *Captivam duxit captivitatem* (Eph. 4.8) is explained in the *Glossa*, *PL*, 114, 595: "Id est eos quos diabolus captivaverat a paradiso, et proprios mundi et inferni fecerat, iterum captivos fecit Christus, dum ad coelum reducuntur." It thus refers to the phrase in the Creed, *Descendit ad inferna*. The "mele tyme of seintes (l. 500) refers to the phrase *sanctorum communionem*. The quotation *Non veni vocare iustos, set peccatores ad penetenciam* (Matt. 9.13) refers to the phrase *remissionem peccatorum*.

[3] See, for example, Grosseteste, *Epistolae* (Rolls Series, 1861), 156-57, and similar admonitions in Wilkins, *Concilia*, I, 732, etc.

[4] On the relative positions of Faith and Charity, cf. Godefroid (Louvain, 1931), 316.

[5] The text is a partial quotation of Ps. 70.20, which continues *et de abyssis terrae iterum reduxisti me*. Peter Lombard comments, *PL*, 191, 655: "Ecce clementia in conversis. *Et de abyssis terrae*, id est de subversione peccati, *iterum* spe *reduxisti me*." The subsequent quotations in the text from Ps. 31.1, and Ps. 35.7 reinforce the idea of the mercy of God.

"vpward to Cryst" for grace "Treuthe to seke." The grace
that they desire is charity.[6] Without it they bluster forth as
beasts, unable to find the true way. They are like the sheep
without a shepherd whom Christ saw and pitied (Matt.
9.36): *Videns autem turbas misertus est eis, quia erant
vexati et iacentes sicut oves non habentes pastorem.*[7] They
meet a worldly pilgrim who does not know the way to
Truth, (532-43) for he has not heard the earlier words
of Reason:

> And ȝe that seke seynte Iames   and seintes of Rome,
> Seketh seynt Treuthe   for he may saue ȝow alle.
>
> (57-58)

In contrast, Piers Plowman, who now makes his first en-
trance (544) shows that he is the true pastor and guide
to Truth. He represents the tradition and ideal of the good
plowmen, the producers of spiritual food: the patriarchs,
the prophets, Christ, St. Peter, the apostles, the disciples,
and those of their followers who actually fulfill the ideal
of the prelatical life. He, like the disciples, has heeded
Christ's call for workers in the spiritual harvest, made
when Christ saw the need of the people lost *sicut oves non
habentes pastorem* (Matt. 9.37, 38):

*Tunc dicit discipulis suis: Messis quidem multa, operarii autem
pauci; rogate ergo Dominum messis, ut mittat operarios in messem
suam.*

As Piers Plowman says, he has served him forever, "bothe
to sowe and to sette" (547) as long as he could. He has
had "huire of hym wel," (557) for as Christ says to his
workers in the harvest (Matt. 10.10): *dignus est operarius*

---

[6] Cf. Peter Lombard, *Sententiae*, II, XXVII, IX, in Bonaventura, *Opera*,
II, 651.

[7] Bede comments, *PL*, 92, 50, "Misertus est eis, constituens pastores,
magistros videlicet, ad viam veritatis ducentes." For the *pastores* see below.
Cf. Mark, 6.34, and Bede, *ibid.*, 191, 192. A similar figure is used by
Chaucer, "Truth," 18: "Forth, pilgrim, forth! Forth, beste, out of thy stal!"

cibo suo.[8] Piers' name and perhaps his first exclamation, "Peter" suggest the first of the workers in the harvest (Matt. 10.2): *primus Simon, qui dicitur Petrus.* The name has important allegorical significance. In commenting on Matt. 10.2, Bede derives the word *Peter* from *petra,* which signifies Christ.[9] The relationship between Peter and Christ is further reinforced by Matt. 16.18-19:

> *Et ego dico tibi quia tu es Petrus, et super hanc petram aedificabo Ecclesiam meam, et portae inferi non praevalebunt adversus eam, et tibi dabo claves regni caelorum, et quodcumque ligaveris super terram, erit ligatum et in caelis et quodcumque solveris super terram erit solutum et in caelis.*

The exclamation "Peter!" thus not only suggests the character of the guide sought by the pilgrims; it also suggests their goal. Piers' statement that conscience and "Kinde Witte" (*scientia*) showed him the way and kept him on it (546-48) was probably meant to suggest the *claves regni caelorum,* which were thought to consist of either the ability or the authority to judge (conscience) and to discern (*scientia*). The seed which he sows are the four cardinal virtues (XIX, 269ff.). The power of the keys, the poet tells us, was left by St. Peter with charity and these virtues (Prol. 100-6), implying perhaps his belief that the power depends more on ability than on status.[10] The beasts Piers follows are the four evangelists (XIX, 256ff). Within and without, he has engaged in the manifold labors of charity (551-55). His reward for these labors is the Heavenly Kingdom to which he offers to

[8] Cf. Luke 10.7, and the surrounding text. An explanation for the appearance of the worldly pilgrims may be found in Matt. 10 and Luke 10. The first has a bag, in violation of the admonition *Nolite portare sacculum;* he mentions other pilgrims with pikes and scrips, in violation of the admonitions *Nolite possidere . . . peram . . . neque . . . virgam.*

[9] *PL,* 92, 51: "Petrus dicitur ad distinctionem alterius Simonis. Idem ergo est Latine Petrus quod Syriace Cephas, et in utraque lingua nomen a petra est derivatum: de qua petra Paulus ait: *Petra autem erat Christus.*"

[10] This is Peter Lombard's position, *Sententiae,* IV, XIX. It was not universally accepted and has been abandoned by the modern church.

76

direct the pilgrims.[11] In his offer to guide the pilgrims to Truth, Piers unmistakably demonstrates his prelatical function. He illustrates the principle of true reward by example; he refuses to accept remuneration for showing the way (III, 250-52). Piers proceeds at once to explain to the pilgrims the one theological virtue they lack, charity. They must begin with humility, the opposite of pride, which will activate conscience so that Christ may be aware that they have fulfilled the two precepts. Since it is from these precepts that the law depends (Matt. 22.37-40), Piers follows them with a generalized exposition of the commandments.[12] These lead to speaking Truth and thus to the Castle of Truth in the human heart, a figure which elaborates in detail Holy Church's instruction regarding the treasure of Truth. The image of the tower appeared briefly in Holy Church's explanation of man's proper use of treasure (1, 54-57). Moreover, just as Will was instructed to look within himself to find the way to Truth through charity (1, 140ff.), Piers tells the pilgrims that they will find Truth in their own hearts "in a chain of charity." Again, the emphasis on Love, Humility, and Loyalty in Piers' directions recalls a similar emphasis not only in Holy Church's discourse, but also in the advice of Conscience to the King. The relation of Piers' directions to the instruction of Will is clear in the fact that the walls

[11] Line 559 suggests strongly the Parable of the Vineyard and the reward indicated there.

[12] Like the Apostles' Creed above, the commandments are rearranged, with some omission. The purpose of the rearrangement is evidently to emphasize the contrast between true mirth and jangling. Piers begins with Beth-buxum-of-speche, which is followed by *Honora patrem*, etc., symbolic of true praise, and Swere-nouȝte. He concludes with Bere-no-false-witnesse. The first and sixth commandments are omitted because they have little thematic relation to the rest of the poem. This does not mean, however, that the author forgot them or expected his audience to forget them; they would be implicit in any suggestion of the law. In general, the author of *Piers Plowman* allows himself liberties with fundamental formulas of the faith, a knowledge of which he could take for granted.

of the castle, Sapience, are designed to curb Will, and in the identification of the fiend with Wrath, the sin for which Will has repented and to which Will as a character in the poem seems especially prone. The figure of the castle embodies more specific directions than any given previously. Here the soul is defended by Mercy, Sapience, and Faith; and it is protected by Love and Humility. One attains mercy through prayer maintained by penance and alms. Before approaching the castle one must have grace, and must perform penance in order to obtain purity. His position must be maintained by a careful avoidance of vices and a reliance on the virtues opposing them.[13]

When Piers warns the pilgrims finally that the way will be especially hard for those who do not practice the virtues (634-38), some sinners, represented by an apeward, a cutpurse, and a waferer, begin to despair. Piers assures them that Mercy is "syb to alle synful" so that they may obtain grace if they set out in time. But a pardoner, one of the worst of the janglers, swears by St. Paul that he may not be known by Truth;[14] and followed by a whore, who will pretend to be his "sustre," he turns deliberately from the way in the sin against the Holy Spirit. Reason has attempted to win the commons to the right road. He has been successful in so far as he has caused them to put their sins aside through confession and repentance. Having repented, the people are prepared for the guidance of Piers, who teaches them that the road leads through obedience to the avoidance of sin. Piers' teaching in this passus typifies the activity of the true members of the prelatical status who give to the people the spiritual food of God's word. Will is shown here the kind of guidance most needed by the Church militant in its struggle against cupidity.

[13] For Scriptural precedents for the individual's tower, see Luke 6.48; Prov. 9.1.
[14] Cf. 2 Tim. 3.1-5.

PASSUS VI

Early in the Prologue, the poet describes the plowmen.

Some putten hem to the plow	pleyed ful selde
In settyng and in sowyng	swonken ful harde,
And wonnen that wastours	with glotonye destruyeth.

(20-22)

In Passus VI, we see these plowmen in the person of Piers, their archetype, hard at work in the field, planting virtues among the folk, and, in contention with wasters, extirpating vices. The folk must prepare the field before they can find the castle of Truth, a construction perhaps suggested to the poet by Prov. 24.27-34:

Praepara foris opus tuum et diligenter exerce agrum tuum, ut postea aedifices domum tuam. Ne sis testis frustra contra proximum tuum, nec lactes quemquam labiis tuis. Ne dicas: Quomodo fecit mihi, sic faciam ei, reddam unicuique secundum opus suum. Per agrum hominis pigri transivi et per vineam viri stulti; et ecce totum repleverant urticae, et operuerant superficiem eius spinae, et maceria lapidum destructa erat: quod cum vidissem, posui in corde meo, et exemplo didici disciplinam. Parum, inquam, dormies, modicum dormitabis, pauxillum manus conseres ut quiescas; et veniet tibi quasi cursor egestas, et mendicitas quasi vir armatus.

Bede's comment on this passage makes clear many of the events of Passus VI; the work of the field is the preparation of the human heart through good works for the building of the tabernacle. Negligence in the work of the field signifies worldly concupiscence:

Quid est praeparato opere agrum diligenter exercere, nisi evulsis iniquitatum sentibus actionem nostram ad frugem retributionis excolere? Et quid est post agri exercitium ad aedificium domus redire, nisi quod plerumque ex bonis operibus discimus, quantum vitae munditiam et in cogitatione constituamus? Ille quippe bene mentis domum aedificat, qui primum agrum corporis a spinis vitiorum purgat, ne si desideriorum sentes in carnis argo proficiant, intus tota virtutum fabrica fame boni crescente destruatur.—*Ne sis testis frustra contra proximum tuum,* etc. Et haec ad exercitium agri nostri, id est, ad cultum bonae actionis pertinent, innocentem

79

videlicet proximum falso testimonio non laedere, peccanti cuilibet, fiduciam amplius peccandi, adulando non tribuere; malum pro malo non reddere; sic enim fit ut cum primo actus exterius bene composueris, postmodum ad interioris quoque hominis excolendam munditiam pertingas, et quasi post exercitium agri, etiam mentis habitaculum piis cogitationibus ornare altiusque constituere incipias. Quod quia reprobi facere dissimulant, recte subditur: *Per agrum hominis pigri transivi,* etc. Per agrum vineamque pigri ac stulti transire, est cujuslibet vitam negligentis inspicere, quam urticae vel spinae replent, quia in corde negligentium prurientia terrena desideria, et punctiones pullulant vitiorum. Juxta quod scriptum est: *In desideriis est omnis otiosus.* Et maceria lapidum in vinea vel agro stulti destructa jacet, cum coepta virtutum munimina, vel improbitate hominum malorum deceptus, vel immundorum spirituum persuasione callida, quisque negligens perdit.[15]

If the commons are to be turned to the highway of Truth, so that Reason and Love may reign in the kingdom, each individual must prepare the field of his own heart for the building of the tabernacle there. In this task it is the function of Piers to assist as guide and counsellor. The confessions showed the course to be taken by the folk as a whole; in the plowing of the half-acre, we see the problem as it involves the individuals in the field.

Piers outlined to the ladies and to the knight the basic principles of their duties in the good community. Women are to sew and to spin for Church and for the needy, helping Piers in his charitable work. He in turn will supply spiritual food for all of them (17-21). The knight is to hunt and to put down those who interfere with the production of spiritual food, the hares, foxes, boars, and bucks, who are transgressors. He is to be generous and merciful to his tenants "maugre Medes chekes," following humility and reason. As for Piers himself, he will dress as a pilgrim in clothing "yclouted and hole," carrying a hopper of bread-corn, the seeds of his calling, instead of a scrip (59-

[15] *PL,* 91, 1010-12. Cf. *PL,* 92, 172-73.

66).[16] When he has finished his sowing he will go on pilgrimage "pardoun for to haue." All those among the folk who help him with his sowing will win pardon with him, except the janglers, who he says, quoting Ps. 68.29, *deleantur de libro viventium.* Jack, Ionet, Danyel, Denote, the Friar, and Robin represent those who think to be saved, but who are immersed in temporal concern so that they wander from the way and are enemies of the Church.[17] Because they do not work in the labor of salvation, they are not true members of the Church, for the name of Holy Church, the bride of Piers, is Dame Worche-whan-tyme-is, and her children, the true faithful, are loyal.[18] The purpose of Piers' testament (88-106) is to show his relation to the church.

Literally the will seems conventional enough, not inappropriate to a plowman with a wife and children about to depart on a pilgrimage. Piers leaves his soul to God, his remains to his parish church where he has paid his tithes faithfully and expects to be remembered in masses. His wife and children shall have his goods, except for those things he needs for his pilgrimage. Allegorically, there is nothing presumptuous in Piers' confidence that God will receive and protect his soul, for as the representative of the spirit of Christian teaching, Piers, like Christ, can place his soul in the hands of the Lord (Luke 23.46). The stipulation that the church will keep his bones refers to the relics

[16] See Chapter 2, notes 5 and 20.

[17] See Peter Lombard's comment, *PL*, 191, 637-41.

[18] On the identification of the wife of Piers with the Church, cf. Bruno Astensis on Matt. 8. 14-15, *PL*, 165, 142: "Scire enim oportet quae sit uxor Petri. . . . Petri namque uxor ecclesia est, quoniam ei a Domino specialiter tradita est; dicente Domino: 'Si diligis me, pasce oves meas (John 21.18).' " On her name see Gal. 6.10: *Ergo, dum tempus habemus, operemur bonum ad omnes.* Peter Lombard comments, in part, *PL*, 192, 165: "Tempus seminandi est praesens vita qua currimus; in hac licet nobis quod volumus seminare. Cum vero transierit, operandi tempus auferetur." Cf. Bede on John 9, *PL*, 92, 758; *Glossa ordinaria*, *PL*, 114, 587.

which were contained in Christian altars. The tithe of "corne and catel" represents the fruit of Piers pastoral labor, and he is commemorated in every mass in the name of Christ. The institution of the church receives from him the Treasury of Mercy to distribute among his "douȝtres" and his "dere Children." Piers has paid his debt to God, and with the remnant of his goods he can plow men's hearts and provide spiritual food for them. Since Piers represents a tradition, the will does not indicate an accomplished act, but a continuing process, an arrangement which the good plowmen of every age make with the church.

Many of the folk assist Piers at his work of sowing, but there are some who "hulpen erie his half-acre with 'how! trollilolli' " (118). When Piers reprimands them, they feign themselves blind or crippled. Piers recognizes them as wasters; they are the wasters of spiritual food whom we saw in the Prologue, false contemplatives and preachers who pretend to pray for Piers but who actually interfere with his work. At Piers' repeated warning "gan a wastoure to wrath hym" (154). A brytoner boasts, "we wil haue owre wille!" (158) reinforcing the pertinence of the figure of the half-acre to the soul of the individual Christian and to Will in particular. Since the wasters are spiritual rather than temporal, the Knight can do no more than warn them; their correction is not really in his province. The literal level of the remainder of the passus is concerned with Hunger's activities and the principles of alms. It shows that Hunger will force men to work through false fear of temporal harm, but that the evocation of such hunger is not ultimately beneficial. Further, Hunger's colloquy with Piers sets the principles of practical charity. Man must work if he is able; if he is unwilling to work, he should be fed with "barley bread and water"; if he is unable to work, he should be fed well. Alms should never be withheld entirely, and the judgment of false beggars should

82

be left to God. The chief significance of the passus, how-
ever, lies on the allegorical level.

Since he is the type of the good priest, Piers wishes all
of the folk to be workers in the field. As St. Gregory puts
it, "Agricolae quippe hujus terrae sunt hi qui, minori loco
positi, quo valent zelo, quanto possunt opere, ad erudi-
tionem sanctae Ecclesiae in praedicationis gratia cooperan-
tur. . . . Pia etenim pastorum mens, quia non propriam
gloriam, sed auctoris quaerit, ab omnibus vult adjuvari
quod agit."[19] The folk are not only assisting in the work
of Piers with regard to the Church; they are helping him
to cultivate their own hearts. The two kinds of sowing are
clarified by Bede: "Homo qui seminat a plerisque Salvator
intelligitur, quod in animis credentium seminet. Ab aliis
homo ipse seminans in terra sive agro suo, hoc est in seme-
tipso, et in corde suo."[20] Piers plants the virtues in the
hearts of the folk while they are at work preparing them-
selves. The wasters neither assist Piers in the Church nor
cultivate themselves. Piers says to them:

> ȝe wasten that men wynnen   with trauaille and with tene,
> Ac Treuthe shal teche ȝow   his teme to dryue,
> Or ȝe shal ete barly bred   and of the broke drynke.
> But if he be blynde or broke-legged   or bolted with yrnes,
> He shal ete whete bred   and drynke with my-selue,
> Tyl god of his goodnesse   amendement hym sende.
>
> (135-40)

The barley bread may be taken to represent temporal
rather than spiritual bread;[21] the water, the opposite of the
honey of sapientia, is "dulcedo hujus vitae."[22] The blind,
the lame and the imprisoned are those who are caught in
the world but who desire spiritual food.[23] God will amend

---

[19] *Moralia*, XXIII, XXIII, *PL*, 76, 247.

[20] *PL*, 92, 172-73.   [21] Cf. Gregory, *PL*, 76, 248.

[22] Cf. Peter Lombard on Ps. 80.15, *Et cibavit illos ex adipe frumenti;
et de petra melle saturavit eos, PL*, 191, 775; and on Ps. 123.2, *ibid.*, 1149.
Here it is compared with the food of hogs, for which see below.

[23] On the blind, see Luke 18.35ff. and Bede, *PL*, 92, 558. The lame are

them. Their wheaten bread is the body Christ, and their drink is the wine of the sacrament; in other words, they receive the spiritual food of the word of God.

We have seen the results of negligence in the work of the field indicated in Chapter 24 of Proverbs quoted above. It leads to temporal desires and dissatisfactions. Moreover, *Parum, inquam dormies . . . et veniet tibi quasi cursor egestas, et mendicitas quasi vir armatus*. Hunger represents tropologically the lack of spiritual food in forgetfulness of the Creator; "Fames . . . indigentia verbi veritatis est, in oblivione Creatoris."[24] Piers calls Hunger to control the wasters, but instead of ridding himself of them completely, Piers threatens to let them eat with hogs, as the prodigal son once did (Luke 15). Those who eat with hogs partake only of the food of the flesh and of the doctrines of the world:

Et cupiebat implere ventrem suum de siliquis quas porci manducabant. Siliquae quibus porcos pascebat sunt doctrinae saeculares, sterili suavitate resonantes, de quibus laudes idolorum fabularumque ad Deos gentium vario sermone atque carminibus percrepant, quibus daemonia delectantur. Unde cum iste saturari cupiebat, aliquid solidum et rectum quod ad beatam vitam pertineret invenire volebat in talibus, et non poterat.[25]

In other words, Piers threatens to excommunicate the wasters so that they may have no access to spiritual food, but only to miserable worldly doctrines and to the discom-

---

in Matt. 15.30 and Bede, *ibid.*, 76. For the chained see Ps. 68.33 and *Glossa ordinaria*, *PL*, 113, 950. In this psalm to which the poet has already referred, these chained prisoners of the Lord are contrasted with those who are deleted from the book of life, that is, with the wasters (ll.77-78). See also Bede on John 9.4, *PL*, 92, 758.

[24] Bede on Matt. 15, *PL*, 92, 522. Ample evidence for the conventionality of this interpretation of hunger may be found in St. Bonaventura, *Opera*, VII, 391ff.

[25] Bede, *PL*, 92, 523. Cf. Bonaventura, *Opera*, VII, 392: "Siliqua . . . designat delectationes vitiorum." Bonaventura quotes the *Glossa interlinearis* to the effect that "Siliqua est genus leguminis sonoris follibus et vacuis, quod ventrem magis onerat, quam reficit." Cf. the phrase in line 218: "benes for bollyng of her wombe."

fort of sin. Under this threat, dissimulators go back to
work,

For a potful of peses that Peres hadde ymaked
An heep of heremites henten hem spades,
And ketten here copes and courtpies hem made,
And wenten as workemen with spades and with
schoueles,
And doluen and dykeden to dryue aweye hunger.

(189-93)

Piers has succeeded where the secular arm represented by
the Knight failed; he has caused those who clothe them-
selves falsely in the habit of a status to which they do not
belong to resume their true labor in the field. Only Piers
can correct dissimulators who usurp positions of spiritual
responsibility for worldly ends. He alone can give the food
of Jerusalem to the Babylonian captives.

To illustrate the use of the weapon with which Piers at-
tacked the wasters, the poet presents a dialogue be-
tween Piers and Hunger. Piers asks what is to be done
with the beggars who will not work; since they are all his
brothers, he does not wish to be too harsh with them. Hun-
ger replies to the effect that excommunication may be used
against those who are able to work but who refuse to do
so:

Bolde beggeres and bigge that mowe her bred biswynke,
With houndes bred and hors bred holde vp her hertis,
Abate hem with benes for bollyng of her wombe;
And ȝif the gomes grucche bidde hem go swynke,
And he shal soupe swettere whan he it hath deseruid.

(216-20)

But those who have been harmed by fortune or by the
counsels of evil men should be treated with love. Hun-
ger quotes part of Gal. 6.2, but the entire passage, 6.1-10,
is relevant, stressing as it does the importance of a chari-
table attitude in Piers.

Fratres, etsi praeoccupatus fuerit homo in aliquo delicto, vos, qui spirituales estis, huismodi instruite in spiritu lenitatis, considerans te ipsum, ne et tu tenteris. Alter alterius onera portate, et sic adimplebitis legem Christi. Nam, si quis existimat se aliquid esse, cum nihil sit, ipse se seducit. Opus autem suum probet unusquisque, et sic in semetipso tantam gloriam habebit et non in altero. Unusquisque enim onus suum portabit. Communicet autem is qui catechizatur verbo ei qui se catechizat in omnibus bonis. Nolite errare: Deus non irridetur. Quae enim seminaverit homo, haec et metet. Quoniam qui seminat in carne sua de carne et metet corruptionem; qui autem seminat in spiritu, de spiritu metet vitam aeternam. Bonum autem facientes non deficiamus; tempore enim suo metemus non deficientes. Ergo, dum tempus habemus, operemur bonum ad omnes, maxime autem ad domesticos fidei.[26]

The attitude here expressed recalls the passage from Proverbs 24: *Ne dicas: Quomodo fecit mihi, sic faciam ei, reddam unicuique secundum opus suum.* Hunger reinforces this principle by quoting part of Rom. 12.19. Again, the surrounding text is relevant (12.16-19):

Nolite esse prudentes apud vosmetipsos, nulli malum pro male reddentes, providentes bona non tantum coram Deo, sed etiam coram omnibus hominibus. Si fieri potest, quod ex vobis est, cum omnibus hominibus pacem habentes, non vosmetipsos defendentes, carissimi, sed date locum irae; scriptum est enim: Mihi vindicta, ego retribuam, dicit Dominus; sed, si esurierit inimicus tuus, ciba illum; si sitit, potum da illi; hoc enim faciens carbones ignis congeres super caput eius. Noli vinci a malo, sed vince in bono malum.[27]

Piers, or the good priest, should supply spiritual food even to his enemies. Finally, Hunger quotes Luke 16.9: *Facite vobis amicos de mammona iniquitatis,* warning Piers to make himself beloved among the humble.[28]

[26] The *Glossa ordinaria, PL,* 114, 585, opens its explanation of this passage with the remark, "Hactenus toti Ecclesiae locutus est improbando legem, et commendando gratiam, modo se convertit ad praelatos qualiter tractent subditos, scilicet leniter, quia etiam fratres sunt, etsi superiores." Cf. Piers in line 210: "They are my blody bretheren." Cf. note 18, above.

[27] Peter Lombard, *PL,* 191, 1502, glosses *locum irae* as "judicio Dei." The Day of Judgment as indicated later in the passus. Cf. Holy Church's parting admonition to Will, Chapter 3, note 17.

[28] On the significance of the verse, see Bede, *PL,* 92, 530-31: "Mam-

Piers still has some doubts concerning the harsh treatment of the beggars, so that he inquires, "Miȝte I synnelees do as thow seist?" (232). Hunger assures him that work in the field is absolutely necessary to salvation, quoting Gen. 3.19: *In sudore vultus tui vesceris pane tuo.* The applicability of the verse is plain in Rabanus' comment: "Illum hic panem intellige qui ait: *Ego sum panis vitae qui de coelo descendi* (John 6). Quo in sudore vultus nostri vescimur, quia ad conspectum divinae celsitudinis non nisi per laborem necessariae afflictionis ascendimus."[29] To reinforce his point, Hunger quotes Prov. 20.4: *Propter frigus piger arare noluit; mendicabit ergo aestate, et non dabitur illi.* Bede's comment on this verse shows that those who do not labor will not be rewarded in Jerusalem:

Qui nunc propter desidiam in Dei servitio laborare neglexit, venturo die regni mendicabit, et non dabitur ei, quia quaecunque seminaverit homo, haec et metet. Bene ergo regnum Dei aestate comparatur, quia tunc moeroris nostri nubila transeunt, et vitae dies aeterni solis claritate fulgescunt, et fructus laboris in gaudio percipitur.[30]

The parable of the talents (Matt. 25.14ff.; Luke 19.11ff.) is used to illustrate the principle that he who works will be rewarded but he who does not work will lose everything.[31] Finally, Hunger quotes Ps. 127.2: *Labores manuum tuarum, quia manducabis: beatus es, et bene tibi erit.* Peter

monam iniquitatis ob hoc appellat istam pecuniam quam possidemus ad tempus, quia mammona divitiae interpretantur. Nec sunt istae divitiae nisi iniquis, qui in eis constituunt spem atque copiam beatitudinis suae. A justis vero cum haec possidentur, est quidam ista pecunia, sed non sunt illis divitiae, nisi coelestes et spirituales. Quibus indigentiam suam spiritualiter supplentes, exclusa egestate miseris, beatitudinis copia ditabuntur. Si autem hi qui praebent eleemosynam de iniquo mammona faciunt sibi amicos a quibus in aeterna tabernacula recipiantur, quanto magis hi qui spirituales largiuntur epulas, qui dant conservis cibaria in tempore suo, certissima debent spe summae retributionis erigi?"

[29] *PL*, 107, 498.
[30] *PL*, 91, 995. Cf. Gal. 6.1-10, quoted above.
[31] Cf. Bruno Astensis, *PL*, 165, 279ff.

Lombard's comment amply illustrates the blessings of those who work faithfully in the fear of the Lord.[32]

Having disposed of the question of the proper handling of spiritual food, Piers asks concerning temporal food and its interference with spiritual work (255-58). Hunger's reply repeats the doctrine of moderation explained by Holy Church in Passus 1 ("mesure is medcyne," 1.35). If it is followed, physicians will change their clothing and learn to labor:

> And ȝif thow diete the thus   I dar legge myne eres,
> That Phisik shal his furred hodes   for his fode selle,
> And his cloke of Calabre   with alle the knappes of golde,
> And be fayne, bi my feith   his phisik to lete,
> And lerne to laboure with londe   for lyflode is swete;
> For mortheres aren mony leches   lorde hem amende!
> Thei do men deye thorw here drynkes   ar destine it
>   wolde. (270-76)

Allegorically, the physicians are those who furnish the food of hogs, the *doctrinae saeculares*. We may compare the physicians in Luke 8.43, whom Bede describes as follows:

Medicos sive falsos theologos, sive philosophos, legumque doctores saecularium, qui multa de virtutibus vitiisque subtilissime disserentes, utilia se vidende credendique instituta mortalibus dare promittebant, seu certe ipsos spiritus immundos significat qui velut hominibus consulendo, se jam pro Deo colendos ingerebant. Quibus vicissim audiendis, gentilitas quanto magis naturalis industriae vires expenderat, tanto minus potuit ab iniquitatis suae sorde curari. Unde bene Marcus de hac muliere scribens, ait (5.26): *Et fuerat multa perpessa a compluribus medicis, et erogaverat omnia sua, nec quidquam profecerat, sed magis deterius habebat.* Sed haec, ubi populum Judaeorum aegrotare, verumque de coelo cognovit adesse medicum, coepit et ipsa languoris sui sperare pariter et quaeritare remedium.[33]

[32] *PL* 191, 1161-64.
[33] *PL*, 92, 442. For the hogs and their food compare verse 32 of this chapter and Bede's comment, *ibid.*, 439. In the poem, it is significant that in

Hunger says, then, that if *temporalia* are used in moderation, one will have no need for false doctrines to make one forget the hunger of the spirit.

Piers thanks Hunger and asks him to leave the field, but having come to the heart of man, Hunger can not leave until it is dismissed through the moderate use of *temporalia* and through spiritual labor. Piers understands the significance of Hunger's refusal to leave. He declares that he has only that food which is necessary to sustain him physically in his spiritual labor, especially in his effort

to drawe a-felde my donge the while the drought lasteth.[34] (290)

His spiritual hunger will be fulfilled at the harvest day; *dignus est operarius*. But the folk of the field make the error of attempting to sate hunger with an over-abundance of temporal food. They wish to "poysoun" Hunger, to kill spiritual Hunger with temporal satisfactions, finally giving themselves up to Gluttony, so that wasters once more thrive in the field. The process is well described by St. Gregory:

Rursum per panem jucunditas humanae delectationis accipitur. Unde Jeremias propheta dum synagogae perditos mores defleret, dixit: *Omnis populus ejus gemens et quaerens panem*: *dederunt pretiosa quaeque pro cibo ad refocillandam animam* (Thren. 1.11). Gemens enim populus quaerit panem, dum prava hominum multitudo affligitur, quia non ad votum de praesentis vitae jucunditate satiatur. Sed et pretiosa quaeque pro cibo dat, quia virtutes menti in appetitum delectationis transitoriae inclinat. Et refocillare animam nititur, quia perversis suis desideriis satisfacere conatur.[35]

The laborers in the field at the close of the passus are in the same condition as those lusting after hot viands at the close of the Prologue:

---

describing the physicians, the poet uses most of the basic images of the Prologue: food, clothing, money, and labor.

[34] For the significance of the drought, see Ps. 142.6: *Expandi manus meos ad te; anima mea sicut terra sine aqua tibi.* See Peter Lombard's comment, PL, 191, 1250.

[35] *Moralia*, XXIII, XXV, PL, 76, 282-83.

Laboreres that haue no lande   to lyue on but her handes,
Deyned nouȝt to dyne a-day   nyȝt-olde wortes.
May no peny-ale hem paye   ne no pece of bakoun,
But if it be fresch flesch other fische   fryed other bake,
And that *chaude* or *plus chaud*   for chillyng of her mawe.
(309-13)

They jangle against God as if he were to blame for the ills of the *civitas terrena* which they have incurred in turning their backs on the *civitas Dei,* where men live in the fear of the Lord. The poet closes with a warning that men work while they may:

Ac I warne ȝow, werkemen   wynneth while ȝe mowe,
For Hunger hiderward   hasteth hym faste. (322-23)

Dum tempus habemus, operemur bonum. The day of judgment approaches; then there will be no more time.[36]

In the episode of the half-acre the poet develops the ideal of the prelatical status. Piers nourishes the folk with spiritual food, checks their inclinations toward the world, and prepares his flock for the Day of Judgment. His problems with wasters and janglers are the problems of the ordinary prelate, and his solutions to those problems, based firmly on the principles of charity, are the solutions which the good prelate should apply. The prelate must make his flock work while there is time in loyalty to the Church, for by their fruits they will be known. Although it is impossible to force any man to take the path to Jerusalem, the prelate should exhort the wicked and make clear their punishment, even to the extent of resorting to excommunication. The events in the episode should not be taken to represent a temporal sequence, nor should the fact that Piers is instructed by Hunger be taken to represent any actual ignorance on his part. By presenting various situations the poet is simply showing what Piers is, or what the good prelate should be. Tropologically, the episode shows

---

[36] Cf. Conscience's prophecy, III, 297ff.

how the individual Christian must follow the promptings
of his natural desire for the good so that he may direct his
will in following Piers and build the tabernacle of the
Holy City in his own heart.

PASSUS VII

In Passus VI the folk of the field have become immersed
in the concerns of the world to such an extent that they seek
to satisfy their longing for the good, their spiritual hunger,
in false worldly doctrines; in other words, they have
turned from the faith. When Truth hears of this condition,
at the beginning of Passus VII, he instructs Piers

To taken his teme   and tulyen the erthe. (2)

That is, Piers is told to preach the faith with the aid of the
four Gospels,[37] just as the apostles were instructed, *Euntes
in mundum universum praedicate evangelium omni crea-
turae.*[38] Faith is a primary requisite to salvation; it must
precede good works,[39] for man is justified by grace and
not by his own efforts to fulfill the law. Without Christ's
Redemption, the law is of no avail (Rom. 3.20-26):

*Quia ex operibus legis non iustificabitur omnis caro coram illo; per
legem enim cognitio peccati. Nunc autem sine lege iustitia Dei
manifestata est, testificata a lege et prophetis. Iustitia autem Dei
per fidem Iesu Christi in omnes et super omnes qui credunt in
eum; non enim est distinctio, omnes enim peccaverunt et egent
gloria Dei iustificati gratis per gratiam ipsius, per redemptionem
quae est in Christo Iesu, quem proposuit Deus propitiationem per
fidem in sanguine ipsius, ad ostensionem iustitiae suae propter re-
missionem praecedentium delictorum, in sustentatione Dei, ad
ostensionem iustitiae eius in hoc tempore; ut sit ipse iustus et iustifi-
cans eum qui est ex fide Iesu Christi.*

[37] For the imagery, see Chapter 2.
[38] Mark 16.15. Cf. Matt. 28.19.
[39] Cf. the *Glossa ordinaria* on Matt. 28.19, *PL*, 114, 178: "Congruus
ordo. Primo enim docendus est auditor. Deinde fidei sacramentis imbuendus,
tunc ad servanda mandata instruendus. Quia nisi prius anima fidem recipiat,
non est dandus baptismus, nec valet mundari, si post non insistat bonis operi-
bus."

To enable Piers and his flock to be saved, therefore, Truth sends a pardon:

> And purchaced hym a pardoun   *a pena et a culpa*
> For hym, and for his heires   for euermore after. (3-4)

And this pardon is the necessary grace *per redemptionem quae est in Christo Iesu.* Those who receive grace, however, must implement their faith, a point which Bede stresses in his comment on the passage from Mark quoted above:

Fortasse unusquisque apud semetipsum dicat: Ego jam credidi, salvus ero. Verum dicit, si fidem operibus tenet. Vera etenim fides est, quae in hoc quod verbis dicit, moribus non contradicit.[40]

It is for this reason that Truth admonishes Piers and his flock to work:

> And bad hym holde hym at home   and eryen his leyes,
> And alle that halpe hym to erie   to sette or to sowe,
> Or any other myster   that myȝte Pieres auaille,
> Pardoun with Pieres plowman   treuthe hath ygraunted.
> (5-8)

The folk who are listed as recipients of the pardon in the succeeding lines are those we have met in the Prologue. In the course of the list, the poet recalls the previous episodes of the poem. Thus Lady Meed appears in *Super innocentem munera non accipies* (1.41), the King in *A regibus et pryncipibus erit merces eorum* (1.43), the tabernacle in *Domine, quis habitabit in tabernaculo tuo* (1.51), Piers' teaching concerning charity in *Quodcumque vultis ut faciant vobis homines, facite eis* (1.61), and the problems of Passus VI are recalled in the remainder of the quotations. Meanwhile, the admonitions addressed to the folk of various types summarize much that has been said about good works. These good works are not uniform among the folk, but are those appropriate to the various

[40] *PL*, 92, 299.

states. A bishop, for example, must exercise prelatical correction to implement his pardon (ll.13-17).

When Piers has been given a pardon, the grace of the Redemption, and a set of instructions by means of which to make that grace manifest, the law, a priest appears and offers to interpret the pardon (106). In Piers he sees only a literal plowman; in Truth's message to Piers he sees only the visible manifestation of grace, good works. He cannot perceive grace, which is invisible except to the eye of faith. He and Will, who looks over his shoulder, see only the law, represented here in the last clause of the Athanasian Creed:

> *Et qui bona egerunt, ibunt in vitam eternam;*
> *Qui vero mala, in ignem eternum.*

Specifically, the priest does not recognize the basic opening statement of the Creed:

> *Quicunque vult salvus esse:*
> *Ante omnia opus est ut teneat catholicam fidem.*

It is for this reason that he says, "I can no pardoun fynde." He sees only the law: "dowel, and have wel and God shal have thi sowle. . . ." The grace of the Redemption is hidden from him, as is the apostolic dignity of Piers. Piers understands his predicament and wishes to instruct him in the primacy of faith in the New Law, *quia ex operibus legis non iustificabitur omnis caro coram ille.* Piers "in pure tene pulled" the visible promise of pardon "atweyne." So Christ, in His sorrowful death on the cross fulfilled the old law by making manifest the two parts of the New Law: *Dilige Deum et proximum tuum.* As the "golden gloss" of Hope in Passus xvii indicates, these precepts underlie and fulfill both the commandments and the promises of the old law: *In hiis duobus mandatis tota lex pendet et propheta.* Through his act Piers in sorrow indicates symbolically why not only a commandment but also a promise of pardon is contained in the New Law for those who have faith in it. His speech reinforces the meaning of his action. He quotes Ps. 22.4, which is, literally, an affirmation of faith: *si ambulauero in medio umbre mortis, non timebo mala; quoniam tu mecum es.* Tropologically, the verse is an assertion of faith and consolation in the face of heresy. Peter Lombard comments:

In umbra mortis non timet mala, id est pravas persuasiones haereticorum et schismaticorum. Quasi dicat: Vere deduxit me *nam* id est quia *et ambulavero in medio umbrae mortis,* id est si conversor inter ignaros Dei.[41]

By implication, therefore, the priest lacks faith and is one with heretics and schismatics. He has the deadly literalmindedness of which Paul spoke when he said, "The letter killeth."

Piers says that he will cease his sowing and devote himself to prayer and penance rather than to labor. Allegorically, with special reference to his prelatical status, his turning from the field symbolizes his recourse to conscience in contemplation which was expected of all those in the prelatical status.[42] He is offering example to the priest, who is in need of contemplation to cultivate his spiritual understanding. Piers quotes Ps. 41.4 to show, literally, his fortitude in earthly tribulation: *Fuerunt mihi lacrimae meae panes die ac nocte.* Again, the allegorical significance

---

[41] *PL,* 191, 243. On the idea of darkness as applicable to true and false priests, see Chapter 2, note 9.

[42] See Bede on Luke 17.7, *PL,* 92, 541, "Servus de agro regreditur cum, intermisso ad tempus opere praedicandi, ad conscientiam doctor recurrit, atque, a publico locutionis ad curiam cordis rediens, sua secum secretus acta vel dicta retractat." The comment on this passage in the *Glossa ordinaria, PL,* 114, 318, elaborates Bede's comment and introduces the conception of Peter the Plowman: "*Quis autem,* etc. Servus arans aut pascens doctor est Ecclesiae, de quo dicitur: *Nemo mittens manum ad aratrum et aspiciens retro, aptus est regno* (Luc. 9) Dei. Et Dominus Petro dicit: *Pasce oves meas* (John 21). Qui servus de agro regreditur, cum intermisso opere praedicandi, quasi ad curiam conscientiae rediens sua dicta vel facta pertractat, cui Dominus non statim jubet ad hac vita transire, et aeterna quiete refoveri, sed domi parare quod coenet, id est post laborem apertae locutionis, humilitatem, propriae conversationis exhibere, in tali enim conscientia Deus coenet."

indicates the shortcomings of the priest, for the tears are caused by the wicked,[43] just as the priest has caused Piers to suffer "pure tene." Since the priest represents a defection resulting from too much concern with the world, the text *ne solliciti sitis* (Luke 12.22), which Piers quotes, is especially appropriate. The effects of neglecting the lesson of this text are amply evident in the Prologue. In response to Piers' efforts to instruct him, the priest shows himself without reverence for the words of Scripture which have been set before him. He asks ironically who has taught the humble plowman. Piers replies in patience that abstinence and conscience, the two principles he has just recommended, have been his teachers. The priest mocks him with the suggestion that if he were a priest Piers could preach on the theme *dixit insipiens* (Ps. 13.1). The irony of the priest's blindness is enforced by the verse which he selects to cap those quoted by Piers. Like Lady Meed, he uses a quotation which reflects on himself rather than on his opponent. For if he had turned the leaf, he would have found that the foolish one is he who says that there is no God: *Dixit insipiens in corde suo: Non est Deus*. The priest is himself one of little faith. Piers replies sharply with a verse from Proverbs which clearly places the priest as a jangler and a false doctor (Prov. 22.10): *Eice derisores et iurgia cum eis, ne crescant.*[44] The priest has seen the visible symbol of the law but has not seen through the eyes of faith the invisible substance of the law (Hebrews 11.1).

The quarrel between the priest and Piers is not concluded when Will awakes. Will ponders on the significance

---

[43] Peter Lombard, *PL*, 191, 417: "Causa vero harum lacrymarum, id est insultatio jugis pravorum." In St. Augustine's commentary, *PL*, 36, 466, those contrasting with the faithful are "obscuratos intelligentia, in tenebris interioribus constitutos, vitiorum cupiditate caecatos." The priest's blindness is implicit in this description.

[44] Indeed, the significance of the verse as Bede interprets it, *PL*, 91, 1003, indicates that Piers may have been warning the priest of excommunication: "Ejice haereticum, quem corrigere non potes, ab Ecclesia; et cum illi libertatem abstuleris praedicandi, catholicae paci auxilium praestas."

of dreams and on the difficulties of interpreting them. In
the stories of Daniel and Jacob, Will reveals his own prob-
lem; he has no sure interpreter to indicate the significance
of what he has seen. He remembers only that the priest
impugned the pardon with Do Well, and considered Do
Well better than "al the pardoun of seynt Petres cherche"
(172). That is, the priest placed the deeds of the law be-
fore the Redemption and the apostolic power of the keys
which springs from it. Like the priest, Will was unable
to see the true pardon, and he has been misled by the
priest's heresy.

In the passage from line 173 to the end of the passus, the
poet states his own view and directly admonishes his
readers. The power of the keys is valid, as Matt. 16.19
proves, but, as Truth has declared at the beginning of the
passus, good works are necessary to faith. To trust in
temporalia to purchase spiritual reward is the highest of
folly. In the concluding lines, he shows the proper relation-
ship between Piers' pardon, or grace, and good works:

> For-thi I conseille alle Cristene   to crye god mercy,
> And Marie his moder   be owre mene bitwene,
> That god gyue vs grace here   ar we gone hennes,
> Suche werkes to werche   while we ben here,
> That after owre deth-day   Dowel reherce,
> At the day of dome   we dede as he hiȝte. (195-200)

There are several considerations which make a distinction
between the dreamer's apparent approval of the priest
and the author's statement at the close necessary. In the
first place, they are contradictory, for the speaker in lines
147, 168-72, does not see the need for grace nor for the
power of the keys, but places all of his trust in the fulfill-
ment of the law. On the other hand, the speaker in 173-
200 asserts his belief in the power of the keys and asks for
grace.[45] Again, the speaker in 177-78 understands

[45] It is significant that the poet introduces himself at those points in the

> That pardoun and penaunce   and preyeres don saue
> Soules that haue synned   seuene sithes dedly,

whereas Will in Passus VIII, 20ff. does not understand how a person who sins seven times a day can be saved. Finally, Will's dream ends when it does precisely because of his untutored state. Holy Church in Passus I has attempted to teach him Truth. He does not understand and asks to be shown the vision of False. This vision properly culminates in the opposition of the priest to Piers, the final and most serious of evils, illustrative of those who place themselves falsely in the prelatical status to the detriment of the folk as a whole:

> And some putten hem to pruyde   apparailed hem there-
> after,
> In contenaunce of clothyng   comen disgised.
> (Prol. 23-24)

The reason for Will's failure to understand Truth has been explained in his vision. Truth cannot be learned as in a book; it must be discovered first in one's own heart and then in the practice of good works. It is now Will's task to leave false teachers and to rediscover Piers Plowman.

At the close of Passus IV, Conscience told the King that the rule of Reason would be impossible without the consent of the commons. In Passus V, Reason urges obedience to the law, which it is the function of the higher reason to discern, and directs the folk toward Truth. Repentance produces a preliminary acknowledgement of sin and a profession of Faith and Hope. Piers, echoing Reason, tells the folk that the road to Truth leads through the law of Charity. But the mere direction to follow the law is ineffective without the leadership of Grace, through its intermediary, Piers. The plea of the folk for guidance is a plea

---

poem where dangerous doctrine is expressed. See Prol. 208-9, III, 278-81; III, 64-86.

for Grace. Piers explains in the figure of the Truth that mercy is attained through prayer, penance, and alms, and that no one can approach the castle without grace, which has been offered freely to all through mercy. In Passus VI, Piers directs the folk in the labor of the field, stressing the necessity for working while there is time. As they begin to become slothful and wrathful, he brings spiritual hunger to them, and threatens the wasters with excommunication. Many of the folk turn to false worldly concerns and teachings in a futile effort to escape from the discomfort of spiritual hunger.[46] In Passus VII, Truth sends the pardon of his Grace to the folk Piers. In the contest with the Priest, Piers emphasizes the necessity for prayer and penance in the attainment of mercy, showing vividly that salvation lies not in the law but in' living faith made manifest in good works. In short, he repeats the lesson of John 6.27-37:

Operamini non cibum qui perit, sed qui permanet in vitam aeternam, quem Filius hominis dabit vobis: hunc enim Pater signavit Deus. Dixerunt ergo ad eum: Quid faciemus ut operemur opera Dei? Respondit Iesus et dixit eis: Hoc est opus Dei, ut credatis in eum, quem misit ille. Dixerunt ergo ei: Quod ergo tu facis sig-

---

[46] The psychological process of this defection is well described by St. Caesarius of Arles, Sermo LXI, *Opera*, ed. Morin, Maretioli, 1937, I, 257-58: "Quomodo enim domos vel stabula nostra si cotidie emundantur, nec horrorem nobis faciunt nec laborem, ita minora peccata si cotidie redimantur, nec desperationem nec dolorem poterunt generare. Si vero ad purgandum negligentes esse volumus, quomodo stabula, quae longo tempore non mundantur, ita computrescunt et foetorem horribilem reddunt stercora ipsa, ut ibi non solum homines habitare, sed nec ipsa animalia stare possint, ita quicumque neglegens in animan suam peccatorum sordes malis actibus longo tempore congregare voluerit, et cotidie bonis operibus emundare neglexerit, non solum deus illum non dignabitur visitare, sed ipse peccator non poterit in se ipso consistere. Denique omnes neglegentes, quorum corda multis peccatis velut a quibusdam bestiis lacerantur, et tamquam a spinis venenosissimis conpunguntur, hoc solent ad sibi similes dicere: Noveritis nos tristes esse vel anxios et ideo venite, dissimulemos nos, aut ad circum aut ad theatrum euntes, aut ad tabulam ludentes, aut in aliquibus nos venationibus exercentes. Isti tales ideo a foris mundi consolationem quaerunt, quia illam a deo intus in anima datur, accipere non merentur."

num, ut videamus et credamus tibi? quid operaris? Patres nostri manducaverunt manna in deserto, sicut scriptum est: Panem de caelo dedit eis manducare. Dixit ergo eis: Amen, amen, dico vobis, non Moyses dedit vobis panem de caelo, sed Pater meus dat vobis panem de caelo verum. Panis enim Dei est qui de caelo descendit et dat vitam mundo. Dixerunt ergo ad eum: Domine, semper da nobis panem hunc. Dixit autem eis Iesus: Ego sum panis vitae; qui venit ad me non esuriet, et qui credit in me non sitiet unquam. Sed dixi vobis, quia et vidistis me et non creditis. Omne, quod dat mihi Pater, ad me veniet; et eum, qui venit ad me, non eiciam foras.

Piers has shown the only method of satisfying spiritual hunger and the only road to Truth.

5. Preparation for Dowel

PASSUS VIII

THE *Visio* is complete. It is complete because the poet
has completed his generalized accounts of the good and evil
which struggle for ascendancy in the world. The principles
set forth by Holy Church represent the divine laws of
Jerusalem, and the activities of Lady Meed reflect the
customs of Babylon. The struggle between the two forces
is centered in the King, whose victory over Meed in alli-
ance with Reason and Conscience typifies the manner in
which this victory must always be won. As the King needed
his confessor to interpret Reason's Law for him, so the
Christian needs Piers Plowman to satisfy his spiritual
hunger for the good and to lead him toward Truth. The
efficacy of Piers' leadership arises from Christ's Redemp-
tion which was a pardon to all sinners. Without it no man,
whatever good works he may perform, deserves to be
saved. But at the end of the vision the first glimpse of the
church militant is introduced, in the person of the Priest.
The Priest of the earthly church fails to recognize Piers,
the Priest of the celestial church, and does not understand
his pardon. It is in the church militant that Will must fare
on his earthly pilgrimage. In the *Vitae* the poet turns from
general principles to the corrupted world around him whose
leaders are typified by the Priest. As the Christian will,
the dreamer is faced with the problem of following the
path to Jerusalem in the face of the misleading doctrines
and temptations of the world. The *Visio* shows generally
in what life of perfection consists, but Will must do more

than learn general principles; he must initiate and carry on his own practical work of charity. He must not only heed the sermon of Reason and weep with Repentance; he must also labor in the field of his heart to build the tabernacle there. For this purpose, he must learn to distinguish the true from the false in the three earthly states of perfection. It is with the practical problems of Christian life in these states that the three *Vitae* are concerned. Thus the *Vita de Dowel* begins with a picture of Will very little changed from his original portrait. At the close of Passus VII, in spite of the dramatic clarity of what he has seen, Will has not achieved a state of grace; far from it, he does not understand the basic doctrine of grace, the true foundation of Dowel, and he is unable to recognize Piers. He has been misled at the beginning of his search by the Priest, whose errors typify those of the earthly church and illustrate the kind of danger Will must face. The visions have not brought about any changes in Will's clothing. He is still "yrobed in russet." He continues to search for the good, but he still wanders, and in his wandering he is "vnholy of workes."

In Passus II Liar, who instigated the marriage between Lady Meed and False-Fickle-Tongue, was ultimately forced to seek refuge with the friars who "coped hym" as one of their order. And in Passus III it was a friar who welcomed Lady Meed as a "sustre," thus admitting the terrible forces of the Whore of Babylon into the structure of the Church. It is not inappropriate therefore that Will should meet first in his earthly search for Dowel a pair of Franciscans. When he asks them the dwelling place of Dowel, they say

'Amonges vs,' quod the Menours   'that man is dwellynge,
And euere hath, as I hope   and euere shal here-after.'
(18-19)

In other words, they refer him to the place where Liar

"is welcome whan he wil and woneth . . . oft." (II, 232)
The reply reveals considerable self-satisfaction and
self-love typical of *homines se ipsos amantes* as William
of Saint-Amour called the friars.[1] Like the priest who
mocked Piers, the friar who speaks seems to glory in his
own goodness, against the specific admonition of Ps.
110.10: *Laudatio ejus manet in saeculum saeculi* which
Peter Lombard explains, "Non ergo glorietur homo in se,
qui justitiam non operatur, nisi justificatus."[2] The Pharisee
of Christ's parable had a similar attitude (Luke 18.11):
*Pharisaeus stans haec apud se orabat; Deus, gratias ago
tibi, quia non sum sicut ceteri hominum. . . .*[3] Although
such self-gratification is inappropriate to the humility req-
uisite of a true spiritual guide, it is consistent with the
attitude held by the friars in the Prologue and in Passus
III. This discrepancy should appear most striking to one
who has understood the meaning of Piers' humility, but
Will, who has already been misled by the presumptuous
Priest, objects not to their attitude but to their words, not
to the *sentence* but to the letter. He introduces a scholas-
tic quibble. The just man falls seven times daily (Prov.
24.16). Whoever sins does evil. Do-evil and Do-wel can-
not dwell together. He concludes with the splendid *non-
sequitur*: Dowel is not always among the Friars. The Friar
replies by explaining the significance of Will's Biblical
quotation so as to support his original proposition that
Dowel lives with the Friars. His argument is that since the
friars are just (the unexpressed main premise), and since

---

[1] See above, Chapter 2, note 22.   [2] *PL*, 191, 1009.

[3] The *Glossa ordinaria* comments, *PL*, 114, 322: "Quatuor sunt species
tumoris: cum vel quis bonum quod habet, a se habere aestimat: aut si datum
a Deo credit, pro meritis datum putat; aut cum jactat se habere quod non
habet; aut cum despectis caeteris appetit singulariter videri habere quae
habet." William of Saint-Amour accuses the friars of the sin of the Pharisee
in his sermon on the parable. As Perrod paraphrases him, *op. cit.*, 143, Wil-
liam affirms that the Pharisee, or friar, "ment enfin dans toutes ses affirma-
tions: en se disant saint, il usurpe sur Dieu qui seul l'est. . . ."

the just man is kept from deadly sin through Dowel, it follows that the friars practice Dowel. The argument is phrased in terms of sound doctrine, that charity is a remedy for sin, but this doctrine has no relevance for the actual proposition the friar is defending. Indeed, he is not above using false doctrine to make his points. Thus he declares that "witte and fre wille" have been given to "foules, fissches, and bestes" (53-54). This teaching is contrary to the accepted proposition that man alone among earthly creatures has free will.[4] His use of a clear and appealing example to support false doctrine enforces the dangerousness of the Friar's gifts.[5] The argument is beyond the dreamer's understanding, so that he takes leave of these unavailing teachers.

At the beginning of Passus VIII, then, Will is without intellectual direction. This lack is of fundamental importance because the first step in the way toward achieving good will is to submit the will to the intellect. The untutored will concomitantly is without grace.[6] Second, in achieving intellectual perception of Truth, Will must learn

[4] Godefroid (1924), p. 174. "Et ex hoc patet responsio ad quaesitum principale, scilicet quod appetitus bruti non est liber." The title of the quaestio is "Utrum appetitus bruti sit liber et sic possit dici voluntas."

[5] The example of the ship represents a gloss on Luke 8.25; cf. St. Bonaventura, *Opera*, VII, 200ff.

[6] Cf. Godefroid de Fontaines (1914), 209: "Nullius enim dominium habet voluntas sola sine intellectu, et nullo etiam utitur sine illo, sed in virtute intellectus, a quo movetur ipsa voluntas." Cf. (1924), 140-76 where intellect as a control over will is discussed at length. Peter Lombard has a valuable discussion of the relations among grace, faith, the intellect and good will, in the *Sententiae*, PL, 192, 710-13: "Ecce his verbis et aliis praemissis evidenter traditur, quia voluntas hominis praeparatur et praevenitur gratia Dei ut velit bonum, et adjuvatur ne frustra velit. . . . Non est libera voluntas, nisi eam liberet gratia per legem fidei, id est, non est libera, sine fide operante per dilectionem; et illa sufficienter et vere bona est. . . . Scimus bonum, nec delectat agere; et cupimus ut delectet. Sic iste olim desiderare concupiscebat, quae bona esse cernebat, cupiens eorum habere delectationem, quorum potuit videre rationem. Ostendit itaque quibus quasi gradibus ad eas perveniatur; prius enim est ut videantur, quam sint utiles et honestae; deinde, ut earum desiderium concupiscatur; postremo proficiente ut gratia delectet earum operatio, quarum sola ratio delectat."

to distinguish between Piers Plowman, the true spiritual guide, who will teach him faith and prepare him for grace, and such false pretenders to the role as are represented by the self-satisfied friars. Much the same introductory purpose is served by Will's first sleeping encounter. Thought represents those ideas concerning the way to achieve Truth of which Will is at the moment capable. Although he desires the good, Will has been misled by the friars. The definitions offered by Thought should reveal something of this difficulty. Indeed Thought describes Dowel, Dobet, and Dobest in terms of externals, with no suggestion of the necessary preparation of the will for good action through faith and grace. Like the Priest who opposed Piers Plowman, Thought defines the good life of Dowel with no reference to grace or to charity, without which it is impossible for will to be good.[7] Without the need for grace and the need to exercise charity the virtues would, indeed, be not far from our grasp, "nauȝte fer to fynde," as Thought declares. Dobet is correctly defined in terms of the religious life, but the religious life is externally characterized by its concern with alms-giving and preaching (i.e. of the friars). No reference is made to contemplation or to the counsels; nor is any emphasis given to the Rule. Furthermore, Thought fails completely to understand the *sentence* of 2 Cor. 11.19, which he cites:

Libenter suffertis insipientes, cum sitis ipsi sapientes.

It is this which Dobet is to preach to the people:

[7] Peter Lombard, *PL*, 192, 743: "Sciendum ergo est, quod ex fine suo, ut ait Aug. voluntas cognoscitur, utrum recta, an prava sit. Finis autem bonae voluntatis beatitudo est, vita aeterna, ipse Deus. Malae vero finis est aliud, scilicet mala delectatio, vel aliquid aliud in quo non debit voluntas quiescere. Finem vero bonum insinuat Propheta dicens: *Omnis consumationis vidi finem, etc.* Charitas ergo cuius *latum mandatum est,* finis *omnis consumationis est,* id est omnis bonae voluntatis et actionis, ad quam omne praeceptum referendum est. . . . His verbis aperte insinuatur quis sit rectus finis voluntatis, sive actionis bonae, scilicet charitas, quae et Deus est."

'And suffreth the vnwise   with ȝow for to libbe,'
And with gladde wille doth hem gode   for so god ȝow
hoteth. (92-93)

But the context of the verse and the gloss on it make clear
that Paul is being ironical in his advice; actually he is
admonishing the Corinthians not to be tolerant of the false
prophets, "insipientia enim est aliquem laudare se."[8] Peter
Lombard explains:

Libenter enim, id est voluntarie, *suffertis insipientes,* in hac gloria,
quod non debetis, *cum ipsi sitis,* id est esse debeatis, *Sapientes,* sed
non estis: quod inde hic probatur, quod tales suffertis.[9]

Thought's error indicates that the misled Will has failed
to understand the fraudulence of the Friars. They are the
preaching members of Dobet; they are those who praise
themselves, but Thought apparently sees nothing wrong
in their distorted Scriptural advice that the people accept
false prophets, that is, the friars themselves (cf. Prol. 58-
67). The poet has cleverly succeeded in satirizing the pre-
tensions of the friars and in showing the superficiality of
Will's thought.

Finally, in his description of Dobest, Thought is again
correct only in externals. He places Dobest in the status
of the bishop, but describes only his obvious corrective
functions (94-97). Nothing is said of his obligation to
supply spiritual food in the tradition of Piers Plowman.
As Dobest leads Dowel and Dobet, the Pope, the highest
of those in the prelatical status is to judge in any appeals
against the authority of the bishop (cf. Prol. 107-11, and
v, 49-52). He is the "kyng" who will rule by the counsel
of the three states of perfection (99-106). Although the
pope ruled by perfection is, of course, the leader of the
church, the difficulty in Thought's proposal is that the three
states as he has described them would offer very poor
counsels of perfection: Dowel, who works without thought

---

[8] *Glossa ordinaria, PL,* 114, 567.   [9] *PL,* 192, 75.

of charity; Dobet, the false preaching friar, and Dobest, who is concerned with correction, not with his positive function of supplying the spiritual food by which man must live.

Like the instruction of the Friars, the conclusions arrived at by Thought, are not satisfying to Will. They have not satisfied his spiritual hunger nor brought him grace. Thought declares that Wit may have the answer to his problem. Will continues his meditation until suddenly Wit comes to him:

> Thouȝte and I thus thre days we ȝeden. . . .
> And ar we were ywar with witte gan we mete.
>
> (112-14)

Wit in his clothing, appearance, and conversation shows clearly his affinity with Reason and with its principle of measure:

> Was no pruyde on his apparaille ne pouerte noyther,
> Sadde of his semblaunt and of soft chiere.
> I dorste meue no matere to make hym to Iangle.
>
> (116-18)

Will asks Thought to be his mean in addressing Wit: that is, Will, filled with the natural desire to know the good, has been directed through the concepts furnished in his thought to the intellect which must prepare the will to desire grace.

It should be understood that although Will as a character in the poem seems distinctly and appealingly human, this humanity arises chiefly from the fact that he represents the human will in general. Similarly, Will's thought is not the thought of any particular individual; it typifies the thought of men in a confusing moral world. The humanity of the allegorical characters in the poem is, in general, representative and not individual.

106

PASSUS IX

Thought has been able to present to Will only such material as "ex notitia simplicis et confusae intelligentiae producitur."[10] If he is to be shown the possible courses of action, he must have recourse to the speculative intellect; he must derive them "ex habituali notitia existente in intellectu possibili." Moreover, before Will can put these possibilities perceived by the speculative intellect into action, the *intellectus agens* must be activated, for it is through this faculty that are produced the "notitia declarativa quae verbum dicitur."[11] Thus Thought directs the inquiring Will to Wit, the speculative intellect. It is the function of Wit, in other words, to present the modes and forms of the notions of thought from which Will may select a variety of courses of action. Wit informs Will accurately of the possibilities inherent in man who was made by God in His image. He describes what man is and what man may do to preserve or to destroy the image of God in him.

Dowel, Wit explains, lives within a castle made by Kind, that is, within man who was created by God from earth and water, air (the breath of life) and wind (the spirit of God).[12] In the castle of man is the soul which is made in God's image. God loves the soul, but the Devil hates her. To preserve the beloved soul God has given her to the care of Dowel, the duke of the marches in which the castle is situated; in her immediate service is Dobet, the daughter of Dowel; Dobest is a peer of the bishops, who rules Dowel and Dobet and leads the soul through his learning. Dowel, that is, is chiefly concerned with the avoidance of

[10] The running quotations in this paragraph are from Godefroid (1914), p. 32. Cf. (1931), p. 362.

[11] The term *word* here indicates overt action, "verbum in actu," by analogy with the *word* or active principle of God.

[12] The commentators distinguish between the animate spirit and the soul. See the *Glossa ordinaria*, PL, 113, 86.

sin in the active status. He is the first guardian of man. Dobet lives more intimately with Anima in contemplation; she serves her spiritually, guarded from external temptation by Dowel, from whom she has sprung. Dobest, the prelate, is concerned both with the spiritual nourishment of the soul through contemplation and with the active struggle against the devil. The watch is kept by Practical Intellect ("Inwit") under whose direction all good works are performed.[13] Practical Intellect with his five sons, by his first wife, Sir Seewell and the others, is to guard Anima until Kind sends for her. The first wife represents the old law and the five sons the obedience to her precepts which results in doing well. Until the pardon of Piers, that is, Divine Grace, in which the Priest had been able to see only the old law, is made finally manifest, Practical Intellect must guide the soul.[14]

Will, betraying his deficiency in the most fundamental matters of faith and doctrine, asks what kind of a thing Kind is. Wit explains that Kind is the Creator, who made the animals with his word, *Dixit, et facta sunt*. When he made man, he did so not only with his word but with his

[13] The *intellectus agens* has as its purpose the guidance of the Will. Cf. Godefroid (1931), p. 354: "Concludendo ergo veritatem quaestionis et ad principale quaesitum revertendo, dico quod intellectus practicus et speculativus non dicunt diversas potentias, sed cuius actus speculativus habens operabile pro obiecto sine habitudine ad voluntatem operandi fit practicus cum tali habitudine." The speculative intellect is not concerned with the Will. Cf. *ibid.*, p. 351: "Et sic intellectus speculativus et practicus videntur differe in hoc quod speculativus id quod considerat non ordinat ulterius ad opus sed sistit in sola consideratione, non includens appetitum vel desiderium finis, licet id ipsum quod est finis consideret; practicus autem quod apprehendit ordinat ad opus." At the same time it must be borne in mind that the will which is not guided by the intellect is necessarily evil. Cf. *ibid.* (1914), 232: "Omnis voluntas discordans a ratione sive recta sive erronea semper sit mala." Thus the active intellect is the true guide of the will in right action.

[14] See our preceding discussion of the pardon episode. The sons are not the five senses; they are the external manifestations of doing well possible even to the righteous heathen. That is, they are the fruits of the practical intellect.

work, for he said *faciamus*. Just as a lord requires pen and parchment to write his word, so the Creator invoked the other members of the Trinity to create man; for in man there is the Holy Spirit and the grace of Christ, which animals lack. In other words, the soul of man, Anima, was created in the image of the Trinity.[15] Traditionally, the image of God in man consists of the mind, whose three parts—memory, intellect, and will—correspond to the Trinity. Peter Lombard gives a brief account of this doctrine based on St. Augustine's *De trinitate:*

Eo enim ipso imago Dei est mens, quo capax ejus est, ejusque particeps esse potest . . . . Ecce enim mens meminit sui, intelligit se, diligit se; hoc si cernimus, cernimus Trinitatem, nondum quidem Deum, sed imaginem Dei. Hic enim quaedam apparet trinitas memoriae, intelligentiae et amoris. Haec ergo tria potissimum tractemus, memoriam, intelligentiam, voluntatem.[16]

Godefroid explains that the *intellectus agens* pertains to the highest or paternal faculty, the memory, and hence guides the others.[17] As the poet expresses it, the soul lives in the heart where it is controlled by the practical intellect.

Ac Inwitte is in the hed   and to the herte he loketh,
What *anima* is lief or loth   he lat hir at his wille;
For after the grace of god   the grettest is Inwitte.
                                          (56-58)

Wit now passes to the form of evil as one of the potentialities that Will may select. He quotes Phil. 3.19, *Quorum deus venter est,* to illustrate the evil of those who disregard the practical intellect. The passage from which the text is taken begins (3.17):

Imitatores mihi estote, fratres, et observate eos qui ambulant sicut habetis formam nos.

Those who are ruled by the practical intellect act in accord-

[15] On the distinction between *Dixit, etc.* and *faciamus* see *Glossa ordinaria, PL*, 113, 80-81, and the references there.
[16] *PL*, 192, 530-31.   [17] Godefroid (1914), pp. 29-32.

ance with the image of God within them;[18] those whose will acts in defiance of it despoil the image of God. Their God is the belly:

> *Finis interitus quorum, Deus venter est, et gloria in confusione ipsorum qui terrena sapiunt.*

As Peter Lombard explains, their end, *finis interitus,* will be eternal punishment, "aeterna poena":[19]

> For þei seruen sathan   her soule shal he haue;
> That liueth synful lyf here   her soule is liche the deuel.
> And alle that lyuen good lyf   aren like god almiȝti,
>   *Qui manet in caritate, in deo manet, &c.* (61-63)

Those who lead the good life are like the *filii altissimi* of Holy Church's sermon on charity, whose theme Wit recalls by citing 1 John 4.16. As Holy Church showed, to be ruled by *caritas* is to follow Truth. As Holy Church warned against drunkenness, symbolic of immersion in *temporalia* (1, 27ff.), Wit laments that drink should destroy the temple of God and cause Him to forsake those who might have shone in His image. Wit's citations are most appropriate. The drunkards are like the five foolish virgins, who were immersed in the pleasures of the five senses and were repudiated by Christ (Matt. 25.12), *Amen dico vobis, nescio vos;*[20] they also resemble the evil characters of Psalm 80 who refuse to hear the word of God in their concern

---

[18] Lombard comments, *PL,* 192, 250: "Id est imaginem vitae nostrae, scilicet qui ita credunt, vivunt, docent." The sequence of ideas in relation to the verse from Genesis on the creation of man is illustrated well by Rupert's commentary on Gen. 1.26, *PL,* 167, 249: "Quid tandem est: *Faciamus hominem ad imaginem et similitudinem nostram,* nisi, faciamus hominem, qui trinae operationis nostrae in semetipso habeat evidentiam . . . faciamus hominem viventem, rationalem, Deo similem. . . . Sed ea, qua carere non potest homo, facultas rationalitatis, instrumentum est sive oculus quidam ad quaerendam similitudinem Dei. Est ergo inexcusabilis, cum ad similitudinem Dei non pervenerit: quia videlicet bono instrumento, ad hoc, propter quod sibi datum est, uti noluit."

[19] *PL,* 192, 257.

[20] Cf. Bede, *PL,* 92, 102-3 and our discussion of Holy Church's use of the symbol of spiritual sleep, Chapter 2, notes 42, 44, 48.

for the world and are cast out, *et dimisi eos secundum desideria eorum* (80.13).[21]

Drunkards "misrule" their inwit, but there are those who are not ruled by practical intellect because they are deficient in it: fools and madmen who do not have it; widows and orphans who have lost their guides to proper action. These Holy Church must protect and cherish. Figuratively, these helpless ones are in want of spiritual food, are in need of the ministrations of Piers.[22] Just as godparents are literally responsible for the spiritual welfare of their godchildren, the prelates are responsible for the welfare of the folk:

> For more bilongeth to the litel barne   ar he the lawe
>   knowe,
> Than nempnyng of a name   and he neuere the wiser!
> Shulde no crystene creature   crien atte ʒate,
> Ne faille payn ne potage   and prelates did as thei shulden.
>   (77-80)

If prelates performed their function, there would be no Christians crying at the gate for crumbs like Lazarus (Luke 16.19).[23] Wit laments the unkindness of Christian prelates. They are like Dives in their disregard for those in need of comfort. A bishop, Wit declares, who gives to a jangler what he should give to the poor is worse than Judas; he does not give spiritual nourishment, but rather comforts

[21] See Lombard, *PL*, 191, 771-74.

[22] Wit, in calling on Luke to witness the truth of his statements, probably refers to Luke 9.2, where the task of healing the sick is laid upon the disciples. Wit may also be referring to the parable of Lazarus. See note 23 below.

[23] Bede's commentary on the parable of Lazarus indicates that the food is to be understood spiritually; that the dogs who lick Lazarus' wounds are the preachers; Dives represents the proud Jews who held the law for selfish ends; Lazarus represents the Gentiles. In the parable Dives, when it is too late, has compassion on his erring brothers, perhaps suggesting the contrast in the poem between the compassionate Jew and the uncharitable Christian prelate. The Jews in the poem are called "owre loresmen," a phrase which suggests the interpretation of Dives and Lazarus as Jew, proud possessor of the law, and Gentile, humble petitioner for the crumbs of enlightenment. Cf. Bede, *PL*, 92, 533-38.

the worldly in their defiance of God. Such a bishop, externally in the status of Dobest, does not even do well; he has no fear of the Lord, the beginning of wisdom (Ecclus. 1.16). Having exemplified the contrast between external representation of status and internal actuality of status, Wit indicates on the basis of the text, *Inicium sapiencie*, the inner development of spiritual perfection. To fear God for fear of pain so that one avoids evil is a good beginning, but it is better to fear him for love.[24] Best of all is to avoid all false speech and waste of time.[25] The image of false speech is that developed in the Prologue and Passus 1. God wishes no false minstrel to serve him; his gleeman is not to be a "goer to tavernes," that is, a glutton abandoned to the world, whose God is his belly. God provides for his workmen; he gives them grace and spiritual food so that they may be able to praise him (104-6). Wit cites Ps. 33.11:

Inquirentes autem dominum non minuentur omni bono.

Those who work when there is time are truly married to Holy Church, the Bride of Piers, Dame Work-when-time-is:

[24] Cf. Rabanus, *PL*, 109, 767: "Unus timor quo timent homines Deum, ne mittantur in gehennam. Ipse est timor ille qui introducit charitatem; sed sic venit, ut exeat. Si enim adhuc propter poenas times Deum, nondum amas quem sic times: non bona desideras, sed mala caves. Sed ex eo quod mala caves corriges te, et incipis bona desiderare. Cum bona desiderare coeperis, erit in te timor sanctus." The commentary succinctly explains how Dobet, the daughter, springs from Dowel, the father.

[25] Here Wit probably refers to Ecclus. 4.23-24: *Fili, conserva tempus et devita a malo.* Rabanus, *PL*, 109, 787, comments; "Ideo exhortans filios suos ipsa docet sapientia, ut conservent tempus, quia 'tempus omni rei sub coelo; et tempus est belli, et tempus pacis,' quoniam quandiu in hoc saeculo sumus, tempus est belli; et pro fide ac justitia standum, et pro salute animae pugnandum. Unde et omne malum, hoc est, vitium nobis est devitandum. Cum autem migraverimus de hoc saeculo, pacis tempus adveniet. In pace enim locus Dei, et civitas nostra Hierusalem de pace sortita vocabulum est." For false speech in connection with fear see Lombard, *PL*, 191, 342, on Ps. 33.11-13.

Trewe wedded libbing folk   in this worlde is Dowel;
For thei mote worche and wynne   and the worlde sus-
                      teyne. (107-8)

In the *status conjugatorum* of the active life, these are the faithful who assist Piers in the eradication of sin and in supplying food and clothing to sustain the body in the work of the spirit. Good folk of all three states spring from Dowel:

For of her kynde [*status conjugatorum*] thei come   that
                      confessoures ben nempned,
Kynges and kniȝtes   kayseres and cherles,
Maydenes and martires   out of o man come. (109-11)

Here Wit uses the symbolic value of marriage as indicative of the external state of Dowel. The three states Dowel, Dobet, and Dobest were conventionally designated as *conjugatorum, viduarum, virginum*. In the subsequent discussion Wit extends the symbolic force of marriage in the equally conventional senses of marriage between Christ and the Church or between the soul of man and God.[26] Those whose souls are truly married to God, in whatever status, are the *filii altissimi* of Holy Church's sermon, or the sons of Adam. Conversely, those who are falsely married to Lady Meed are sons of Satan or of Cain. Wit, the speculative intellect, is concerned with the ultimate alternatives of good and evil which face the will, not with particular problems of pastoral theology. Maidens and martyrs who lead the life of perfection may be said to come out of one man, as the poet says, since God created Adam in the image of the Trinity, and the good are of his generation. As Adam was made in the image and likeness

---

[26] See, for example, Hugh of St. Victor, *Miscellanea*, v, xxv, *PL*, 177, 765: "Triplex igitur est desponsatio: in misericordia, in justitia, in fide, quae in fide conjugit sponsum et sponsam; quae in misericordia, Christum et Ecclesiam; quae in justitia, Deum et animam."

of God, the good are made in the image and likeness of Adam.[27]

Holy Church, the wife, was made by God as Eve was made to be the helpmate of Adam (Gen. 2.18-25), "for to help worche." Holy Church is espoused to Christ as Eve was to Adam and as the soul of the good Christian is married to Holy Church.[28] The marriage of the "mene" person of the Trinity, Christ, is made "bi the faderes wille," the council of the Holy Ghost, "the frendes conseille," and the "assent of hem-self," Christ and the will of the individual member of the Church:

And thus was wedloke ywrouȝte   and God hym-self it
                                                  made;
In erthe the heuene is   hym-self was the witnesse.

(116-17)

Unlike the marriage of Lady Meed, the marriage of Holy Church, made in earthly paradise, was witnessed by God Himself.

Those who are not of this marriage are, like Lady Meed, bastards born out of true wedlock. They, the faithless, the liars, the wasters, are the descendants of Cain, born "out of wedlock" as was he (1 John 3). Cain, in the commentaries, is the first in the generation of the wicked, as is

[27] See Rabanus Maurus, *PL*, 107, 509-10: "*Vixit autem Adam centum triginta annis, et genuit filium ad similitudinem et imaginem suam* [*vocavit nomen ejus Seth.*] Nota quia Adam ad imaginem et similitudinem Dei factus est, homines autem ad similitudinem Adae facti sunt." See also Rupert, *PL*, 167, 323: "Quis inter haec aestimare sufficit constantiam propositi Dei in eos, quos praescivit et praedestinavit, quos jam proposuerat vocare sanctos, cum diceret primis duobus masculo et feminae, quos creaverat: Crescite et multiplicamini? (Gen. 1) Quomodo? nisi per multam virtutem benedictionis et bonae voluntatis ejus, in tanta multiplicate adversae generationis, tam ante quam post diluvium, vigere vel superesse usquam potuit genus electorum? Vicit Dei bonitas iniquitatem nostram, et ad hunc Abram locutus repromisit ei, quod benedicerentur omnes gentes in semine ejus, quod est Christus." See also *Glossa ordinaria*, *PL*, 113, 102-3.

[28] This is a standard signification of the marriage of Adam and Eve; see Augustine, *PL*, 34, 215-16. The marriage of Adam and Eve was considered to be not only the archetype for human marriage but also of the marriage of the soul to the Church.

114

Abel (actually Seth who replaced him) the first in the generation of the righteous; Rupert says:

Nam generationis electorum causa ex gratia Dei est, dicentis: *Crescite et multiplicamini, et replete terram* (*Gen.* I), etc. Generationis autem reproborum ex ira ejusdem dicentis ad mulierem: *Multiplicabo aerumnas tuas et conceptus tuos* (*Gen.* III). Quae prior jussa est nasci, ipsa praepediente fluxu peccatorum, tardius crevit. Primo enim sic scriptum est: *Adam vero cognovit Evam uxorem suam. Quae concepit et peperit Cain dicens: Possedi hominem per Deum. Rursumque peperit fratrem ejus Abel* (*Gen.* IV). Ille primus in generatione iniquorum, iste primus computatur in generatione justorum.[29]

To describe the generation of Cain, Wit adduces the text Ps. 7.15:

> *Concepit in dolore, et peperit iniquitatem, &c.*

As Peter Lombard explains, they conceive in the misery of appetite for temporal things and bring forth injustice.[30] The Psalm continues:

Lacum aperuit et effodit eum et incidit in foveam quam fecit. Convertetur dolor ejus in caput ejus; et in verticem ipsius iniquitas ejus descendet.

Peter Lombard commenting on *dolor ejus* indicates that the unjust are those who misuse Reason:

Dolor ejus, quod concipitur, *convertetur in caput ejus,* id est in mentem, *et iniquitas ejus* quam peperit *descendet in verticem ipsius,* id est rationem, quam dixerat caput. . . . Hoc ideo, quia noluit ipse peccatum evadere, sed servus esse peccati, libidine dominante rationi. . . . Et postea dolor et iniquitas, descendat, scilicet cum impetu, super caput et verticem, cum poenis aeternis subjicent eum.[31]

> And alle that come of that Caym   come to yuel ende.
>
> (122)

The sons of Seth[32] must keep themselves from the sons of

---

[29] *PL*, 167, 322. Rupert continues by discussing the allegorical meaning of the names Cain, Abel, and of Seth who takes the place of Abel.

[30] *PL*, 191, 118.   [31] *PL*, 191, 119.

[32] The ms. readings of line 123 are divided between Shem and Seth. Seth is clearly demanded by the meaning. Cf. Skeat, II, 144.

Cain; that is, must not turn from the marriage with Holy Church to the marriage of Lady Meed. But the sons of Seth mingled with the daughters of men, that is, according to Rupert, with the generation of Cain:

Filii Dei et filii hominum hoc loco differunt, quia filii Dei de generatione Seth, filii autem hominum de generatione sunt Cain.[33]

The generation of the just was thereby corrupted and became filled with the pride of life; the sins of the corrupt generation led God to repent the making of man: *Penitet me fecisse hominem* (Gen. 6.6).[34] In the flood the generation of Cain and the corrupted generation of Seth were destroyed. The flood symbolizes Baptism, which saves the faithful within the Church, but destroys the wicked. As the *Glossa ordinaria* on Gen. 7.10 puts it:

Cumque transissent [*septem dies, aquae diluvii inundaverunt super terram.*] (Isid.) Quia in spe futurae quietis, quam significat septimus dies, baptizamur, omnis caro extra arcam diluvio consumpta est; quia extra Ecclesiam aqua baptismi, quamvis eadem sit, non valet ad salutem, sed ad perniciem.

The sin of Cain is visited upon the children of his generation and upon those of Seth who are corrupted by it; that is upon those who fall from grace in sin.

Wit now explains the significance of the eternal punishment of the generation of Cain, the apparent inequity in the "barne" suffering the "belsyres gulte." He states the problem in terms of the reconciliation of the doctrine of original sin with the text of Ezek. 18.20:

Filius non portabit iniquitatem patris,
& pater non portabit iniquitatem filii, &c.[35]

[33] *PL*, 167, 338.

[34] The proud are signified by the "mighty men" who resulted from the union of the two generations (Gen. 6.4). Cf. Rupert, *PL*, 167, 339-41. The text, *Penitet*, etc., is not that of the modern Vulgate, but that quoted, for example, in Peter Comestor's *Historia scholastica.*

[35] The same problem is discussed by Peter Lombard, *Sententiae*, II, Dist. XXXIII.

He adduces the text, Matt. 7.16:

Numquam colligimus de spinis uvas, nec de tribulis fycus.

The *Glossa ordinaria* explains that the spines and thistles are heretics from whom no good may be expected.[36] They are without grace, through lack of baptism or through the regression from grace; their wills are not directed toward good. Grace was lost to man through the fall of Adam, but the sons of Seth pass through baptism to salvation; the sons of Cain are not saved.

From the symbolic development of marriage in Biblical history, Wit turns to a similar symbolic development of marriage in the present. On the literal level his discussion is pastoral, but in terms of the general purpose of Wit's discourse, the *sentence* elaborates the meaning of what has preceded. The historical past makes clear the historical present, but both reveal the fundamental truth that man in the image of his Creator is spiritually married to Him; but in the corruption of this image is spiritually married to False. Corrupt modern marriages, Wit continues, reflect the symbolic evil marriage of the two generations of Seth and Cain, the violation of the precept that "goode shulde wedde goode" and not for the good of this earth. In them is celebrated the marriage of Lady Meed with the sons of Cain, whose name signifies *possessio*; the marriage of Christ with his Church is not celebrated, in spite of Christ's admonition: *Ego sum via et veritas et vita. Nemo venit ad Patrem nisi per me* (line 159). Marriages of young girls to old men for concupiscence, marriages for wealth, marriages of convenience symbolize the turning from the way to Jerusalem. Wit warns:

> For no londes, but for loue   loke ʒe be wedded,
> And thanne gete ʒe the grace of god   and good ynogh
>   to lyue with. (175-76)

[36] Cf. *Glossa ordinaria, PL*, 114, 110, on verses 16 and 17.

117

Grace comes only to those truly wed to Holy Church who in charity use the goods which God has given them. Everyone in the active life "every maner seculer," should wed before "leccherye" destroys him. This lechery, which symbolizes *amor saeculi* may be avoided if he works "in tyme . . . in parfyte charitee," in his marriage to the Church, avoiding sin and following the precepts of charity. This marriage was created by God, as St. Paul said (1 Cor. 7.2):

> *Bonum est ut unusquisque uxorem suam habeat, propter fornicacionem.*

Fornication with Lady Meed is the great and pressing temptation facing man; in faithfulness to Holy Church, man may avoid falling.[37] Those born out of spiritual wedlock are the false folk:

> Vngracious to gete goode   or loue of the people,
> Wandren and wasten   what thei cacche mowe.
> Aȝeines Dowel thei don yuel   and the deuel serue,
> And after her deth-day   shulle dwelle with the same,
> But god gyue hem grace here   hem-self to amende.
>
> (194-98)

Finally, Wit comes to the answer to Will's question about Dowel and the other states of perfection. He has established a firm basis of doctrine, and proceeds to the definitions. Dowel is not only to follow the law, as the Priest thought, but also to "drede God." From such fear comes *sapientia* and ultimately charity. Dobet is not only to love friend and foe, but "to suffer," to share in Christ's passion for humanity. Dobest is not only to heal and help, *sanare infirmos*, but partaking of both the active and contemplative states ("cometh dobest of bothe"), it reforms the proud, the "wikked wille," the corruption of which, inherited from the Fall, "dryueth away dowel through dedliche synnes."

If Wit's instruction is compared with that of Holy

---

[37] See our discussion of II, 5-48, above.

Church in Passus I, the manner in which it develops her lesson is striking. The literal level of the allegory, for example, the discussion of marriage, takes up the contrast between the two marriages with which Holy Church concluded her instruction. The image of the castle of Caro develops concretely the idea of the treasure of truth which is found in man's heart. The manner of Wit's lesson, with its foundation in Biblical texts, is almost identical with that of Holy Church. It is, in fact, in the use of the Biblical texts that the meaning of the allegory rests. The literal level of the allegory serves to summarize the tradition of pastoral teaching on the Sacrament of marriage, which developed in England from the time of the Fourth Lateran council (1215). On this level the instruction is appropriate as an answer to Will's question about the meaning of Dowel, the active status, the *status conjugatorum*. But this explanation leaves much to be desired; it is an answer to the whole by the part. Certainly it ill prepares Wit to make the simple and unexplained definitions at the end of the Passus. Again the allegorical level supplies the answer; marriage has both literal and allegorical meaning. The allegory advances from and expands the teaching of Holy Church, which Will has already received; it indicates the relevance to the will of this teaching in insisting on the internal, not external, reality of the good life, the necessity for the will to act in accord with reason. This allegorical teaching may be briefly summarized.

Dowel is essentially a function of the soul, not merely an external compliance with the law. To do well is to act in accordance with the true nature of man, formed in the image of the Trinity, to be governed, that is, by the active intellect, not by the whims of the will. One function of the priest, of Piers, is to nourish and to correct those lacking in reason, to admonish and to warn those who live in defiance of reason. Those who obey reason are the generation of the just who share in the grace of God. Only through grace, through the true marriage of the soul with the Church, can man achieve salvation and avoid eternal punishment. Those of the generation of Cain are the faithless janglers:

> Ac iapers and iangelers   Iudas chylderen,
> Feynen hem fantasies   and foles hem maketh,
> And han here witte at wille   to worche ȝif thei sholde.
> (Pro. 35-7)

> Fauel thorw his faire speche   hath this folke enchaunted,
> And al is Lyeres ledyng   that [Lady Mede] is thus ywed-
> ded. (II, 41-2)

> Aȝeines Dowel thei don yuel   and the deuel serue,
> And after her deth-day   shulle dwelle with the same,
> But god gyue hem grace here   hem-self to amende.
> (IX, 196-8)

PASSUS X

Suddenly Wit's wife, Dame Study, with violence and at length, condemns him for his instruction of Will. Her attack is not directed at his doctrine, but at its lack of appropriateness to his audience, Will, who is still without grace. Will has not put aside his hermit robes; there is no suggestion that he has become holy of works. Dame Study perceives Will's state; she perceives the danger in treating difficult matters of doctrine before Will has shown his loyalty to the Church, before he has learned through the practical intellect the discipline of faith which will keep him from using his intellect wrongfully to defend an evil course. She cites Matt. 7.6. *Nolite dare sanctum canibus, neque mittatis margaritas uestras ante porcos, etc.* Bede's comment makes clear the aptness of the verse to Study's condemnation of Wit for the inappropriateness of his discourse:

Canes et porcos pro contemptoribus accipimus; non convenit igitur istiusmodi in luto infidelitatis manentibus porcis vel haereticis, vel hominibus ad vomitum peccatorum revertentibus, evangelicum pandere margaritam. Ne conculcent, id est contemnant illud, et conversi incipiant vos dissipare.[38]

It should again be noted that Wit is not Will's wit. The allegorical faculties are the faculties as such; the generalizations may be applied to the individual, but are not themselves of the individual. Thus Wit gives instruction to Will which is beyond his grasp, for Wit is truly married to the study of the Faith and the Law, whereas Will is without grace; the well-wed intellect is necessary to his recovery of grace, but he too must be properly wed to the Church before the lesson of the intellect may be efficacious. The swine, Study declares, are those:

'that sheweth bi her werkes,
That hem were leuer londe   and lordship on erthe,
Or ricchesse or rentis   and reste at her wille,
Than alle the sothe sawes   that Salomon seyde euere.'
(13-16)

Will, by implication, has a tendency to care more for temporal reward than for wisdom; he has been unholy of works; he agreed with the mouse who defended a policy of slothful peace in the Prologue; he failed to understand both the heretical doctrine of the priest and the true nature of Piers. For this reason, Dame Study proceeds to a long and spirited denunciation of janglers, of those who misuse their intellect for gain.

As the world now is, wisdom is loved only for the wealth which may be gained thereby. She cites Scripture to the effect that only worldly wisdom prospers in the world; those who have "holy writte" in their speech are disregarded. Japers, who distract the worldly from the pangs of spiritual hunger, are in vogue; true mirth and minstrelsy are forgotten. If holy writ comes to the lips of worldly clerks, it is for the purpose of distorting the letter

[38] *PL*, 92, 36.

until it gives comfort to those who wish to forget their hunger for God in their worldly pleasures. But the sheep are unfed; Piers has gone:

> Ac the careful may crye   and carpen atte ȝate,
> Bothe afyngred and a-thurst   and for chele quake;
> Is none to nymen hym nere   his noye to amende,
> But hoen on hym as an hounde   and hoten hym go
> thennes. (58-60)

With Piers, charity has gone—or has almost gone: it still lingers with Christ's poor. Christ is on the lips of the doctors, but He is in the heart of the humble, the temple of God.[39] The misuse of intellect for temporal ends, Study says, is well illustrated in the works of the friars, whose evil is corrupting the world so that prayer is no longer efficacious (71-77). The doctrine of original sin and the problem of evil are especially dangerous in the hands of those of little faith. These problems were among those explained to Will by Wit (110ff.) She advises Will to

---

[39] Study cites Ps. 131.6, the relevance of which is not immediately apparent: *Ecce audiuimus eam in effrata, inuenimus eam in campis silue.* We give the following tentative explanation. The commentaries make the distinction between the receiving of Christ by the Jews and by the gentiles through faith, whereas we should expect reference to the masters and the poor. Cf. *Glossa ordinaria*, PL, 113, 1054. The answer rests in Wit's passing use of the parable of Lazarus in the preceding Passus: there Dives, who was without charity, was contrasted to Lazarus, the poor man with charity. Dives stands for the Jews who possessed the word of God, the proud doctors; Lazarus for the gentiles who waited at the gate for crumbs from the table ("carpen atte ȝate"). Lines 69-70

> Clerkes and other kynnes men   carpen of god faste,
> And haue hym moche in the mouthe   ac mene men in herte.

are not intended to paraphrase verse 6, but continue the quotation by a paraphrase of verse 7:

Introibimus in tabernaculum ejus: adorbimus in loco, ubi steterunt pedes ejus.

The *Glossa* has the following: "Ad hanc domum pertinet, qui aliis tanquam vivis lapidibus charitate compaginatus est. Intrat ergo qui diligit, et qui intrat, domus Dei efficitur. *In loco.* Domus Dei est, ubi debet adorari: praeter quam non audit Deus ad vitam aeternam. Ille ad domum pertinet, qui est charitate compaginatus aliis. Vel locus in quo stant pedes domus Domini, Christus est, in quo perseverant." The poor with charity worship in the temple of God which is in their hearts, not on their lips.

put aside questions on such matters until "ymaginatif shal answere to ȝowre purpos." In the words of Saint Augustine, she warns that it is wrong to know more than is fitting for a man to know:[40] man must "beleueue lelly in the lore of holicherche" and pray to God;

> Al was as thow wolde   lorde, yworschiped be thow,
> And al worth as thow wolte   what so we dispute!
>
> (127-28)

In conclusion, she exclaims against Will: may he be deaf since he wishes to know what are Dowel and Dobet without learning first to live the life of Dowel, that is, to be guided by the *intellectus agens*. She swears that this Will will never learn Dobet unless he lives Dowel, though Dobest attempt to instruct him "day after other."

Wit is abashed at the condemnation of Study; he remains silent. He will give Will no further instruction unless Study approves, that is, until Will is prepared to receive it. Will humbles himself; there is in the will the natural desire to know good. Study perceives this and directs Will to his proper guides, Clergy and Dame Scripture, another truly married couple. Will asks the way to the instruction of Clergy; that is, he asks concerning the manner in which he must receive it. He must learn to endure fortune and misfortune in the world and to refrain from concern for wealth; he must avoid lust, false speech, and gluttony until he learns faith, "kepe wel thi tonge." His sobriety and simplicity of speech will cause in others the desire to instruct him. Study tells Will that he is to greet Clergy with the evidence of his own understanding of the true function of study, which, at some length she explains to him. True study in whatever field is governed

---

[40] Cf. Lombard, *Sententiae*, II, Dist. XXIII, 1, *PL*, 192, 700, where Augustine on Genesis is quoted to this effect in connection with the problem of why man is tempted.

by charity and the desire to know Truth;[41] it has no con-
cern with false argument, even though this argument be
intended to confound the evil:

> And alle that lakketh vs or lyeth vs   owre lorde techeth
>   vs to louye,
> And nouȝt to greuen hem that greueth vs   god hym-self
>   for-badde it.
>   *Michi vindictam, & ego retribuam.*
> For-thi loke thow louye   as longe as thow durest,
> For is no science vnder sonne   so souereyne for the soule.
>   (203-6)

Concern with astronomy, with sorcery, with alchemy, with
worldly sciences deceives man (207ff.)

Will hastens to Clergy, who here represents spiritual
learning, not the priesthood, since unlike Piers who is
married to the Church, Clergy is married to Dame Scrip-
ture. Will greets him and his wife, Dame Scripture, as
Study has taught him, declaring that he wishes instruction
so that he may learn charity. When they learn that Will
has come from Wit and Study, Clergy and Scripture wel-
come him. Will declares that he has been sent to learn
Dowel, Dobet and Dobest, although Study has made clear
that he should not be enquiring of Dobet until he has
learned to do well. In humility, he should be asking simply
to be shown the law so that he may learn to perform good
works. Clergy, however, apparently impressed by Will's
credentials, proceeds to explanation. He defines Dowel
in terms of the elements of the Faith (the creed); Dobet
in terms of obedience to counsel as well as to precept (doing
all that the book commands); Dobest in terms of the per-
sonal purity requisite to those who would correct others.
Clergy recurs to the theme of the wolf in sheep's clothing,

---

[41] Cf. Augustine, *De Doctrina*, PL, 34, 34: "Omnium igitur quae dicta
sunt, ex quo de rebus tractamus, haec summa est, ut intelligatur Legis et
omnium divinarum Scripturarum plenitudo et finis esse dilectio (Rom. 13.10;
et Tim. 1.5) rei qua fruendum est, et rei quae nobiscum ea re frui potest;
quia ut se quisque diligat, praecepto non opus est."

declaring the dangers inherent in the lack of personal perfection in those who lay claim to the prelatical status. The religious, including the friars, are similarly admonished. Clergy prophesies the destruction of wicked religious on the day of doom.[42] The King of Heaven will come, but before that day, Cain, the Antichrist, will appear, only to be put down by Dowel, the congregation of the loyal faithful.

Will mistakes Clergy's meaning; he understands him completely on the literal level:

'Thanne is Dowel and Dobet . . . . *dominus and kniȝthode.*'

(331)

Scripture patiently attempts to correct his absurd error. Kings and knights, no matter how good, can never help a man gain heaven. She declares that temporal wealth and power are, in fact, hindrances not aids to salvation; the love of temporal wealth is the height of iniquity (Ecclus. 10.10). Again pretending to clerical learning, Will replies, "Contra," saying that baptism is sufficient to salvation. Scripture explains that this is true *in extremis,* but for the Christian more is necessary: faithfulness to Holy Church and the observance of the precepts of Charity.[43] Without these things, earthly possessions will prove a heavy burden on the Day of Judgment. All Christians should love one another, putting wrath aside, leaving judgment to God.

In opposition to Scripture's teaching, Will develops his argument that salvation is the result of predestined grace. It is clear enough that he is talking nonsense; he argues with Scripture herself on the basis of Scripture; he violates the basic principle of humility in speech which has been

---

[42] Cf. similar warning on a literal level contained in Reason's sermon, v, 46-48; see also the Prophecies of Conscience and of Hunger, III and VI.

[43] On the appropriateness of Scripture's citation of Col. 3.1-2 (l. 355), on the level of the *sentence,* see Lombard, *PL,* 192, 279-80.

enforced by his instructors more than once. In doctrine he has shifted from acquiescence in the extreme doctrine of Piers' priestly opponent that good works are alone necessary for salvation to an equally extreme predestinarianism. Wit attempted to show Will the true inwardness of Dowel; Clergy specifically indicated the basic position in Dowel of faith, referring to the opening articles of the Creed, those articles which the priest and Will had failed to take into account:

> 'It [Dowel] is a comune lyf. . . . on holycherche to bileue,
> With *alle* the artikles of the feith   that falleth to be
>   knowe.
> And that is to bileue lelly   bothe lered and lewed,
> On the grete god   that gynnyng had neuere,
> And on the sothfaste sone   that saued mankynde. . . .
>   *Deus pater, deus filius, deus spiritus sanctus.*' (230-38)

They have been unsuccessful: as Dame Study feared, Will has simply followed the letter of their teaching to the insistence that faith is alone necessary to Dowel, that salvation is granted through predestined grace. This refusal to see and to acknowledge the truth is caused by Will's human sloth, his shrinking from spiritual labor. Misled by the friars, he seeks easy paths. He wants Dowel without having to work for it; if Dowel simply represents good works, that is well enough. He can do good works without any necessity to trouble himself with matters of faith, of inward grace. If Dowel is simply faith, and salvation simply a matter of grace given by God independent of good works, his spiritual responsibility is also nil. In short, in looking for Dowel he is trying to find a convenient formula for living in the world with as little discomfort as possible: his doctrine of predestination serves excellently well; he may now do as he wishes. The rest is up to God.

His argument against Scripture consists of a series of half-truths and *non-sequiturs*. He begins by declaring that man is placed either among the elect or among the damned long before his birth. He uses as his authority, John 3.13: *Nemo ascendit ad celum, nisi qui de celo descendit.* Will interprets the verse apparently to indicate that the man who ascends to heaven has been sent to earth for the specific purpose of returning. But the commentaries offer no justification for this heretical view; rather they indicate that Man will ascend to heaven only when he has become a true member of Holy Church.[44] Will then attempts to show that he has no need for instruction in Faith and precept, for learning and wisdom are futile; moreover, clerks like those who helped build the ark, which represents Holy Church, are often damned; furthermore many clerks are evil and to follow them is to follow them to damnation:

And if I shulde worke bi here werkes   to wynne me heuene
That for her werkes and witte   now wonyeth in pyne,
Thanne wrouʒte I vnwysely   what-so euere ʒe preche.
(387-89)

Here Will states a principal tenet of the Donatist heresy. Without good works, the thief on the cross was saved. In spite of their most evil works, Mary Magdalene, Paul and David, were saved through grace. All are in the hands of God, those who love and those who hate. In support of this doctrine Will cites Eccles. 9.1 : *Sunt iusti atque sapientes & opera eorum in manu dei; [et tamen nescit homo utrum amor an odio dignus sit.]*

There aren witty and wel-libbynge   ac her werkes ben yhudde
In the hondes of almiʒty god   and he wote the sothe
Wher for loue a man worth allowed there   and his lele werkes,
Or elles for his yuel wille   and enuye of herte,
And be allowed as he lyued so. . . . (431-35)

[44] See, for example, Bede, *PL*, 92, 670-71. In sharply ironic contrast to Will's self-assurance in answering Scripture, Innocent III takes the verse as an admonition to humility, Sermo XIV, *PL*, 217, 525-26.

In the citation of this verse to support his argument Will betrays his own continuing inability to distinguish Dowel from Doevil (cf. Pass. I, 136). In the Biblical text, people in the position of Will are ironically admonished to eat and drink and clothe themselves well, to make the most of the world since the future in the next world is uncertain. In his commentary on this passage Rupert makes clear Will's folly in defending neglect of spiritual responsibility on the basis of his ignorance of God's purpose:

Quae gravior vanitatis species, quae cura sciendi vanior esse potest? Ecce ex persona alicujus intenti vanitati tractat scire quis Domini dignus, quis indignus amore. Quod nullus invenire potest quidnam prodest quaerere? Et quis homo intelligere potest mentem Domini? Sunt justi et sapientes, sunt et eorum opera in manu Dei, qui velle gubernat, et posse, ne plus velint scire quam necesse est. Et quis homo intelligere non potest, amore Dei illos esse dignos, qui juste vivunt et sapienter operantur?[45]

Will, having been misled, is like a foolish man who cannot perceive that living well and working wisely make one worthy of the love of God. In his confusion he falsely imputes to God responsibility for evil men, who, he says, exist, so that one may know good from evil: if there were no black how could we know white?[46] Nothing can be done about evil men in the world; there are many of them and few good. Will quotes approvingly, *nemo bonus*, Luke 18.19, with the implication that since God Himself declares the world to be entirely evil, we may as well resign ourselves to it:

Quant Oportet vyent en place   yl ny ad que Pati.[47]

---

[45] *PL*, 168, 1278. Cf. Bonaventura, *Opera*, VI, 71-73.

[46] This is in direct violation of the accepted principle that God does not create evil; cf. Peter Lombard, *Sententiae*, Dist. XXXVII, 4: "Deus fecit hominem substantiam, sed per iniquitatem lapsus est homo a substantia in qua factus est; iniquitas quippe ipsa non est substantia. Non enim iniquitas est natura quam formavit Deus, sed iniquitas est perversio quam fecit homo." The material is from St. Augustine.

[47] The full text of Luke 18.19 is: *Dixit autem ei Iesus: Quid me dicis bonum? nemo bonus nisi solus Deus.* The implication of the verse is that all

He concludes with a further attack on clerical learning and a commendation of the ignorant who "percen with a *paternoster* the paleys of heuene," simply because of "her pure byleue." The unlearned do not fall so far as do the clerks who are entrusted with God's treasure, the salvation of souls; as authority he quotes Matt. 20.4: *Ite vos in vineam meam*, probably with the implication that the learned and unlearned are rewarded alike.[48]

PASSUS XI

Scripture "scorns" Will. She recognizes his wrongfulness, which is to attempt an external understanding of Dowel, without any effort at spiritual comprehension. Until he looks in his own heart—as Holy Church and the others have told him—he will not find Dowel. Once more to teach him this principle Scripture quotes the opening lines of *Meditationes Piissimae*, attributed to Bernard; the passage teaches precisely what Will must learn:

Multi multa sciunt, et se ipsos nesciunt. Alios inspiciunt, et se ipsos deserunt. Deum quaerunt per ista exteriora, deserentes sua interiora, quibus interior est Deus. Idcirco ab exterioribus redeam ad interiora, et ab inferioribus ad superiora ascendam: ut possim cognoscere unde venio, aut quo vado; quid sum, vel unde sum; et ita per cognitionem mei valeam pervenire ad cogitationem Dei. Quanto namque in cognitione mei proficio, tanto ad cognitionem Dei accedo.[49]

Will is heedless; he becomes wrathful and falls into spiritual slumber:

And in a wynkyng wratth   wex I aslepe.
A merueillouse meteles   mette me thanne,

---

goodness comes from God, not what Will has taken it to mean. Cf. Bede, *PL*, 92, 554.

[48] Although the laborers in the vineyard are rewarded in the same coin, their status in heaven is dependent on the character of their work. St. Augustine, *PL*, 38, 533. For arguments which "ad sonos vocum pendent" like Will's here, see the *Miscellanea*, ascribed to Hugh of St. Victor, *PL*, 177, 543-44.

[49] Bernard, *PL*, 184, 485.

That I was rauisshed riȝt there and fortune me fette,
And in-to the londe of Longynge allone she me brouȝte,
And in a myroure that hiȝt Mydlerd she mad me to bi-
holde. (4-8)

This sleep within a sleep recalls Holy Church's first greet-
ing of Will after she had descended from the mountain
to him: "Sone, slepestow?" The spiritual slumber is here
characterized in the manner of Saint Augustine:

Amaverunt praesentia, et dormierunt in ipsis praesentibus. . . .
venerunt in hanc vitam, et per cupiditates temporales quasi ob-
dormierunt hic.[50]

Will becomes like one of those in Isa. 65.11, who abandon
the Lord, forget the Holy Mountain, and prepare a table
for Fortune: They are described allegorically in the *Glossa
ordinaria* as those who have abandoned Holy Church in
error:

Et vos qui dereliquistis, etc. Allegorice. Omnes qui Ecclesiam dese-
runt, et obliviscuntur montem sanctum Dei, tradentes se spiritibus
erroris, vel immundis doctrinis daemoniorum, parant fortunae
mensam, et nihil ad Deum pertinere credentes, sed vel stellarum
cursu vel varietate fortunae omnia gubernari, hi tradentur aeternis
supliciis, ut nullus eorum possit evadere.[51]

Finally, Will's refusal to labor spiritually, his jangling,
his wrath at Holy Scripture, his gazing into the mirror of
Fortune, and his falling into worldly concupiscence all may
be reflections of James 1.19-27. The deceiving mirror of
James 1.23 is made particularly relevant to the poem by
the *Glossa ordinaria,* which takes it to represent false and
unguided interpretation of Scripture whereby it becomes
a mirror in which only the fickleness of Fortune is per-
ceived. This perception leads to a weak and temporary
compunction which easily succumbs to concupiscence. The
commentary precisely describes Will's situation.[52]

---

[50] *PL,* 36, 963. See also Chapter 2, note 44.
[51] *PL,* 113, 1310. Fortuna, as such, appears only in the verse cited.
[52] *Scitis, fratres mei dilectissimi. Sit autem omnis homo velox ad audien-
dum, tardus autem ad loquendum et tardus ad iram. . . . Estote autem*

Fortune has three followers: *concupiscentia carnis, concupiscentia oculorum, superbia vitae.* This combination is ultimately derived from 1 John 2.16: *Quoniam omne quod est in mundo, concupiscentia carnis, et concupiscentia oculorum est, et superbia uitae: quae non est ex Patre, sed ex mundo est.* The three errors, which are held to spring from *amor sui* and to be the source of all sin, must be overcome before one can begin the life of perfection.[53] They promise him enduring earthly joy; Fortune promises to be his friend and to bring him perpetual bliss. Age warns Will against this absurdity as does 1 John 2.17: *Et mundus transit, et concupiscentia eius.* But Recklessness defies Age, which seems far away; there will be a time for stooping. Plato, the poet, reaffirms Will in his slothful predestinarianism: "Lat God done his wille." If Truth declares it well done to follow Fortune, worldly concupiscence will never grieve you unless you let it. The *doctrinae saeculares* are reduced to absurdity—though not to such an absurdity that they do not convince Will. Childishness agrees with the doctrine and leads Will to *concupiscencia carnis.* Age laments:

---

factores verbi et non auditores tantum fallentes vosmetipsos. Quia, si quis auditor est verbi et non factor, hic comparabitur viro consideranti vultum nativitatis suae in speculo: consideravit enim se et abiit et statim oblitus est qualis fuerit. . . . Si quis autem putat se religiosum esse non refrenans linguam suam, sed seducens cor suum, huius vana est religio. Religio munda et immaculata apud Deum et Patrem haec est: visitare pupillos et viduas in tribulatione eorum et immaculatum se custodire ab hoc saeculo.

The comment in the *Glossa ordinaria, PL,* 114, 673, is as follows: "*Consideranti vultum.* Qui proponit in animo suo considerare in Scripturis quasi in speculo vultum nativitatis, qualiter homo sit natus, quam fragilis, vel quid futurus, quam brevis aevi, in quantis miseriis positus, conpunctionem magnam et voluntatem poenitendi contraxit; sed statim, aliqua tentatione seductus, obliviscitur compunctionis, et ad peccata redit. Hujus inconstantiae comparat eum qui libenter verbum audit, et implere negligit. Et est similitudo inter illum qui sponte sua, sine doctore se ad Scripturas applicuit, et illum qui ab alio Scripturas audit, cum neuter impleverit. . . . *Et immaculatum se custodire ab hoc saeculo.* Per saeculum intelligit mundum, seu omnia quae sunt in mundo, ut sunt concupiscentia carnis, et oculorum, et superbia vitae.*"

[53] See *PL,* 217, 979.

'Allas, eye!' quod Elde   and Holynesse bothe,
'That witte shal torne to wrecchednesse   for wille to haue
his lykynge!' (43-44)

Concupiscencia oculorum comforts him in his youth, tells
him to give conscience no thought and to turn to the friars
for spiritual food. While Fortune is his friend, he will
find the friars ready to befriend him. Their spiritual food
is bought for money. But with age, Will learns that the
world betrays. With the turn of Fortune, the friars also
turn. Will alienates them further by refusing to be buried
in their house, loyally heeding the teachings of conscience
that where a man was christened, there he should be
buried:[54]

And for I seyde thus to freres   a fool thei me helden,
And loued me the lasse   for my lele speche. (68-69)

He accuses the friars of concern for *temporalia* under the
figure of the man who courted a widow for her wealth (cf.
IX, 161-62). He ironically wonders why the friars should
be eager to confess and bury, but not to baptize, although
baptism is the first essential to salvation. There is no tem-
poral profit in baptism. Will has at last come to understand
the agency through which the evils of Lady Meed are
spread through the world. Since the *intellectus agens* is
the faculty which makes judgments of this kind so that
the will may act reasonably, it is clear that the stage of the
poem has been reached in which this intellect is operative.
The result is that henceforth Will acts with increasing
reasonableness.

His loyal speech brings Loyalty to his side. Will has

[54] The avarice of the friars for burial fees was one of the points brought
against them by the seculars under William of St.-Amour. As a result, Hum-
bert de Romans felt it necessary to correct his Dominicans on this point. See
Denifle and Chatelain, *Cartularium*, I, 288. The secular position was main-
tained by Godefroid de Fontaines (1904), 154. Later it was re-emphasized
by Jean de Pouilli. See A. Gwynn, *op. cit.*, p. 81. A general account of the
subject may be found in J. R. H. Moorman, *Church Life in England in the
Thirteenth Century* (Cambridge 1945), pp. 390-93.

perceived the wolfishness of the false doctors, the friars; he yearns to speak his mind, but his experience has apparently taught him something of humility. He does not speak out in the old manner; rather he exclaims: "if I durste . . . amonges men this meteles auowe!" Loyalty gives him permission to express his loyal speech with the important provision that his admonition be spoken not in hatred, but in charity, with the sincere desire for the correction of the individual reproved. He declares that the complaint must involve only what is openly known—as, we understand, the evil-doing of the friars is openly known —that the complainant must not be the first to speak out, and that prelates may not tell tales touching sin. The counsel to charity is contained in the texts adduced by Loyalty. *Non oderis fratres secrete in corde tuo, set publice argue illos* (Lev. 19.17), as "witnessed" by Saints Peter and Paul, is an admonition to charity. Thus Rabanus commenting on the verse cites St. Paul:

Est autem confirmatio haec: *Et diliges amicum*, sive, ut Septuaginta, *proximum tuum sicut teipsum*: habens in modico totam legem, et per unum tibi hoc mandatum omnia custodire facile est. *Charitas enim*, ait Paulus, *proximo malum non operatur. Plenitudo* ergo *legis charitas est* (1 Cor. 13).[55]

Will replies that the friars will answer this admonition with Matt. 7.1, *Nolite iudicare quemquam*. The objection is specious; it is a reply by the letter, not by the spirit. The *sentence*, as revealed, for example, in the commentary of Bruno Astensis, confirms the opinion of Loyalty:

Dicatur ergo: nolite injuste et contra legis praeceptum aliquem judicare, et non judicabimini de injusto judicio. . . Et de occultis quidem judicare Apostolus prohibet dicens: "Nolite itaque ante tempus judicare, quoadusque veniat Dominus qui et illuminabit

[55] *PL*, 108, 452. For Peter's "witnessing," see 1 Peter 1.22: *animas vestras castificantes in oboedientia caritatis, in fraternitatis amore, simplici ex corde invicem diligite attentius.*

abscondita tenebrarum, et manifestabit consilia cordium (1 Cor. 4.5)."[56]

The commentaries cited indicate the force of Loyalty's answer to Will:

> And wher-of serueth lawe. . . . if no lyf vndertoke it,
> Falsenesse ne faytrye;   for sumwhat the apostle seyde,
>   *Non oderis fratrem.* (89-90)

Of what force would be the love of one's neighbor if no one revealed falseness so that it might be corrected? The "somewhat" which the apostle said on the verse from Leviticus has been indicated above.[57] Psalm 49.21, *Existimasti inique quod ero tui similis, &c.*, which Loyalty also cites, indicates that the evil have seen consent to their evil doing in the silence of God (verse 20: *haec fecisti, et tacui*).

Scripture agrees with Loyalty and preaches on the theme, Many are called, but few are chosen (Matt. 22.14), the parable of the marriage feast. Augustine's sermon on the parable makes clear its use in the poem. The good and the bad, according to Augustine, are invited to the feast by the servants of God; it is God Himself who casts out the evil, symbolized by the one guest who was without the proper marriage garment. This garment is not the act of baptism; rather it is charity. In the imitation of Christ and in obedience to the precepts of charity, one must attempt to lead one's enemies to good:

Dic plane, dic etiam hoc, dic ut inimicum tuum persequaris: sed scienter dic; distingue quod dicis. Ecce homo est inimicus tuus: responde mihi, quid in illo inimicetur tibi; numquid hoc quod homo est, inimicatur tibi? Non. Sed quid? Quod malus est. . . . Audio enim hominem, et malum: unum nomen est naturae, alterum culpae: sano culpam, et servo naturam.[58]

[56] *PL*, 165, 125.
[57] See also 1 John 3.12-15 and 1 John 4.20 for the admonition against hatred of one's brother and toward charity. In general Loyalty's remarks concerning fraternal admonition are similar to the conclusions expressed by Godefroid (1932), 121-24.
[58] *PL*, 38, 565.

Augustine also explains that charity is necessary to faith, a point of importance in view of Will's lapse into predestinarianism. Will must learn to wear the marriage robes of charity, of humility, and of faith. Scripture's sermon causes Will to tremble in his heart and to consider whether or not he is of the elect. Holy Church has received him at baptism, as Christ receives all who turn to him. He cites Isa. 55.1, *Omnes sitientes venite,* but not exactly. Will's version is *O vos omnes scicientes, venite, &c.* This modification is not due to carelessness but represents a play on the words *sitientes,* "thirsting," and *scientes,* "knowing." The wordplay indicates that Will not only thirsts after Truth, but also knows what his thirst implies. Jerome comments on the verse which Will cites:

De quo lacte dicebat et Paulus: *Lac vobis potum dedi, non solidum cibum* (1 Cor. 3.2), Et Petrus: *Quasi modo nati parvuli, rationale lac desiderate* (1 Pet. 2.2). Unde et Moyses vinum et lac in Christi intelligens passione.[59]

Will sees the folly of his predestinarianism:

'Thanne may alle crystene come. . . . and cleyme there entre,
By the blode that he bouȝte vs with   and thorugh bap-
                                                          tesme after,
  Qui crediderit & baptizatus fuerit, &c. (118-19)

Bede's commentary on the verse, Mark 16.16, indicates its connection with Will's renunciation of his false views and his acceptance of the true:

Fortasse unusquisque apud semetipsum dicat: Ego jam credidi, salvus ero. Verum dicit, si fidem operibus tenet. Vera etenim fides est, quae in hoc quod verbis dicit, moribus non contradicit.[60]

Utilizing the same image of the servant and the lord with which he concluded his false argument (x, 467-74), Will now indicates his understanding of the proper use of God's gifts (122-31). No man may dispose of the spiritual gifts given him because they are not in his gift; he may misuse

[59] *PL,* 24, 549.   [60] *PL,* 92, 299.

them, however, and turning his back on God, "as a reneyed caityf recchelesly gon aboute" (125), to fall more and more in debt to God. His debts must be paid in the after life until the Day of Judgment, when he will be finally doomed unless, while there was time, contrition has come to obtain mercy for him. He must, that is, handle *temporalia* to the end that God may be worshiped, and in so far as he fails, he must make amends through the stages of contrition.

Scripture assents to this doctrine, asserting the universal efficacy of mercy, but with the caution that meekness must accompany its operation, a point of special importance for Will. She cites Ps. 144.9: *Misericordia eius super omnia opera eius.*[61] Since there is no sin too great for the mercy of God, whatever hardness of punishment exists, exists only in the hardness of the sinner's heart. The promise of mercy is a call to repentance and to charity. As Peter Lombard says, commenting on the verse:

Et in hoc quod exspectat in peccato manentes et monet converti, bene omnibus facit, et miserationes omnibus exhibet. Quod si punit, severitas est, non in ejus, sed in tua opera; si enim tollas opera tua mala, et non in te remaneant nisi opera ejus, non te dimittet miseratio ejus; si autem tu non dimittas opera tua, erit ejus severitas in opera tua.[62]

To illustrate the efficacy of mercy and charity, Scripture introduces dramatically the figure of Trajan, who was saved from Hell through the prayers of Gregory the Great. Scripture asks lords to witness how Trajan, the non-Christian, was saved through his loyalty to the precepts of charity, which enabled him, through mercy, to achieve salvation. Law without love, declares Trajan, is nothing. What man does he must do for charity. The old law is fulfilled

---

[61] The Vulgate reads *miserationes*, not *misericordia.*
[62] *PL*, 191, 1265.

in the new law of charity.[63] Poverty, along with age, turned Will's mind toward humility:

And pouerte pursued me   and put me lowe.   (61)

This humility prepared him to receive the further instruction of Scripture, which had been interrupted through his presumption. Scripture's lesson is a lesson in charity as the fundamental and necessary adjunct to faith. The lesson of charity is of fundamental importance to Will, for without charity perception of the Truth is impossible. As Holy Church has shown, the law is learned through charity (1, 140-50). Scripture for this reason now turns to an elaboration of the meaning and operation of charity. God has commanded the Christian to love his neighbor, that is, his fellow Christian:

Operemur bonum ad omnes, maxime autem ad domesticos fidei, id est, ad christianos. Omnibus enim pari dilectione vita aeterna optanda est, etsi non omnibus eadem possunt exhiberi dilectionis officia; quae fratribus maxime sunt exhibenda, quia sunt sibi invicem membra, qui habent eumdem Patrem, scilicet Deum.[64]

It is especially meritorious for the Christian to love his enemy (Matt. 5.4). As Peter Lombard states,

Illud vero August., novissime positum, de perfecta charitate dictum intelligitur, quae tantum est perfectorum; qui non solum amicós, sed etiam inimicos perfecte diligunt, eisque benefaciunt. Quae perfectio dilectionis non est tantae multitudinis, quanta exauditur in oratione Dominica, et hoc revera grande est et eximiae bonitatis, perfecte diligere inimicum. Ita et cum dicit impleri verba illius sponsionis ab homine qui non ita profecit ut diligat inimicum, de dilectione perfecta accipiendum est.[65]

The poor people are the poor in spirit, the children of Christ, our fellow Christians, whom we should love first, and after them our enemies:

[63] Cf. Peter Lombard, In Ep. II Ad Cor, PL, 192, 24, "Lex ergo bona est, sed cum gratia, ut cum charitate scientia prodest, sine ea occidit. Ita lex sine gratia occidit, cum sit virtus peccati, non tamen etiam sic, mala est."
[64] Peter Lombard, Sententiae, III, Dist. XXIX, 2, PL, 192, 816.
[65] Ibid., III, Dist. XXX, 1, PL, 192, 819.

> And comaundeth eche creature   to confourme hym to
>   louye,
> And souereynelyche pore poeple   and here ennemys after.
>   (175-76)

The humility of Christ, figured in his poverty, is an example to all of us:

> For owre ioye and owre hele   Ihesu Cryst of heuene,
> In a pore mannes apparaille   pursueth vs euere,
> And loketh on vs in her liknesse   and that with louely
>   chere,
> To knowen vs by owre kynde herte   and castyng of owre
>   eyen,
> Whether we loue the lordes here   byfor owre lorde of
>   blisse. (179-83)

Augustine's explanation of Christ's assumption of poverty explains the doctrine underlying the passage:

Verus pauper. Christus pauper et dives. Invenimus verum pauperem, invenimus pium humilem, non de se fidentem, pauperem verum, membrum pauperis qui propter nos pauper factus est, cum dives esset.[66]

Christ calls to us, testing the truth of our hearts, when those in need of food, drink, and clothing (figuratively or literally) call to us. If we heed them, we heed Christ; if we do not, we deny Christ (Matt. 25.34-46). The poor whom we should heed are the members of Christ, that is, the faithful of the Church:

Et respondens rex dicit illis: Amen, amen dico vobis, quandiu fecistis uni de his fratribus meis minimis, mihi fecistis. [Matt. 25.40] In membris suis suscipitur Christus: membra enim, sua sunt omnes Christiani; ideo enim Christiani dicuntur, quia membra sunt Christi. . . . Christus igitur in esurientibus esurit, in sitientibus sitit, in infirmis aegrotat, et in aliis similiter patitur. Magna ergo reverentia suscipiendi sunt pauperes Christi; cum magna veneratione serviendum est eis; si quidem Christus in eis suscipitur, et honoratur in eis.[67]

[66] *Sermo de versu 14 Psalmi 9, PL,* 38, 115.
[67] Bruno Astensis, *PL,* 165, 285. Some significance may be attached to the

We should invite the poor, that is, the members of Christ, to our feasts, not our friends, that is, those of the world (Luke 14.12):

Cum facitis conuiuia, nolite inuitare amicos.

Those of the world, our friends, repay us with temporal reward; Christ rewards us with salvation (Luke 14.14):

Et beautus eris, q'ria non habent retribuere tibi; retribuetur enim tibi in resurrectione iustorum.

Ac for the pore I shal paye   and pure wel quyte her trau-
                                                                                    aille,
That ȝiueth hem mete or moneye   and loueth hem for my
                                                                                    sake. (189-90)

The poor in spirit may or may not be rich or poor in the sight of the world, but they are all brothers in Christ in the new law of charity.[68] Through sin we become poor in the things of the spirit; we become false beggars, not the poor in spirit who are the members of Christ:

No beggere ne boye amonges vs   but if it synne made;
    Qui facit peccatum, seruus est peccati, &c. (197)

The text cited is John 8.34. Bruno comments:

Peccavit enim primus homo, et factus est servus peccati. Ejectus igitur de paradiso, ejectus de domo Domini, non mansit ibi in aeternam. Qui simul cum tota sua posteritate, nisi per Dei Filium, ab originali peccato liberari non potuit.[69]

Thus we were called the sons of men, of the issue of Adam, until the Saviour came, when we, his brothers became the sons of God, in loving and helping one another (Gal. 6.2):

Alter alterius onera portate (205)

We must be humble, like the common woman, whom Christ

---

fact that Bruno takes up the problem of predestination in his commentary on the passage. It is in the acts of charity that man of his own will acknowledges Christ: in the recognition of this truth lies the answer to Will's predestinarianism.

[68] Cf. Jerome's commentary on Isa. 55.1, quoted above, p. 135.
[69] *PL,* 165, 522.

saved through her faith (Luke 7.50). The passage cited is significant because read simply *ad litteram*, it could be misinterpreted:

> *Dixit autem ad mulierem: Fides sua te salvum fecit; vade in pace.*

But it was not her faith alone which saved her; it was her charity as well:

> Vide ergo quid fides et dilectio operetur.[70]

Faith, Scripture says, is a "lele helpe above logyke or lawe," but the message of Faith, "faithes techynge" is to be found in Luke 6.38:

> *Eadem mensura qua mensi fueritis, remecietur vobis*

As Bede says concerning the verse:

> Huic simile est, quod alibi dicit: *Ut et ipsi recipiant vos in aeterna tabernacula* (Luke 16.9). Non enim pauperes ipsi, sed Christus mercedem his [cf. Luke 14.14 and line 189 cited above], qui eleemosynam fecere redditurus est. Quam tamen in sinum dare dicuntur, quia promerendae illius occasionem dedere, cum vel egentes misere, vel improbe saevientes, fortiorum sunt et tolerati patientia, et beneficentia sustenati, et ad ipsam aliquoties fidem dulci gratia provocati.[71]

Scripture summarizes:

> For-thi lerne we the lawe of loue as owre lorde tauȝte,
> And as seynte Gregory seide for mannes soule healthe,
> *Melius est scrutari scelera nostra, quam naturas rerum.*[72]
>   (222-23)

[70] Bruno, *PL*, 165, 382. See also Bede, *PL*, 92, 425-28, for an extended discussion of the allegorical significance of the acts of the woman in bathing the feet of Jesus.

[71] *PL*, 92, 409. Saint John is said (221) to bear witness to this verse. There are cross references in some commentaries to the Apocalypse, but we have not been able to determine with any assurance the exact verse or verses intended by the poet in the Gospel, the Epistles, or the Apocalypse. Father J. B. Dwyer, S.J., suggests that 1 John 3 may be relevant here as a good summary of St. John's teaching on charity. Professor Gerould suggests to us that the poet simply mistook his Evangelist.

[72] The source for this in Gregory we have not found; the *sentence* is the same as that in the beginning of the meditations of Bernard with which

Scripture then develops the allegorical symbol of poverty.
Christ appeared as a poor man and a pilgrim to Cleophas
on the way to Emmaus. (Luke 24.13ff.) He was not rec-
ognized until later when he broke bread with the disciples:

So bi his werkes thei wisten that he was Iesus;
Ac by clothyng thei knewe hym nouȝte ne bi carpynge
of tonge. (230-31)

These lines reflect the traditional interpretation:

Fregit, etc. Quem in expositione Scripturae non cognove-
runt, in fractione panis noverunt, quia non auditores legis,
sed factores justificabuntur, et veritas melius operando
quam audiendo intelligitur.[73]

The poet continues,

And al was in ensample to vs synful here,
That we shulde be low and loueliche of speche,
And apparaille vs nouȝte ouer proudly for pylgrymes ar
we alle. (232-34)

Bonaventura's commentary on Luke 24.18 illustrates the
meaning:

Recte autem *peregrinus* eis apparebat, quia *peregrinus* erat *in
mundo;* Ioannis primo: "In mundo erat, et mundus eum non
cognovit." . . . *Peregrinus* erat *in oculis discipulorum* non creden-
tium. . . *Peregrinus* etiam *in membris;* ad Hebraeos undecimo:
"Confitentes quasi peregrini et advenae sunt super terram"; et
secundae ad Corinthios quinto: "Dum sumus in hoc corpore, pere-
grinamur a Domino." Et ideo primae Petri secundo: "Obsecro
vos tanquam advenas et peregrinos."[74]

---

the Passus begins. Lombard, *PL,* 191, 1601, quotes a very similar statement
from Augustine.

[73] *Glossa ordinaria, PL,* 114, 352. Note that the *Glossa* quotes Jas. 1.22,
a passage of importance in the episode of Will's falling into the Land of
Longing (page 130 above). The contrast is enforced by the commentary on
the subsequent verse, Luke 24.31: "*Aperti sunt,* etc. Subtrahitur carnalibus
oculis species infirmitatis, ut mentibus incipiat apparere gloria resurrec-
tionis." So Will's eyes were blinded by the mirror of middle-earth, and are
now learning to see the light of grace.

[74] *Opera,* VII, 593. The reference to Christ's incarnation in the Virgin
Mary (240-41) is appropriate to the discussion of poverty, not only for
the obvious reason that Joseph was a poor carpenter, but also for a more
significant reason which Augustine has stated, *PL,* 38, 115 (see note 66):
"Paupertatem cogitemus, ne forte pauperes vel ipsam capiamus. Concipitur

As Mary showed no concern for the world, so ought the poor in spirit to suffer the tribulations of the world in patience and with a lifting of the spirit to God. All the wise "preysen pouerte for best lyf if pacience it follow."[75] The reward for patient suffering of poverty is great, in evidence of which Scripture adduces several texts.[76] The doctrine is especially applicable to the priesthood in its function of supplying spiritual food. Scripture cites Ps. 42, which contains the verse, *Spera in Deo*. Verse 4, *Et introibo ad altare Dei*, Peter Lombard says, makes the Psalm peculiarly appropriate to the priesthood:

Nota quod altare missam celebraturus sacerdos ascendens, ait: *Introibo, etc.* Desiderio enim et amore superioris et invisibilis altaris, hoc visibile cum modestia adire debet, aeterna non caduca petiturus, ut Christi celsitudinem humilis sequatur.

Spera in Deo (verse 6) is said to give further counsel:

Haec vox, fratres, tuta est, sed vigilate in operibus bonis, tangite psalterium obediendo, et tangite citharum passiones tolerando, frange esurienti panem tuum. . . . Aliis ergo da quod tibi denegasti. Quam multos enim pauperes saginare potest intermissum hodie prandium!

The Psalm, again according to Peter Lombard, contains the general admonition to resist the world:

---

utero feminae virginali, includitur visceribus matris. O paupertas! In angusto diversorio nascitur, etc." The instance of Martha and Mary (242-46) is appropriate to Scripture's discussion because it is taken as illustrative of the doctrine of charity: *Glossa ordinaria*, PL, 114, 287: "Habito sermone de dilectione Dei et proximi, supponitur exemplum utriusque dilectionis, non tam in solo verbo, quam in operibus exhibitione." Mary seated at the feet of Jesus serves as an example of humility: "Quanto humilius sedet, tanto amplius cadit." Matthew's testimony is probably to be found in Matt. 6.33, which explains why Mary has selected the better part, "Quaerite ergo primum regnum Dei."

[75] The doctrine is found, for example, in Ps. 9.19: *Quoniam non in finem oblivio erit pauperis, patientia pauperum non peribit in finem*. Compare Ecclus. 2.4: *Omne quod tibi applicitum fuerit accipe et in dolore sustine et in humilitate tua patientiam habe*.

[76] Matt. 19.21; Ps. 36.25; Matt. 17.20, Ps. 33.11, Ps. 42.1.

142

Et est iste psalmus contra pressuras saeculi, ne et ipsae retrahant nos a Deo. Intentio. Monet ne in pressuris deficiamus.[77]

This poverty, Scripture makes clear, does not imply want or destitution; the priest must have the means to carry on his work, but he must use what he is given in the service of God.

The priest who does not live up to this obligation is a jangler, with no claim to the sustenance of the priesthood. He betrays his flock. The jangling priest violates the law of charity as is indicated by the citation of Jas. 2.10, which refers to the offense of the tongue and its serious consequences:

Qui offendit in uno, in omnibus est reus, &c.

Bede comments:

Offendens quippe in uno, factus est omnium reus. Quaerendum est ergo, unde sit omnium reus, si in uno offenderit, qui totam legem servaverit. An forte quia plenitudo legis est charitas, qua Deus proximusque diligitur, in quibus praeceptis charitatis, tota lex pendet et prophetae, merito fit omnium reus, qui contra illam facit in qua pendent omnia?[78]

The discussion of priesthood was suggested by Will's own contumacious attack on the priesthood. Scripture indicates that the discussion was digressive and affirms that her subject has been the praise of spiritual poverty. She began by explaining the precepts of charity: love God and thy neighbor. Among our neighbors we should love first the poor in spirit, who are our neighbors in Christ. To practice charity well, we should ourselves be among them. Poverty of spirit is thus one of the fundamental principles Will must learn if he is to understand the basic doctrine of the eternal Church, *Deus caritas*.

[77] Peter Lombard, *PL*, 191, 423-27.
[78] *PL*, 93, 19. The chapter of the Epistle from which the verse is cited contains much that is relevant. It is significant that Holy Church, after citing Jas. 2.20, proceeded to attack priests who had chastity but not charity (1, 187-97).

Nature now appears to show Will a vision of the world, not in the mirror of cupidity, but clearly so that Will may build upon the fear of the Lord which he has felt (110-12), the beginnings of the wisdom which will lead him to the love of God:

I was fette forth by ensaumples to knowe,
Thorugh eche a creature and Kynde my creatoure to
               louye. (316-17)

He has seen the evil in the world in the episode of Lady Meed; he has himself experienced the evil of the world: he must learn that this evil is present in the world for a divine purpose, to test the hearts of men, who must learn to suffer evil patiently. The proposition is implicitly proved by Will's own beginnings of reasonableness, occasioned by his discovery of the transparent evil of the friars. In the vision he sees the birds and beasts acting in apparent accord with Reason, whereas men often do not. When he sees men, he also sees the opposites that have come into the world through evil; he sees the alternatives that Wit presented to him, and he also sees that men often choose the wrong alternative:

Man and his make I myȝte bothe byholde;
Pouerte and plente bothe pees and werre,
Blisse and bale bothe I seigh at ones,
And how men token mede and mercy refused.
               (322-25)

The beasts and birds follow the law of Kind, the order of Reason: They do not work out of season. Will's mind is troubled by the problem of why the beasts act in apparent accord with Reason whereas men often do not. He is troubled to the point that he ceases to look for the lesson which will teach him to love God; instead he loses his newly acquired humility and questions God's Providence by reproving Reason for permitting evil to exist:

144

Ac that moste moeued me   and my mode chaunged,
That Resoun rewarded   and reuled alle bestes,
Saue man and his make;   many tyme and ofte
No resoun hem folwed   and thanne I rebuked
Resoun, and riȝte   til hym-seluen I seyde,
'I haue wonder of the,' quod I   'that witty art holden,
Why thow ne suwest man and his make   that no mysfait
                   hem folwe.' (360-66)

Reason rebukes Will sharply for his presumption. He has raised a question the answer to which he can understand only after he has learned true humility: what Reason "suffers" or does not suffer is beyond Will's question. Let Will amend while there is time; Reason's time of Judgment is yet to come.[79] To suffer is a sovereign virtue for man; God's sufferance entails swift vengeance after man's time for suffering has passed. God suffers evil to try men, to reward the good:

'Who suffreth more than god?' quod he   'no gome, as I
                                     leue!
He miȝte amende in a minute while   al that mys standeth,
Ac he suffreth for somme mannes good   and so is owre
                         bettre.' (371-73)

Will has been at fault because he has spoken before he should (Ecclus. 11.8):

Prius quam audias, ne respondeas verbum, et in medio sermonum ne adjicias loqui.

He is himself guilty because he has defended evil in blaming Reason, not the evil-doer, for its existence (Ecclus. 11.9, cited by Reason, 385):

De ea re quae te non molestat ne certeris; et in judicio peccantium ne consistas.

Rabanus comments:

Admonet ut in superfluis rebus non nimis simus curiosi, et peccantium pravitati non consentiamus. Docet enim Apostolus. . . . 'Non

---

[79] Cf. Holy Church, II, 47-48; Reason's retinue, IV, 16-22; the prophecy of Conscience, III, 297.

solum, inquit, qui faciunt mala, sed et qui consentiunt facientibus, digni sunt morte (Rom. 1.32).'

For God created only good, as the *sentence*, not the *letter* of Ecclus. 11.14 indicates:

Bona et mala, vita et mors, paupertas et honestas a Deo sunt. . . . Unde quaeritur quomodo bona et mala a Deo sint, et vita et mors? cum Scriptura dicat: 'Vidit Deus cuncta quae fecit, et erant valde bona.' [Gen. 1.31., cited by Reason, 388.] . . . Non enim Deus alia fecit nisi bona; sed tamen justo judicio suo peccantibus provenire permittit adversa. Facit ergo ipse Deus res intra se contrarias, lucem et tenebras, id est, diem et noctem, pacem et malum, hoc est, otium et bellum.[80]

In this way the opposites which Will had observed (322-25) are to be explained. The beasts of the world were placed here for the pleasure of man, who must suffer because of the flesh and the devil:

For man was made of such a matere   he may nouʒt wel
                                                  astert
That ne some tymes hym bitit   to folwen his kynde.
                                                     (392-93)[81]

[80] Rabanus, *PL*, 109, 840-42. The verses in question and their commentary are most significant in that they deal with the question of spiritual poverty; thus verse 11: *Est homo laborans*, etc . . . . "Terrarum siquidem divites, et pauperes Christi, magnifica contrarietate distinxit. Ait enim: 'Divites eguerunt et esurierunt.' Quando egent divites? quando fidem non habent rectam. Quando esuriunt? quando pastu corporis Dominici minime satiantur. . . . 'Inquirentes autem Dominum non deficient omni bono' [Ps. 33.11, cited line 273]: quia nullo bono deficiunt qui spiritali perfruuntur; nam cum diligimus Dominum, in ipso omnia reperimus." The *Glossa ordinaria* on Gen. 11.31, *PL*, 113, 81, takes up the problem of evil: "Quaeritur, cum singillatim caetera bona dicantur, cur homo ad imaginem Dei factus cum caeteris hoc dicatur? Sed forte praesiebat Deus eum peccaturum, nec in perfectione imaginis mansurum. Qui enim singillatim bonus est, magis cum omnibus, sed non convertitur . . . . Deus autem omnia ordinavit, ut si qua singillatim fuerint deliquendo deformia, semper tamen cum eis universitas sit formosa."

[81] Cf. Peter Lombard, *Sententiae*, II, Dist. XXIII, 1, *PL*, 192, 700: "Praeterea quaeri solet cur Deus hominem tentari permiserit, quem decipiendum fore praesciebat. Sed non esset laudabile homini, si ideo bene vivere posset, quia nemo male vivere suaderet, cum in natura posse, et in potestate habere vellet non consentire suadenti, Deo juvante; et est gloriosius non consentire quam tentari non posse . . . . Item inquiunt: Posset Deus voluntatem eorum

Will blushes in shame and awakes. He recognizes his lapse
from humility; he realizes that he has wished to know
more than he should know, that it is sufficient for him to
know that evil has not come from God but from the evil
will of man. Now that he has awakened from his spiritual
slumber, signified by his dream within his vision, he finds
Imaginative, whose teaching had been promised to him by
Dame Study:

> Ymaginatyf her-afterward   shal answere to ȝowre pur-
> pos.
> Augustyne to suche argueres   he telleth hem this teme,
>   *Non plus sapere quam oportet* (x, 115-16)

With the fear of God has come the beginning of the wis-
dom, that is the *intellectus agens,* which enables him to
feel shame and to distinguish between evil and good:

> 'Now I wote what Dowel is,' quod I   'by dere god, as me
> thinketh. . . .'
> 'To see moche and suffre more, certes . . . is Dowel.'
> (399, 402)

With the guidance of the active intellect it is possible for
Will to look into his own heart, to follow the advice Scrip-
ture has given him, *Multi multa sciunt, & seipsos nesciunt*
(xi, 3), and again, *Melius est scrutari scelera nostra, quam
naturas rerum* (xi, 223). He is prepared to receive the
teachings of Imaginative, the virtue through which the
active intelligence is provided with materials for its func-
tion as the guide to moral action.[82]

Imaginative proceeds to indicate Will's sin of presump-
tion which has lost for him the teaching of truth. His was

---

vertere in bonum, quia omnipotens est; posset revera. Cur non fecit? Quia
noluit. Cur noluit? Ipse novit. Non debemus plus sapere quam oportet." See
x, 116-28.

[82] Cf. Godefroid (1914), p. 172: "Dico quod actio intellectus agentis
proprie dicta est circa phantasmata quae non sunt in intellectu possibili sed
in virtute phantastica."

the sin of Adam in avoiding spiritual responsibility by attributing evil to God, not to man:

Et dixit Adam, Mulier quam dedisti mecum, haec mihi dedit a ligno, et edi. Eia superbia! numquid dixit, Peccavi? Habet confusionis deformitatem, et non habet confessionis humilitatem. Ad hoc ista conscripta sunt, quia et ipsae interrogationes nimirum ad hoc factae sunt, ut et veraciter et utiliter scriberentur; quia si mendaciter, non utique utiliter: ut advertamus, quo morbo superbiae laborent homines hodie, nonnisi in Creatorem conantes referre si quid egerint mali, cum sibi velint tribui si quid egerint boni.[83]

As Satan had corrupted Adam and Eve through the promise that they would be equal in knowledge to God, so Will has sought to know that which God alone may know. But the shame which has come to Will is good:

Shal neuere chalangynge ne chydynge chaste a man so
                sone
As shal Shame, and shenden hym, and shape hym to
              amende. (415-16)

Like the drunken man who has fallen blindly into a ditch, Will since he has awakened himself, may now amend himself through shame. Will acknowledges his sin:

'Why ȝe wisse me thus. . . . was for I rebuked Resoun.'
         (428)

He has finally come to understand what Holy Church taught him

For riȝtful reson shulde rewle ȝow alle (I, 54)

Wit also had admonished him

Moche wo worth that man that mys-reuleth his Inwitte,
And that be glotouns globbares her god is her wombe;
      Quorum deus venter est.
For thei seruen sathan her soule shal he haue;
That liueth synful lyf here her soule is liche the deuel.
And alle that lyuen good lyf aren like god almiȝti,
Qui manet in caritate, in deo manet, &c. (IX, 59-63)

[83] Augustine, *De Genesi ad litteram*, PL, 34, 449.

Will is prepared to learn to bow to Reason, to learn Dowel by allowing his active intellect to guide him in the practice of patience and humility.

PASSUS XII

Imaginative, in answer to Will's question concerning his identity, reveals that he is that faculty which enables Will to think of his inevitable death in the future and of his misspent past, precisely those thoughts which are conducive to moral action. He has warned Will to amend in youth and in middle age, since in old age he may not be able to suffer "pouerte or penaunce or preyeres bidde" (9).[84] Diseases and poverty have also warned Will, and these represent the admonitions of God who chastises those He loves.[85] The chastisement of God is a consolation to the sinner, directing him to reform, as Ps. 22.5 witnesses: *Virga tua et baculus tuus, ipsa me consolata sunt, etc.*[86] But Will, instead of leading a life of contemplation, has concerned himself with "makynges," although there are books enough already to teach men Dowel, Dobet, and Dobest, and

---

[84] The statement is almost a paraphrase of the *Glossa ordinaria* on the text which Imaginative quotes (Luke 12.38): *Si non in prima vigilia, nec in secunda, etc.* The gloss, PL, 114, 298, reads: "Vigilias vocat a similitudine excubantium. In nocte hujus mundi semper debemus esse contra hostem solliciti, et exspectare lucem venturam, id est adventum judicis. Prima ergo vigilia custodia pueritiae est, secunda juventutis, tertia senectutis. Si quis vero in pueritia vigilare neglexerit, non tamen desperet, sed etiam in juventute vel saltem tandem in senectute resipiscat, quia pius judex moras nostras patienter exspectat."

[85] Imaginative quotes *Quem diligo, castigo*, which represents a conception found in various Scriptural passages. Prov. 3.12, for example, runs, *Quem enim diligit Dominus, corripit.* Bede, PL, 91, 951, comments: "Tanto ergo minus de flagello quo castigamur murmurare debemus, quanto certius in eo paternae dilectionis pignus tenemus."

[86] The interpretation of this line required in the poem is that given by Peter Lombard, PL, 191, 243-44: "Virga dicit, disciplinaque est levis, quae sit quasi ad oves. Baculus dicitur disciplina quae est fortis, quae fit ad grandiores filios. Quasi dicat: Non timebo mala, et vere, *nam virga tua et baculus tuus, id est disciplina . . . . ipsa me* non afflixerunt, sed potius *consolata sunt* erudiendo me, quia in his intelligo te esse memorem mei."

preachers enough to make the ideas clear (16-19). Will replies with an excuse from Cato, *Interpone tuis interdum gaudia curis,* and an assertion to the effect that if anyone will teach him Dowell, Dobet, and Dobest, he will devote the remainder of his days to prayer. The object of Imaginative's rebuke is the same as that of Dame Study. He is reproving the unlearned for their proneness to declare their own minds. It is significant that Will's defense shows a new humility; he does not argue but deprecates his own frailty. As he says, "I seigh wel he sayde me soth." (20)

Imaginative answers his request for further instruction concerning the three states by emphasizing the importance of charity. He quotes 1 Cor. 13.13, which recognizes the importance of faith and hope, but places charity above them, since it necessarily includes them.[87] Dowell consists in doing "as lewte techeth," that is, in being obedient to the precepts of charity. Those in the *status conjugatorum* should "lyue forth as lawe wole," observing the duties of true wedded folk as outlined previously by Wit. The religious, as Reason advised, should not run to Rome but should take their pilgrimage in obedience to the rule. Those who are chaste and who can remain continent should seek "neuere seynt forther" (40) but embrace the religious life, voluntarily renouncing "catel and kynde witte" which deceived Lucifer, Solomon, and many others who occupied themselves with the wealth and wisdom of the world.[88] Riches are a hindrance unless they are based on charity whence springs grace.

> Ac grace ne groweth nouȝte   but amonges lowe;
> Pacience and pouerte   the place is there it groweth,
> And in lele-lyuyngemen   and in lyf-holy (62-64)

[87] On the inclusiveness of charity, see Peter Lombard, *PL*, 191, 1663.

[88] We take no account here of ll. 57-59 since there is some doubt as to whether they should be properly included in the B-text. The meaning seems clear enough. *Sapiencia* is used in place of *scientia*, but it is clear that worldly wisdom is implied.

Grace comes through the gift of the Holy Spirit; no one knows where it will fall (John 3.8): *Spiritus ubi vult spirat.* The verse continues, *et vocem eius audis, sed nescis unde veniat aut quo vadat.* Clergy arises from *quod scimus,* knowledge from *quod vidimus* (John 3.11), but grace comes from God.

Even though clergy does not know how grace comes forth, and knowledge cannot trace its path, both clergy and knowledge are commendable. That is, clergy which is based on Christ's love is good. With this preliminary limitation, Imaginative describes Dobest in terms of the dignity and worth of Clergy whom Will had attacked violently (x, 372ff.). Imaginative here reiterates a point made by Study (x, 180ff.). In general, he recalls and reinforces lessons to which Will has been exposed earlier. The worth of Clergy is attested in the example of Moses, in Christ's saving the adulterous woman:

So clergye is conforte   to creatures that repenten,
And to mansed men   myschief at her ende. (85-86)

Without clergy, the sacrament of the eucharist, which is a help to the righteous[89] and death to the evil[90] would be impossible. Thus Clergy and Kind Wit should be respected,

For bothe ben as miroures   to amenden owre defautes,
And lederes for lewed men   and for lettred bothe.
                                                    (97-98)

Clerks can know only what they learn in books, which, although they were made by men, were directed by God and inspired by the Holy Spirit. Clergy holds the keys to the coffer of Christendom

To vnlouken it at her lykynge   and to the lewed peple
ʒyue mercy for her mysdedes   if men it wole aske

[89] Participation in the sacrament increases grace, is efficacious against venial sin, and strengthens against temptation.
[90] Cf. R. Mannyng, *Handlyng Synne,* 10075-78; 10143-56.

151

Buxomelich and benygneliche   and bidden it of grace.
(112-14)[91]

The dignity of clergy is further attested in the example of the Levites.

Kind Wit, the speculative intellect, alone is insufficient for salvation; it comes "of alkynnes siʒtes, of bryddes and of bestes, of tastes of treuthe, and of deceytes." It is concerned only with things in themselves, not with the object of action.[92] Although the ancients set great store by it, it was reproved by patriarchs and prophets (1 Cor. 3.19): *Sapiencia huius mundi, stulticia est apud deum.* Heaven shall be opened by the Holy Spirit so that Love may leap out to earth to be caught by cleanness and found by clerks. That is, literally, Christ shall be born to Mary ("clennesse") and discovered by the shepherds. Imaginative quotes Luke 3.15: *Pastòres loquebantur ad inuicem.* In his comment on this chapter, Bruno identifies those who find Christ with those who are able to penetrate the letter of Scripture to the underlying meaning:

Quamvis enim pannis sit involutus et sub velamine litterae jaceat occultus, invenierent tamen, si eum quaesissent, et intelligerent, si credidissent. Quicunque igitur es qui vis videre Jesum, accede ad hoc praesepe, scrutare Scripturas, remove pannos, pelle litteram: "Littera enim occidit, spiritus autem vivificat," et tunc videbis, quod videre non poteras. Sic enim Ecclesiae pastores eum quaerunt, et quaerentes inveniunt, et invenientes venerantur et credunt.[93]

The tradition of the Biblical shepherds who found the infant Christ is continued by the modern clergy:

Beati isti pastores, qui Christum Dominum videre meruerunt, et Deum laudantes, et glorificantes ea quae audierant et viderant

---

[91] Cf. Prol. 100ff.

[92] See Godefroid (1914), 203: "Ens enim secundum se est obiectum intellectivi speculativi; ens secundum quod conveniens cognoscenti est obiectum intellectus practici; et obiectum voluntatis se habet per additionem ad obiectum intellectus practici, quia est conveniens sub ratione convenientis apprehensum."

[93] *PL*, 165, 354.

crediderunt. Beati illi pastores, qui usque hodie in Ecclesiae prae-
sepio, id est, in sacris voluminibus Christum quaerunt, et in eum
fideliter credunt, ejus nativitatem nuntiantes, ejus fidem praedi-
cantes, et eum ubique laudantes et glorificantes.[94]

The magi (Matt. 2.1) also represent the tradition of cler-
ical learning.[95] These who are truly learned are those who
find Christ. The poet ironically exclaims,

> If any frere were founde there   ich ȝif the fyue shillynges;
> Ne in none beggares cote   was that barne borne,
> But in a burgeys place   of Bethlem the best;
> *Set non erat locus eis in diuersorio; et pauper non habet*
> *diuersorium.* (146-48)

The friars seek Christ not among the poor, as they should,
but in the houses of wealthy burgesses. There was no room
for Christ in the diversorium, and similarly, the friar
"pauper" finds no room among the poor.[96] Imaginative
reminds Will of his abuse of clerks, and assures him that
learning is valuable. By analogy, just as of two swimmers
cast in the Thames, the one who had been trained to swim
would have a better chance of survival than the one un-
trained, so the clerk has a better opportunity to survive
the temptations of the world than the lewd man. With
knowledge comes the ability to identify sin when it occurs;
with such knowledge the clerk is able to comfort his soul
with contrition and to preserve himself from despair. The
unlearned man must wait until the time of confession at
Lent to feel contrition, and then the extent of his sorrow
is dependent on the skill of his priest, who may be unwise.

---

[94] *Ibid.*, 356.
[95] They are called *magi* because they are philosophers. See Bede, *PL*,
92, 12.
[96] The interpretation given here is tentative. We believe that the passage
probably reflects some document in the controversy between the regulars
and the seculars which we have not seen. Father J. B. Dwyer suggests a
possible reference "to the condemnation of the Franciscan teaching that the
way of Christ and his apostles in poverty was exactly that of the Francis-
cans." He refers to the condemnation of Franciscan doctrine by John XXII,
Cum inter nonnullos.

Learning saves the sinner just as the neck verse, *Dominus pars hereditatis mee* (189) saves the condemned clerk.

Will has alluded to the salvation of the thief on the cross (x, 414-21),[97] saying that in spite of his evil works he was saved sooner than John, Adam, or Isaiah, or any of the prophets. Imaginative replies, pointing out that the thief "hadde none heigh blisse" as John or other saints. He sits "by hym-self as a soleyne and served on the erthe" (205), and he enjoys only a precarious place in Heaven. The sinner is forever in danger, especially if he delays contrition (Ecclus. 5.5): *De peccato propiciato, noli esse sine metu.*[98] Thus the thief is not a good example for the ordinary Christian. He occupies the lowest place in Heaven where we are rewarded according to our works. Why one thief should be saved and the other damned is a question which no clerk can answer.

Will has, in his blindness, sought "after the whyes," rebuking Reason. He has wished to know about matters known only to Kynde, the Creator: the colors of the flowers, the habits of the birds. As Dame Study has pointed out, many such false questions confuse mankind. Ignorant persons are curious about the position of Adam's fig-leaf, for example. The birds and beasts do have a spiritual or moral significance, however. The peacock with his clumsy tail can fly only feebly. His flesh and feet are foul, his voice harsh. He is like rich men with their encumbrance of worldly concupiscence, their harsh voices when they finally repent, and their foul carrion at the end. The peacock's feet are like the false executors of the wealthy. On the other hand, the lark, a small bird, betokens humility. The peacock and the lark illustrate the problem of earthly treas-

[97] It should be observed that Imaginative systematically corrects the errors that Will has fallen into.

[98] For the interpretation of this verse a warning against delayed contrition, see Rabanus, *PL*, 109, 791.

ure concerning which Will asked Holy Church in Passus I.

Another problem about which it is futile to argue is that of the salvation of the heathen. Aristotle can teach us about larks, but the problem of his own salvation is one we cannot solve. Will objects to this leniency with the heathen by saying that clerks maintain that no one can be saved "with-outen Crystendome" (277).[99] Imaginative replies with a *Contra* (1 Peter 4.18): *saluabitur vix iustus in die iudicij.* The *Glossa ordinaria* explains that it is not difficult for God to save anyone, but that we all deserve damnation. We are saved only through love, which is granted by God.[100] Trajan was saved, even though he was not a Christian. There are three kinds of baptism: by water, by blood, and by fire. When baptism by water is impossible, one of the other varieties will suffice.[101] Imaginative describes baptism by fire in some detail, expressing what is substantially the doctrine still held in the matter. He who never trespasses against God or His law but lives according to law and believes that there is no better, or that he would amend if there were, and dies with this mode of conduct and belief has considerable claim to salvation. The verse *si ambulavero in medio vmbre mortis,* quoted previously by Piers himself, is a consolation to those of the faithful who must live among the heathen.[102] Imaginative closes his discussion by pointing out the virtue of *sapientia,* a virtue once greatly reverenced and, as Holy Church indicated in Passus I, a virtue necessary to those who are to pursue the true way.

At the beginning of Passus VIII, Will was not yet guided by the practical intellect and thus was unable to penetrate

[99] Will is reflecting his misunderstanding of Scripture's instruction, X, 318-48.

[100] *PL,* 114, 688. Cf. the pun on *vix* called attention to by Skeat, II, 189.

[101] St. Bonaventura advances a *quaestio* similar to Will's and a reply similar to that given by Imaginative, *Opera,* VI, 280.

[102] See above, Chapter 4, p. 94.

the sophistry of the two Franciscans. Still under the in-
fluence of the Priest in Passus VII, he was looking for an
external Dowel by means of which he could obtain salva-
tion without any inner effort on his part. He was spiritually
lazy. Thought described the three states to him in terms
of externals, giving him an impression which Wit, the
speculative intellect, was unable to correct because he could
present only possibilities which Will was not in a position
to evaluate. Nevertheless Wit established in terms of the
poem the true function of the practical intellect and through
the symbol of spiritual marriage the principle of the pres-
ervation or corruption of the Image of God in man. Dame
Study pointed out the dangers of unwise speculation to
which Will, guided only by the *intellectus possibili*, might
be subject, but sent him on to Clergy and Scripture. In
the encounter with Scripture, Dame Study's fears became
justified. Will misinterpreted Scripture, seeing it only
per se on the literal level, and fell into the error of predes-
tinarianism. He attacked clerical learning and succumbed
to a sleep within a sleep, a spiritual slumber in the Land
of Longing. He was stupidly contentious with Clergy and
Scripture. In evidence of God's providence he began to
gain judgment when he perceived the evil of the friars.
He began to see the wolf under the sheep's clothing for
the first time. Scripture's theme, "many are called, but few
are chosen," brought Will the fear of the Lord, the begin-
ning of wisdom. He recognized his error of predestinarian-
ism and began to understand the proper use of *temporalia*.
He achieved a certain humility so that Scripture was able
to instruct him at length in spiritual poverty, or Christian
humility. Nature showed Will a vision of good and evil
in the world, thinking to inspire in him the love of God.
But Will relapsed into an unreasoning preoccupation with
the problem of evil. Reason rebuked him successfully so
that he awakened from his spiritual slumber and was able,

with the aid of Imaginative, to survey his errors one by one. He learned from Imaginative to have a firm respect for clerical learning, which he had condemned in his attack on Clergy. At the end of Passus XII, Will has learned humility and cleared his mind of heretical tendencies. He is now prepared to seek Dowel in the church militant.

6. Dowel

PASSUS XIII

WHEN Will awakes at the beginning of Passus XIII, his condition is somewhat improved, although he has by no means gained perfection. He is "witles nerehande." His hermit's robes have been discarded for those of a mendicant, although he has not submitted himself to any regular discipline and is still "fre." As he wanders about, he considers the lesson of the vision he has just experienced. Fortune has failed him when he most needed assistance, and age has menaced him, although he has not yet come face to face with its problems. He has seen the friars seeking only the rich to the neglect of the poor and corrupting with their "coueitise" other clerks and priests so that the unlearned are frequently at the mercy of blind leaders. Imaginative has shown him the solicitousness of Nature for the birds and beasts and has explained, before he vanished, that *Vix justus saluabitur*. Not yet fully aware of the spiritual significance of what he has seen, Will again falls asleep.

Since the *intellectus agens* has been brought into contact with the *vis imaginativa* it is now possible for the will to be influenced by the conscience. Conscience is an activity of the mind, mediate between the practical intellect and the will. Its function is to bring syllogistic evidence of right action from the intellect to the will.[1] Accompanied by

---

[1] Cf. Godefroid (1932), p. 83: "Per conscientiam intelligimus notitiam practicam alicuius operabilis particularis per syllogismum practicum deductam ex aliquo fine volito a quo ratio practica sumit initium sui processus in syllogizando, ita tamen quod principium talis processus sit aestimatio de aliquo sub ratione boni simpliciter et honesti et legi divinae et mandatis eius convenientis."

Conscience, Will can now see the earthly Church in its true perspective. In his new vision, Will meets Conscience who asks him to dine at "his courte" (23) with Clergy. Showing that he has learned something from Imaginative's eulogy of learning, Will has a special interest in meeting Clergy (24). The court of Conscience represents the Church militant; there Will will have an opportunity to see Clergy as he actually exists rather than as an ideal. At the court of Conscience the first figure Will sees is a "maistre" (25). The title should be considered in the light of Matt. 23.8-10:

Vos autem nolite vocari rabbi; unus est enim magister vester, omnes autem vos fratres estis. Et patrem nolite vocare vobis super terram; unus est enim Pater vester qui in caelis est. Nec vocemini magistri; quia magister vester unus est Christus.

The Scribes and the Pharisees called themselves "masters" in vain glory;[2] and it soon becomes obvious that this master shares this as well as other characteristics with them. In hypocrisy, the master bows humbly to Scripture. Conscience, who knows him well, welcomes him.[3] Patience appears as a poor pilgrim and is also welcomed. The order at the table is significant:

> This maister was made sitte   as for the moste worthy,
> And thanne Clergye and Conscience   and Pacience cam
>   after.
>
> Pacience and I   were put to be macches,
> And seten by owre selue   at a syde-borde. (33-36)

Will sits humbly with Patience, as he should, but the master friar is made ironically to take the place of honor. The poet may have had in mind William of Saint-Amour's

---

[2] See Bruno, *PL*, 165, 263: "Quia enim omnis vana gloria peccatum est; peccat utique qui pro vana gloria sic vocari desiderat."

[3] Conscience's familiarity with the friar is probably an ironical allusion to the activity of friars as confessors. That the church militant is involved is clear from the dominant part played by Conscience, which, as we have seen before, is fallible without the guidance of Reason. Reason does appear in the C-text, but only to disappear shortly in pursuit of Piers.

sermon on the parable of the Pharisee. Perrod's paraphrase of a portion of this sermon is strikingly similar to the poet's ironical portrait: "Pour reconnaitre ses Phariseiens, [sc. friars] Dieu donne quatre signes: ils aiment les premieres places a table, les premieres chaires dans les synagogues, les salutations sur la place publique et ils veulent qu'on les appelle maitres. . . ."[4] The poet probably also had in mind Luke 14.7-11:

Dicebat autem et ad invitatos parabolam, intendens quomodo primos accubitus eligerent, dicens ad illos: Cum invitatus fueris ad nuptias, non discumbas in primo loco, ne forte honoratior te sit invitatus ab illo, et veniens is qui te et illum vocabit dicat tibi: Da huic locum, et tunc incipias cum rubore novissimum locum tenere. Sed, cum vocatus fueris, vade, recumbe in novissimo loco, ut, cum venerit qui te invitavit, dicat tibi: Amice, ascende superius. Tunc erit tibi gloria coram simul discumbentibus. Quia omnis qui se exaltat humiliabitur, et qui se humiliat exaltabitur.[5]

As St. Bruno interprets it, the gospel feast is that celebrating the marriage of Christian souls in the church. All are invited, but all should come in humility. The food served is remarkably like that in the poem. Scripture serves Clergy "of sondry metes manye, of Austyn, of Ambrose, of alle the four euangelistes" (38-39).[6] Except for the friar,

---

[4] *Op. cit.*, p. 141.

[5] It is interesting that the beginning of Will's conversion to the true way is based on the theme (Matt. 22.14): *Multi enim sunt vocati, pauci vero electi.* This theme is also based on a parable of a feast. The earlier feast involves the celestial church; the feast in this passus involves the earthly church.

[6] *PL*, 165, 406-7: "Sed quia parabola dicitur, aliquid aliud praeter litteram significat. Videamus igitur, quae sunt istae nuptiae, qui sint et illi, qui ad nuptias invitantur. Istae enim nuptiae quotidie in Ecclesia fiunt. Quotidie Dominus nuptias facit, quia quotidie fideles animas sibi conjungit, aliis ad baptismum venientibus, aliis hinc ad coelestia regna migrantibus. Ad has enim nuptias omnes invitati sumus, quicunque Christi fidem, et signaculum suscepimus. Hic illa mensa nobis apponitur, de qua dicitur: 'Parasti in conspectu meo mensam adversus eos qui tribulant me (Ps. 22.5).' Hic panes propositionis, hic vitulus saginatus, hic agnus, qui tollit peccata mundi . . . apponitur nobis hic, Evangelia et apostolorum Epistolae, hic Moysis et prophetarum libri, quasi quaedam fercula deliciis omnibus referta apponuntur nobis. Quid igitur amplius quaerimus? Quid primos accubitus eligimus?

those served are satisfied. They are like the disciples of
Luke 10.7, *Edentes et bibentes que apud eos sunt,* a verse
which was taken to mean that the priest should be content
with what he is given for his services.[7] The friar is not
content with spiritual food; nor does he seek to follow the
tradition of the disciples:

Ac this maister ne his man no manere flesshe eten,
Ac thei ete mete of more coste mortrewes and potages;
Of that men mys-wonne thei made hem wel at ese.

            (40-42)

He accepts misgotten *temporalia,* delighting in reward
against the innocent like a true follower of Lady Meed.
It is clear, however, that he shall suffer for his misdeeds
(43-45). Patience and Will are served penance, persever-
ance, humility and contrition (48-58). Patience delights
in his food, but Will is disturbed by the friar's drinking.

The friar in his drunkenness merits the admonition
(Isa. 5.22): *Ve vobis qui potentes estis ad bibendum vinum.*
Jerome indicates that this verse refers to those who simu-
late virtue but who deceive mankind.[8] It is emphasized
that the friar is concerned only with temporal food:
"mortrewes and puddynges, wombe-cloutes and wylde
braune & egges yfryed with grece" (62-63). Will calls
attention to the fact that this very friar has preached before
the Dean of Paul's on the sufferings of Paul the Apostle
(2 Cor. 11.23-28). He has apparently made these suffer-
ings the subject of a discourse on penance. Ironically, he
has omitted one of the chief perils which Paul endured,
that occasioned by false brothers, *Periculum est in falsis*

Ubicunque enim sedemus, omnibus abundamus, et nihilo indigemus. Verum-
tamen quicunque es qui primos hic accubitus quaeris, vade, et recumbe in
novissimo loco. Non te superbia elevet, non scientia inflet, non nobilitas ex-
tollat; sed quanto major es, humilia te in omnibus et coram Deo invenies
gratiam, ut suo tempore dicatur tibi: *Amice, ascende superius.* . . ."

[7] See the *Glossa ordinaria, PL,* 114, 284. Both heavenly and earthly re-
wards are implied.

[8] *PL,* 24, 89.

fratribus (v. 26). The friar has shown himself a false preacher since he has preached penance but is himself a glutton.[9] Will declares to Patience that he will question "this Iurdan" concerning the meaning of the penance he has preached, but Patience bids him be still and observe. The friar will suffer on appropriate penance in time for his gluttony; he will "haue a penaunce in his paunche and puffe at ech a worde." Meanwhile he will soon drink enough to be able to divine, and to prove that in feasting delicately he has actually suffered penance. Then it will be time for Will to question him. Finally the good doctor finishes, coughs, clears his throat, and is ready to act the part of the master. Conscience looks toward Will and Patience. Will then asks, "What is Dowel? sire doctour, . . . is Dowel any penaunce?" The friar's answer is merely negative and is prefaced by a drink:

> 'Dowel?' quod this doctour—— and toke the cuppe and dranke——
> 'Do non yuel to thine euenecrystene nouȝt by thi powere.'
> (103-4)

Like Will in his spiritual slumber, the friar finds that the best precepts are those which require the least effort. Will replies that the friar harms others in his gluttony, referring to the fraternal habit of eating sumptuously in the infirmary rather than frugally in the refectory:

> And if ȝe fare so in ȝowre fermorie   ferly me thinketh,
> But chest be there charite shulde be   and ȝonge children
> dorste pleyne! (108-9)

Gluttony has supplanted charity with contentiousness, so that even children may complain. Conscience silences Will

---

[9] The friar does not follow the admonition to the disciples in Luke 10, so that he becomes like those described by St. Augustine, Sermo CI, *PL*, 38, 610: "Praedicantes, non habent; laudant, et non amant; dicunt, et non faciunt." In the words of the poem (79), "that he precheth he preueth nouȝt." The character and influence of such preachers are well described by Bede on John 10.12, 13, *PL*, 92, 767.

and asks the friar about Dowel and Dobet. The friar in reply defines the three states:

'Dowel,' quod this doctour   'do as clerkes techeth,
And Dobet is he that techeth   and trauailleth to teache other,
And Dobest doth hym-self so   as he seith and precheth:—
Qui facit et docuerit, magnus vocabitur in regno celorum.[10]
(115-17)

The limitations of these definitions are at once obvious. That of Dowel takes no account of the possibility of false friars or of "vnkonnynge curatoures"; that of Dobet says nothing of the rule, and it is only Dobest who must practice what he preaches. By implication, since the friar is a regular and under Dobet, he has no obligation to practice what he preaches; he has only to teach or to try to teach. When Will sought Dowel under the guidance of the friars, doing "as clerkes techeth," he lived in the Land of Longing.

Conscience turns to Clergy for his definition of the three states, but Clergy finds himself puzzled, since Piers Plowman has impugned his sons the sciences, holding that none is of value "saue loue one." Piers has taken as his texts *dilige deum*, the first of the precepts of charity, and *domine, quis habitabit, &c.*[11] Dowel and Dobet, Piers says, are "two infinites" which "fynden oute Dobest, which shal saue mannes soule" (127-29). Since they are infinites, Dowel and Dobet are not comprehensible to the *scientia*; they are ideals which cannot be defined in a few words, and which cannot be fully exploited in human action. Their task, as Piers has already shown, is to seek out Dobest:

[10] The text is from Matt. 5.19. The friar omits the first part of the verse which is more appropriate to himself: *qui ergo solverit unum de mandatis istis minimis et docuerit sic homines minimus vocabitur in regno caelorum.* The *Glossa ordinaria*, PL, 114, 92, comments: "Moraliter autem solvit qui non implet, sed tenet sicut infirmis data sunt. Vel qui non intelligit spiritualiter. Solvere, non est agere, Quod recte intelligit, vel non intelligere quod non depravat, aut minuere integritatem superadditionis Christi."

[11] See above, Chapter 3, p. 53.

And if Grace graunte the   to go in in this wise,
Thow shalt see in thi-selue   Treuthe sitte in thine herte,
In a cheyne of charyte   as thow a childe were,
To suffre hym and segge nouȝte   aȝein thi sires wille.

(v, 614-17)

It is significant that Piers' texts are those of Holy Church, the Church celestial, in Passus I, and that the Clergy of the church militant does not quite understand them. As this passus makes evident, the earthly church does not perfectly reflect its heavenly counterpart.

Conscience does not understand Piers' doctrine either and suggests that it be passed over until Piers arrives. Meanwhile, he says that Patience may know what no clerk can, a suggestion which reinforces the impression of the incompetence of the earthly clergy. Patience replies that Love has taught him to think of Dowel as *Disce*, Dobet as *Doce*, and Dobest as *Dilige inimicos*. These are the three states as they should appear in Clergy. A teacher should learn, teach, and be guided by love. That the final admonition is of fundamental importance is clear in the remainder of Patience's speech. She admonishes that enemies be overcome with kindness, and presents the idea of Christ's New Law in the form of a riddle, asking the friar whether Dowel is not bound up in it. The friar finds very little use for Patience or for charity. "It is but a Dido," he replies, asserting that it is impossible to substitute charity for strife in the world. He takes Clergy and Conscience to one side, directing them in consultation, but judging that Patience should leave, "for pilgrimes kunne wel lye" (178). But Conscience refuses to come under the domination of the friar, asserting that he will go with Patience to be a pilgrim until he has learned more. The friar has openly flaunted the admonition of Christ (Luke 21.19): *In patientia vestra possidebitis animas vestras.*[12] He has failed

---

[12] This verse may be the basis for *Pacientes vincunt* (164, 172).

to understand the connection between patience and charity (1 Cor. 13.4): *Charitas patiens est.* Conscience sees through his shallowness, realizing that true learning shows itself in patience (Prov. 19.11): *Doctrina viri per patientiam noscitur.* St. Gregory's comment on this verse emphasizes the viciousness of the friar's position: "Tanto ergo quisque minus ostenditur doctus, quanto convincitur minus patiens."[13] It is not surprising that Conscience leaves him to seek true learning with Patience. Clergy, now corrupted by the friar's gluttony, attempts to interest Conscience in "ʒeres ʒyues or ʒiftes" and in reading riddles (184). Since he is unfamiliar with charity, he can offer only "a boke of the olde lawe" (185). Here we find the actual source of the Pelagianism of the Priest who impugned the pardon of Piers. The love of Lady Meed fostered by the friar has blinded Clergy to all spiritual truth. But Conscience, moved by Patience and by "the wille of folke here," or Will himself, has determined to mourn for his sins and to continue to direct his steps toward charity. He takes leave of the friar and whispers to Clergy that he would rather have patience than "half thy pakke of bokes!" Clergy refuses to take leave of Conscience saying

> 'thow shalt se the tyme,
> When thow art wery for-walked   wilne me to consaille.'
> (203-4)

Neither Clergy nor Patience is sufficient in itself and both realize their interdependence. Conscience replies to the effect that if Patience were between them, they could soon amend the world's woes. Clergy, in half recognition of the truth, agrees, saying that he will perform his educational duties as best he can until Conscience has been perfected through Patience. In effect, the poet says that the clergy has been corrupted by the avarice of the friars, so that it has lost Christian patience and been deserted temporarily

---

[13] *PL,* 76, 1262. The interpretation below is supported by C XVI, 176-84.

by Conscience. Since the restoration of Patience is necessary to Clergy's efficacy, Will must resume his search for Dowel with Patience and Conscience as his guides; the worldly clergy is not adequate.

The lesson given Will in his vision of the Church militant should be considered in the light of the lesson he obtained from Holy Church in Passus I. There the celestial Jerusalem directed him to the marriage of the soul to the Church, a theme elaborated by Wit. In the course of the poem, Will learned that in turning to God he must learn to suffer in patient humility. This fact enabled Conscience to lead him, in company with Patience, to the Church militant. But they found it corrupted by the false friars so that Conscience himself had to direct Will independently of the Church and of its clergy. Neither Clergy nor Conscience fully understood the mission of Piers. It is significant that Piers does not appear at all in the earthly Church.[14] His place has been taken by the friar. Although Clergy realized the importance of Piers and did not wish to part from Conscience, he was caught in a net of *temporalia*, "ȝeres-ȝyues or ȝiftes," and in a preoccupation with the Old Law. We are faced again, at the beginning of Passus XIII, with the corruption of the ecclesiastical hierarchy depicted in the Prologue. On the negative side that corruption is seen to be due to the operations of Lady Meed; positively, it is due to the absence of Piers Plowman, the spiritual foundation of Dobest. Just as Holy Church finds her opposite in Lady Meed, Piers finds his opposite in the friar.

Having shown the corruption of the shepherds, the poet turns to the resulting corruption of the flock. The flock is made up of those in the active life, the status of which Dowel is the ideal. They are typified by Hawkin,

---

[14] He appears momentarily in the C-text only that his separation from the church may be emphasized. There Reason leaves the church also to follow him. The fact that the name of Piers is introduced in the text at all here is indicative of Will's progress on the path of righteousness.

a composite picture of those who "chosen chaffare" (Prol. 31). Conscience and Patience go forth from the church of the friar as pilgrims, taking with them victuals of "Sobrete, and symple-speche, and sothfaste byleue" (217), and talking of Dowel as they walk. They meet with one who seems outwardly to be a "minstrel," one of those who truly praise the Lord:

> And somme murthes to make   as mynstralles conneth,
> And geten gold with here glee   synneles, I leue.
> (Prol. 33-34)

Patience asks him to tell Conscience "what crafte he couthe an to what contree he wolde" (223). Hawkin assures Conscience that he is a minstrel, *Actiua-vita*, a waferer or purveyor of worldly food. If he could be a jangler, he might, but he does not know how to "Farten, ne fythelen at festes, ne harpen" (231), so that he gets no rich robes or gifts from lords. As a true helper of Piers, however, he is blessed by the priest. He provides earthly food for all: beggars, liars and friars, monks, and the Pope himself. All he has of the Pope in return is a pardon which, he says, will not cure the pestilence. If it would, he could use it to be "prest to the peple." Hawkin quotes, to show the power of the Pope to cure, Acts 3.6: *Argentum et aurum non est mihi; quod autem habeo, hoc tibi do; in nomine domini, surge et ambula.* The reference is not to the actual cure of earthly ills, but to the salvation of souls through the New Law on the part of those who teach by good example like St. Peter.[15] Misinterpreting the passage grossly, Hawkin asserts that the failure of the pardon is not due to the Pope, but to the unworthiness of the people who receive it. Until they amend and cast out pride no blessing will benefit them. Hawkin is quite ready to excuse himself and the Pope in the same breath. He is a hard working man who suffers to supply the people with bread. London

---

[15] See Bede, *PL*, 92, 951.

likes his food well, and in time of dearth, there is much suffering for lack of it.

Will and Conscience are not deceived by Hawkin's appearance. As Will observes,

> He hadde a cote of Crystendome   as holykirke bileueth,
> Ac it was moled in many places   with many sondri
> plottes. (274-75)

His clothes are especially befouled with pride, which shows itself in various ways: proud speech, boasting and bragging, lack of conformity to any standards. His singularity makes him seem to be

> Y-habited as an hermyte   an ordere by hym-selue,
> Religioun sanz reule   and resonable obedience. (285-86)

Thus in his clothing he is reminiscent of Will as he has been previously described. And he is reminiscent of him in his actions; in his pretentiousness he criticizes learned and unlearned alike, condemning true loyalty. He puts on a great show of wisdom, strength, beauty, and so on. In general, the description of his clothing in lines 276-313 resembles closely the lists of everyday manifestations of pride in the manuals used by priests to guide them in the analysis of sin at confession.[16] At the instigation of Conscience, Hawkin continues to describe his clothing, going through the other vices in the same manner.[17] The result is a kind of general confession of sins of all types not necessarily consistent with a single personality, as though the poet had described all of the sins applicable to the active life which he found either in a confessional inquiry or in

---

[16] See D. W. Robertson, Jr., "The Cultural Tradition of *Handlyng Synne*," *Speculum* XXII (1947), 176-81, where several examples are given.

[17] The textual tradition in lines 400-57 is not clear. Certain lines appear only in one MS cited by Skeat, and there is considerable variation among the MSS. Concomitantly, there is a certain inconsistency in point of view in the description of the sins. We believe that the basic problem is here textual rather than critical.

a manual for penitents.[18] Hawkin thus represents the typical layman, who is outwardly holy but actually guilty of constant lapses into sin. He has failed to preserve the whiteness and purity of the spiritual clothing cleansed at baptism.[19] The Passus as a whole indicates that the sins of the ordinary layman are attributable to the corruption of the church militant, which in turn is due to the presence of the friar and the absence of Piers Plowman.

PASSUS XIV

Passus xiv is essentially an elaboration of the traditional concept of the cleansing of spiritual clothing. In reply to Conscience's question asking why he has not cleaned his garments, Hawkin says that he has only one "hool hatere," and that moreover he has a housewife, possessions, "hewen," and children. He quotes Luke 14.20: *Vxorem duxi, et ideo non possum venire.* This text, together with the general excuse, places him among those who refuse to attend the Lord's wedding feast. They are detained from a true marriage with Christ by love for terrestrial goods, by the attractions of the senses, and by the pleasures of the flesh. When they ask to be excused, they reveal a fundamental lack of true humility. As Bede explains it, "Dum enim dicit *rogo*, et tamen venire contemnit, humilitas sonat in voce, superbia in actione."[20] In the version of the parable in Matt. 22. 1-14, one guest attends the wedding feast without the proper garments, only to be cast out. His garments have been soiled by violation of the precepts of the Law and the Evangelists.[21] St. Bruno says of the garments:

---

[18] It is significant that in the C-text this material is transferred to the confessions of the folk of the field earlier in the poem.

[19] The clothing is explained below. Cf. the poem "Over the Bier of the Worldling."

[20] *PL*, 92, 515. For the allegorical meanings of the excuses, see cols. 514-15.

[21] See above, p. 134.

Veste autem nuptiali indutus non est, qui fidem non habet et Christum non imitatur: unde Apostolus ait: "Exuite vos veterem hominem, et induite novum" (Eph. 4.22). "Quincunque enim baptizati estis in Christo Jesu, Christum induistis" (Gal. 3.27).[22]

In St. Bonaventura's comment on Luke 14.23, it is said that we are given spiritual garments from the beginning. These are soiled by original sin, but are cleansed at baptism. When they become soiled after baptism, they may be cleansed only through the sacrament of penance.[23] Hawkin, led by the attractions of the world, has fallen into pride, but he has a seeming humility consonant with his excuse. Although his robes were once clean at baptism, he has soiled them with the sins he confesses. Only through true penance, based on humility and completed through charity, will he be able to cleanse them again. Then he may be a welcome guest at the Lord's feast.

Hawkin says that his coat has been cleaned with sickness and loss of property; moreover, he has cleaned it at confession, but to no avail:

And was shryuen of the preste   that gaue me, for my synnes,
To penaunce pacyence   and pore men to fede,
Al for coueitise of my Crystendome   in clennesse to kepen it.
And couthe I neuere, by Cryste   kepen it clene an houre,
That I ne soiled it with syȝte   or sum ydel speche,
Or thorugh werke or thorugh worde   or wille of myn herte,
That I ne flober it foule   fro morwe tyl eue. (9-15)

He has made the mistake of falling again into the sins which he confessed, so that his penance was invalid.[24] Medieval writers were careful to distinguish between true penance based on contrition and humility and the outward

[22] *PL*, 165, 233.
[23] *Opera*, VII, 396. Cf. Peter Lombard, *Sententiae*, IV, XIV, *PL*, 192, 868.
[24] Cf. Peter Lombard, *Sententiae*, IV, XIV, PL, 192, 869, where several authorities are quoted condemning false penance of this sort.

form of penance which is in itself of no value. Thus Peter Lombard wrote:

Sacramentum enim signum est sacrae rei. Quid ergo hic signum est? Quidam dicunt, ut Grandulphus, sacramentum hic esse quod exterius tantum geritur, scilicet exterior poenitentia quae est signum interioris poenitentiae, scilicet, contritionis cordis et humilitatis.[25]

Hawkin has been without inner penance.

Conscience exhorts Hawkin to true penance at some length. He tells him about contrition, which, in analogy with Dowel, will begin by brushing his coat. Confession will wash it through a wise confessor acting his part as Dobet, the contemplative teacher. Finally satisfaction will beat it bright and preserve it through the good prelate, Dobest, who will lead Hawkin to the practice of charity.[26] If Hawkin undergoes true penance, his garment will remain unspotted; he will become a true harper and through his influence his wife will become a good minstrel.[27] Patience offers to supply him with spiritual food, much more profitable than temporal food. Hawkin laughs at Patience's offer. Seeing that he does not understand, Patience shows him some spiritual food, the *paternoster*. This, he says, will save Hawkin from all sorts of tribulation and worldly care. He cites examples to show that the Lord cares for the faithful so that solicitude for *temporalia* is futile. As Holy Church explained in Passus I, the use of *temporalia* should be governed by moderation. Through faith comes contrition,[28] which affects conscience and so drives away sin. Without true contrition the person in the active status can maintain nothing but an outward show of sanctity. Contrition is completed by confession and satisfaction, which heals the wounds of sin. Since satisfaction is based on

[25] *Ibid.*, IV, XXII, *PL*, 192, 898-99.
[26] Contrition, confession, and satisfaction were traditionally regarded as the three parts of penance. See Peter Lombard, *ibid.*, IV, XVI, *PL*, 192, 877.
[27] Cf. V, 28-41.
[28] See Luke 7.48, and XI, 211.

charity, Hawkin asks "Where woneth Charite?" (97). Patience answers,

> 'There parfit treuthe and pouere herte is   and pacience of
> tonge,
> There is Charitee, the chief chaumbrere   for god hym-
> selue!' (99-100)

This definition is probably a reflection of 1 Tim. 1.5-6, altered somewhat to make it appropriate to the character of Patience:

Finis autem praecepti est caritas de corde puro et conscientia bona et fide non ficta; a quibus quidam aberrantes conversi sunt in vaniloquium.

Hawkin replies by offering a scholastic *quaestio*:

> 'Whether paciente pouerte,' quod Haukin   'be more ples-
> aunte to owre driȝte
> Than richesse riȝtfulliche ywonne   and resonablelich
> yspended?'

Patience bases his solution on Ecclus. 31.8-9:

Beatus dives, qui inventus est sine macula et qui post aurum non abiit nec speravit in pecunia et thesauris: quis est hic et laudabimus eum?

He explains that the rich in general have difficulty with their consciences at the day of death, whereas the poor who have little joy on earth may look forward to joy in heaven. The fallen angels and Dives had joy once, but they suffer for it now. The rich make a heaven of earth and so lose heaven, as Ps. 75.5 shows: *Dormierunt somnum suum, et nihil invenerunt omnes viri divitiarum in manibus suis.* Peter Lombard's comment sheds considerable illumination on Patience's meaning:

In his praesentibus quiescentes, quae eis facta sunt deliciosa, id est a bonis aeternis refrigescentes carni acquieverunt, profutura non praevidentes, somnum suum, qui distat a quiete bonorum, quia iste fallax est. Vident enim per somnum se habere thesauros; sed dum evigilant, nihil inveniunt. Unde dicit: Et nihil invenerunt omnes viri divitiarum. Ecce diffinitio avarorum, id est studentes divitiis. Unde non ait: Habentes divitias. Multi enim habent qui non amant; sed *viri divitiarum,* qui totam scilicet spem suam ponunt in incerto divitiarum, *nihil invenerunt,* dico *in manibus suis.* Ita hoc dicit, quasi adhuc in manibus quaerunt cum se nihil tenuisse cognoscant. Somnium ergo praesentis vitae illos divites facit. Evigilatio autem post hanc vitam pauperes prodit. Alludunt enim haec verba actionibus somniantium, qui evigilantes quaerunt in manibus quae dormientes videbantur tenere et amisisse dolent: quod tamen nequaquam se possedisse cognoscunt. Tales sunt isti qui venerunt in hanc vitam, et per cupiditates temporales quasi obdormierunt. Hic excipiunt illos divitiae et vanae pompae volaticae, et transierunt omnia. Et ita nihil invenerunt in manibus suis, quia nihil posuerunt in manibus Christi, qui dicit: *Esurivi,* etc. (Matt. 25) In pauperibus namque esurit, qui in coelo dives est.[29]

As a supporting text, Patience uses Ps. 72.20: *Velut somnium surgentium, Domine, in civitate tua imaginem ipsorum ad nihilum rediges.*[30] The workman must labor for his reward; so, by implication, must the true Christian suffer on earth for his reward in heaven. It is difficult to pass from joy in *temporalia* on earth to the joys of heaven.[31] But if the wealthy man is lawful, charitable, and contrite, he shall be justly rewarded.[32] Patience stresses the fact that wealthy men of this type are rare, so that few attain "double rest." Just as the animals suffer in winter and enjoy the following summer, so the poor suffer on earth

[29] *PL,* 191, 706, 707. Cf. Chapter 2, note 14.

[30] Peter Lombard's comment, *ibid.,* 676, is very similar to the one just quoted. It adds the notion of the celestial city: "Et est, imaginem ipsorum, id est gloriam temporalem, quam ipsi quaerunt, rediges ad nihilum in civitate tua, id est in coelesti Jerusalem, quia cum deerit eis veritas supernae civitatis, peribit etiam imago, quia nec similitudinem, retinebunt qui de aeterna beatitudine nil habebunt."

[31] The text *De delicijs ad delicias, difficile est transire* probably represents the *sentence* of Matt. 19.23 adapted to the terms of the argument.

[32] See the passage quoted from Lombard in the text above. The distinction between the merely wealthy man and the man who puts his faith in wealth is very important. Cf. Chapter 2, note 14. This distinction is used to explain the text cited in line 211, Matt. 19.23-24. Thus St. Bruno, *PL,* 165, 234, wrote: "Prius difficile, deinde impossibile dixit: impossibile est enim ut divites in divitiis spem habentes intrent in regnum coelorum."

to be made worthy of the joys of heaven. Patience asks mercy for God's prisoners, the poor,[33] calling attention to the fact that Christ promised reward to all who turn to him. He taught them to be clean through baptism, and to maintain themselves in cleanliness through penance. In putting off the devil through shrift, we prove ourselves to be beneficiaries of the pledge of the Redemption.[34] In other words, we come under the pardon of Piers.

> Ac the perchemyn of this patent   of pouerte be moste,
> And of pure pacience   and parfit bileue.
> Of pompe and of pruyde   the parchemyn decorreth,
> And principaliche of alle peple   but thei be pore of herte.
> (191-94)

In the active life, as we learned in Passus VII:

> Alle lybbyng laboreres   that lyuen with her hondes,
> That trewlich taken   and trewlich wynnen,
> And lyuen in loue and in lawe   for her lowe hertis,
> Haueth the same absolucioun   that sent was to Peres.
> (VII, 62-65)

Humility, poverty of spirit, is necessary to the efficacy of confession, and pride destroys it.[35] Without humility our good works are in vain, like the proud inscriptions on the windows of the friars' houses.[36] Christians should hold the wealth of the world for the common good without covetousness, in "trewe wille." Patience explains at some length that riches in the sense of love for wealth leads to all the seven vices;[37] conversely, riches are inconsistent with patient humility.

Hawkin, impressed by the sermon of Patience on poverty, asks for further instruction on "Pouerte with pacience." In reply, Patience explains in detail a commonplace

[33] See above, p. 138.   [34] Cf. XI, 189-97.
[35] Cf. Gregory, *Moralia*, PL, 76, 232-33; Peter Lombard, *Sententiae*, IV, XVII, cap. 5.
[36] See Passus, III, 64-75.
[37] The general principle involved is *radix malorum cupiditas*.

formula in praise of poverty, showing it to be efficacious against pride and the cares of the world. It allows one to possess what goods he owns honestly and without calumny; it is a gift of God which protects both the spirit and the flesh. It promotes health, security, and wisdom. It permits temporal business without loss and eradicates temporal solicitousness. With spiritual humility, in short, the cares of the world become trivial and one is assured of an eternal reward. This is the final answer to Will's own question in Passus I, "What of the money of this world?" It moves Hawkin to lament his sins in true contrition:

'I were nouȝt worthy, wote god,' quod haukyn   'to were
                                           any clothes,
Ne noyther sherte ne shone   saue for shame one,
To keure my caroigne,' quod he   and cryde mercye faste,
And wepte and weyled   and there-with I awaked.

                                       (329-32)

Like Adam before him, when he came to his first realization of sin, Hawkin wishes clothing only to hide his shame.[38] In his humility, he realizes that he is unworthy of the robe of grace which he soiled in his pride. In the past he has confessed to the priest in pride, just as Adam has confessed his sin to God in pride.[39] He has not learned the contrition and humility necessary to valid confession. Just as Will learned that Dowel is to suffer, Hawkin learns that Dowel is spiritual poverty.

The predicament of Hawkin is the predicament of those in the active state whose consciences have been corrupted by the easy confessions made popular by the Friar and his followers. The lesson he learns is very much like that learned by Will. Only through humility is true confession

[38] Adam clothed himself when he realized that the law of his members was contrary to that of his mind. Thus St. Bruno wrote, PL, 164, 169: 'Sed quia comedisti, jam nunc vides aliam legem in membris tuis repugnantem legi mentis tuae," paraphrasing the Lord's address to Adam in Gen. 3.11.

[39] Cf. Gregory, quoted PL, 93, 281.

possible. Since the Friar has taken the place of Piers Plowman in the Church, however, there is no one to teach Hawkin. The poet indicates what must be done. Those in the active state must be taught patience if they are to be saved. But he also implies at the same time that in the church militant there is no one to do it. Hawkin learns from an abstraction, Patience itself, just as Will learns from Conscience. Hawkin's own priest like the Priest of Passus VII cannot teach charity. In other words, the Hawkins of the world are doomed to wear their filthy rags unless the spirit of Piers may be revived and they may learn the lesson of patience. Will has found that in the church militant the ideal of Dowel has disappeared as a natural result of the substitution of the Friar for Piers. It is Dobest who must lead Hawkin to the practice of charity, but the place of Dobest has been taken by a false Dobet, the Friar. Thus the search for Dowel is but a part of the larger search for Piers Plowman.

7. Dobet

PASSUS XV

THE episode of the Friar and Hawkin demonstrated the weakness of the church militant. In Passus xv the poet elaborates this theme, describing in some detail the corruption of spiritual guides generally and the result of that weakness. If he is to learn Dowel perfectly, Will must have before him the examples of Dobet, the teacher, and of Dobest, the incarnation of charity, but these examples are difficult to find in actual life. When Will awakes at the end of Passus xiv, therefore, he has still not learned Dowel perfectly:

> Ac after my wakyng   it was wonder longe,
> Ar I couth kyndely   knowe what was Dowel. (1-2)

He has learned not to be deceived by externals of dress and worldly status, but his knowledge does not yet extend to a reasonable behavior with regard to those who glorify temporal clothing around him. In his confusion, he gives the impression of being a fool, until Reason has pity on him and puts him to sleep for further instruction.

Since to know Dowel "kyndely" the whole man is required, Will meets Anima, a combination of mind, memory, reason, the senses, love, and the spirit, all various aspects of the soul.[1] With these faculties, Will is able to see in one glance the laws of God and the imperfect reflection of those laws in the world; he can evaluate the world in the perspective of eternity. Anima explains her

---

[1] See below, note 58.

own compound nature, using for the purpose a definition from the *Etymologiae* of Isidore of Seville. Will jokes about the manifold names for the soul:

> 'ʒe ben as a bisshop,' quod I   al bourdynge that tyme,
> 'For bisshopes yblessed   thei bereth many names. . . .'
>
> (40-41)

Detecting an unhealthy curiosity about the causes of things in Will's remarks, Anima questions him so that he confesses a desire for "Alle the sciences vnder sonne." In this desire, Anima says, Will is like Lucifer; only Christ should know everything. Will has been warned about improper learning by Study (x, 9-16; 116) and by Scripture (xi, 1-2); but in his eagerness to learn Dowel, he turns in all possible directions. Without Piers to guide him, he cannot be sure of the way. Anima quotes Solomon against those who desire too much learning (Prov. 25.27): *sicut qui mel comedit multum, non est ei bonum: sic qui scrutator est maiestatis, opprimitur a gloria.* Good doctrine, she explains, is harmful unless one works in accordance with it.[2] Lust for knowledge expelled Adam and Eve from Paradise; in short, as Study has explained, *non plus sapere quam oportet sapere.*[3] The harmful character of doctrine that cannot be absorbed is illustrated in the erudite popular sermons of friars and others. Instead of abstract and misleading discussions of matters like the Trinity, which often lead to doubts and heresy, preachers should offer explanations of the commandments and the vices,[4] emphasizing the effects of temporal lust. Friars and others spend

---

[2] Rabanus, *PL*, iii, 765, wrote: "Non hoc autem solum quisque sapiens attendere debet, ne altiora se quaerat, et ne fortiora se scrutatus sit, verum etiam ne ea quae recte utiliter scire potuit, immoderatis sermonibus sibimet minus utilia reddat."

[3] Cf. above, p. 123.

[4] These lines (68ff.) reflect a long series of thirteenth century episcopal decrees on preaching. See D. W. Robertson, Jr., "Frequency of Preaching in Thirteenth Century England," *Speculum* XXIV (1949), 376-388.

In housyng, in haterynge   and in-to hiegh clergye shew-
                                            ynge,
More for pompe than for pure charite   the poeple wote
                                  the sothe. (76-77)

They seek to please lords and reverence the rich, fall-
ing into idolatry. Their position is that described in Ps.
96.7: *Confundantur omnes qui adorant sculptilia.* Augus-
tine says that these men "Sunt etiam homines non boni,
qui suam gloriam quaerunt, et Dei gloriam contemnunt."[5]
They are those addressed in Ps. 4.3: *Vt quid diligitis vani-
tatem, et queritis mendacium?* "Go to the glose," Anima
admonishes. In Peter Lombard we read:

Ut quid diligitis, quasi dicat: Vere gravi corde estis, quia vos diligitis,
id est voto amplexamini, *et quaeritis,* cum labore *vanitatem et men-
dacium,* id. est idola, quae vana sunt, scilicet, a vero esse aliena et
mendacia, quia non sunt Deus ut dicuntur. Et ut quid hoc facitis,
vel diligitis, vel quaeritis, vanitatem et mendacium, id est terrena,
quae sunt vana, quia ut umbra transeunt? Omnia enim quae sub
sole sunt vanitas sunt et mendacia, quia non faciunt quod promit-
tunt, scilicet beatos. Et ut quid hoc facitis, scilicet cur de terrenis,
quae vana sunt et transeunt, vultis esse beati? Sola veritas facit esse
beatos, ex qua vera sunt omnia. Ut quid igitur temporalium rerum
amore detinemini? ut quid tanquam prima extrema sequamini?[6]

The friars and their followers accept alms from sinners of
all sorts "and louten to this lordes" (84). In doing so they
violate Christ's admonition to his disciples *ne sitis persona-
rum acceptores,* the sense of James 2.1: *Fratres mei, nolite
in personarum acceptione habere fidem Domini nostri Iesu
Christi gloriae.*[7] The appropriateness of the *sentence* is clear
in Bede's comment:

Ostendit quod hi quibus scribebat fide quidem evangelica imbuti,
sed operibus erant vacui. Et quia mandata Domini eleemosynis
Pauperum docuerat implenda, vidit illos e contra, quod pauperibus

---

[5] *PL,* 37, 1245. Cf. Chapter 2, note 20.
[6] *PL,* 191, 85.
[7] Cf. Col. 3.25. See Holy Church's complaint, II, 20-22.

erat propter aeterna praemia faciendum, divitibus potius propter terrena accommoda fecisse, ideoque eos prout erant digni redarguit.[8]

Just as holiness and honesty spread from the church "thorw lele libbyng men that goddes lawe teachen" (91), so also all evil spreads from the church "There imparfyt presthod is prechoures and techeres." As an example, we may consider the trees in summer, some bare and some green with leaves. The bare boughs are like evil "persones and prestes and prechoures" whose works are unfruitful. To preach "and preue it nouȝt" is hypocrisy, which makes one like a dunghill full of snakes but covered with snow, or a foul wall whitelimed. Evil priests, preachers, and prelates are "emblaunched with *bele paroles*" but underneath "ful vnlouelich." (113-14)[9] Anima describes the activities of wicked priests at some length, showing, for example, that avaricious bishops enjoy the inheritances of niggardly priests. Good men, on the contrary, are reverenced in charity (115ff.).

At the mention of charity, Will asks, "What is Charite?" Anima replies in terms of Matt. 18.3, which stresses the patience and humility necessary to true charity: *Nisi efficiamini sicut parvuli, non intrabitis in regnum celorum.*[10] Will says that although he has lived "in londe," he has never seen the kind of charity that St. Paul praised. The Friar has referred to patient charity as a Dido, as fiction in the light of the warfare that characterizes the world;

[8] *PL,* 93, 18.

[9] The image of the tree appears in the quotation attributed to Chrysostomos in ll. 115ff. See Skeat's note. Cf. Bruno on Matt. 7.15-17, *PL,* 165, 130-31; and on Matt. 21.12ff., *ibid.,* 245-46. The whitelimed wall appears in Matt. 23.27. The dunghill is a medieval commonplace. Cf. Ps. 13.3.

[10] Patience and humility are implied here, see Bruno, *PL,* 165, 223: "Merito parvulum Dominus vocat, ut ejus exemplo instruantur qui majores videri volant. Videtis, inquit, hunc parvulum? Nisi ab hac stulta sublimitate, quae vestros animos perturbat, ad hujus patientiam et humilitatem conversi fueritis, et efficiamini sicut parvuli, sine invidia, sine odio, sine superbia, sine ambitione; non solum majores in regno coelorum non eritis, verum etiam illuc non intrabitis."

Will does not deny such charity, but he has not been able to find it around him. For the ideal charity he has in mind, he refers to 1 Cor. 13.4-7, part of which he quotes: *Caritas patiens est, benigna est; caritas non aemulatur, non agit perperam, non inflatur, non est ambitiosa, non quaerit quae sua sunt, non irritatur, non cogitat malum, non gaudet super iniquitate, congaudet autem veritati: omnia suffert, omnia credit, omnia sperat, omnia sustinet.* In so far as the actual world is concerned, Will has never seen a man who did not "aske after his." Clerks have told him that Christ or charity is in all places, but he has never seen him, except darkly, as himself "in a miroure." He quotes 1 Cor. 13.12: *Ita in enigmate, tunc facie ad faciem.* Peter Lombard explains that we see God only obscurely as he is reflected in creatures, or the mirror may be the soul in which God may be seen "aliquo modo."[11] Will knows only that charity "is nought championes fyʒte ne chaffare." Anima agrees, elaborating Paul's definition and concluding with the statement that charity

> Coueiteth . . . none erthly good   but heuenriche blisse.
>
> (170)

Will wants to know whether charity has rents, riches, or rich friends. Anima assures him that charity has no need of wealth; he has a friend who supplies him with spiritual sustenance. When Charity is not supplying this sustenance to the poor in spirit, he is working in the laundry of Ps. 7.6, where the sins of the penitent are washed away: *laboraui-in-gemitu-meo.*[12] While he works, he sings (Ps.

---

[11] *PL*, 191, 1662.

[12] The significance of this quotation is made clear in Peter Lombard's comment, *PL*, 191, 107: "*In gemitu meo,* id est cordis. Gemit iste, dum videt quid egit, et quae poena sit futura. Et quasi parum profuerit, addit. Et post, *lavabo per singulas noctes lectum meum,* ad litteram, per noctes in lecto plorabo pro peccatis. Quod idem repetit allis verbis *lacrymis meis stratum meum rigabo.* Idem accipitur his stratus quod supra lectus, quasi dicat vestem superpositam lecto rigabo lacrymis meis, id est multum lacrymabor. Vel lectum vocat conscientiam, quae quibusdam est quies, quibusdam

50.19): *Cor contritum et humiliatum, deus, non despicies.*
Charity not only satisfies spiritual hunger; it inspires contrition, which leads to humility and the washing away of sin.[13] This definition of charity obviously suggests Piers Plowman, whom we saw turning from the work of supplying spiritual food to penance in Passus VII. Will has himself seen the identity of charity and Christ, whose life exemplifies Piers, and at the same time supplies a pattern to be followed in the three states. When charity has no need of riches, but receives spiritual food from God, he is Dowel (171-75). When he prays, goes on pilgrimage, and feeds God's prisoners, he is Dobet (176-80). Finally, when he washes away the sins of mankind, he is Dobest (181-88). The last embraces the other two, but these are themselves, as Piers has said, "infinites," in that each is capable of infinite development so that neither can be precisely defined.[14] Although the three states are not mentioned here in the poem, this is the first elaboration of the concept of charity which implies them. It is here that the poet's doctrine of charity first coalesces with the doctrine of the three states of perfection.

Will, who has now become absorbed in his quest for charity,[15] exclaims,

---

tormentum. Ibi enim mundi corde quiescunt. Ibi male cordati cruciantur. Stratum dicit sensualitatem. Et est sensus: *Lavabo lectum meum,* id est mundabo conscientiam meam. Per singulas noctes, id est per singula peccata. Et lacrymis meis, id est amaritudine poenitentiae, stratum meum, id est sensualitatem, rigabo, id est fertilem faciam, quae prius erat arida a bonis operibus. Vel, lectus est voluptas corporis et delectatio saeculi, in qua aeger animus quiescit; in qua homo resolvitur. Stratus est, cumulus peccatorum, ut vestium, etc."

[13] Cf. the gloss in Peter Lombard on Ps. 50.19, *PL,* 191, 491-92: "Sequitur hujus sacrificii promissio, o Deus, *non despicies cor contritum poenitentia.* Spernit Deus taurum et hircum, etc. Quae tempus habuerunt, dum aliquid promitterent futurum; *et humiliatum* Deo confitendo, non elatum peccatum excusando. Prius dicit contritum, et post humiliatum: Quia non potest humiliari, nisi prius contritum sit."

[14] See above, p. 163.

[15] For the significance of this fact, see Chapter 5, note 7.

'By Cryst, I wolde that I knewe hym,' quod I   'no crea-
                     ture leuere!' (189)

But Anima tells him that only Piers Plowman can show
him charity. Clerks can judge the presence of charity by
words and by works, but only Piers can see beneath ex-
ternals into the will.[16] He can penetrate hypocrisy. Proud
hypocrites and false beggars can deceive clerks; only Piers
understands them, *Petrus, id est, Christus*. This phrase is
not meant to express complete identity. Christ established
the power of apostolic discernment into the hearts of men.
This function of his divinity he transmitted to Peter, and
through him to his successors. As a part of the apostolic
tradition, it is a function of Piers Plowman; in so far as
Christ and Piers share this power, they are the same.[17]
Charity, Anima warns, is not in "lolleres ne in lande-
leperes hermytes," nor in false anchorites. He is God's
champion, courteous and merry, light in heart and conver-
sation; he is not among those who are sad in hypocrisy
(Matt. 6.16): *Nolite fieri sicut ypocrite, tristes*, etc.[18] He
walks in clothing of all kinds,

Ac biddyng as beggeres   bihelde I hym neuere. (221)

Will's own inability to find charity is probably suggested
by his mendicant's robes. Charity is soonest found "in riche
robes":

Ac in riche robes   rathest he walketh,
Ycalled and ycrimiled   and his crowne shaue,
And clenlich yclothed   in cipris and in Tartaryne.
                                (222-24)

[16] The text *Et vidit deus cogitationes eorum* is probably a reflection of
Matt. 9.4.

[17] See above, p. 76.

[18] The *Glossa ordinaria*, PL, 114, 103, comments: "Bonum est jejunio
pro peccatis tristes esse ad poenitentiam, et humiliare animam nostram; unde:
Cor contritum et humiliatum, Deus, non despicies (Ps. 50). Sed tristitiam
quae pro laude est, prohibet. Unde non ait simpliciter: Nolite jejunare, sed
addit: sicut hypocritae, tristes." There is no contradiction between the pic-
ture of merriment given here and that of contrition above.

These are the robes of the Bride of Christ, of the Church Triumphant, of the Christian wedded to Christ in charity.[19] Actual clothing is not itself important, since it is not indicative in any way of spiritual poverty or humility. A bishop may have such poverty, for all of his rich robes, sooner than a beggar. Charity once walked in a mendicant's robes in St. Francis's time, but he has seldom done so since. The wealthy may have charity; charity may appear in the King's court if there is no covetousness there. He seldom appears "in courte amonge Iaperes" or at the consistory. At one time, he walked among archbishops, bishops, and seculars who gave "Cristes patrimonye to the pore," but now avarice has the keys. Charity is not contentious or covetous, as Ps. 4.9 shows: *In pace in id-ipsum dormiam et requiescam.* The thought is completed in verse 10: *Quoniam tu, Domine, singulariter in spe constituisti me.* The implications of these verses appear in Peter Lombard's comments:

In pace in idipsum. Quasi dicat: Dedisti mihi laetitiam utique de hoc quod in pace quae est *in idipsum,* id est, immutabilis, *dormiam* ab omni strepitu mundi secretus. Et hoc erit, cum mortale hoc induerit immortalitatem; et *requiescam* id est fruar vita beata. Et hoc vere, quae jam est spes quae non confundit. *Quoniam tu, Domine,* etc. Vel ita, in pace. Quasi dicat: Illi laborant multiplicari his temporalibus, ego autem in pace mentis dormiam, hic oblitus mundi tendens in idipsum,—id est quod manens immutabili perennitate consistit. . . .[20]

Charity is not interested in the transitory things of the world:

> The moste lyflode that he lyueth by is loue in goddis
>   passioun,
> Noyther he biddeth, ne beggeth ne borweth to ʒelde;
> Misdoth he no man ne with his mouth greueth.

(250-52)

[19] See Prov. 31.22 and Bede's comment, *PL*, 91, 1047-48.
[20] *PL*, 191, 89.

All good Christians should suffer in patience after God's example.[21]

Anima cites several examples from the *Legenda Sanctorum* and from Scripture to illustrate the "penaunce and pourete and passioun" of "holy seyntes." These people had no care for physical sustenance,

Ac god sent hem fode bi foules   and by no fierse bestes,
In menynge that meke things   mylde thinge shulde fede.

(300-1)

Thus righteous men should provide for the religious. Lords and ladies would not assess their tenants for purposes of extravagant gifts to the friars if the latter would return their alms to the poor who supplied them in the first place. Anima makes a contrast between the true contemplatives and the mendicant friars by presenting a typical fraternal argument. She speaks ironically as if she were a friar:

For we ben goddes foules   and abiden alwey,
Tyl briddes brynge vs   that we shulde lyve by. (308-9)

The ordinary religious should be content with alms enough for a sufficiency, as their rule shows. Job 6.5 is cited in support, with an elaboration:

Nunquam, dicit Iob, rugiet onager cum herbam habuerit? aut mugiet bos cum ante plenum praesepe steterit? Brutorum animalium natura te contempnat, quia cum eis pabulum commune sufficiat; ex adipe prodijt iniquitas tua.[22]

For the purpose of the argument, the text must be taken literally, but the commentaries of Gregory and Bruno interpret the food to be spiritual not temporal food.[23] Bruno interprets the *praesepe* to represent Scripture, which is empty "quando ad litteram solummodo intellegebatur."

[21] See above p. 138.

[22] Skeat points out the similarity between the elaboration and Bruno's comment.

[23] See the *Moralia, PL*, 75, 773-74; Bruno, *PL*, 164, 574.

In other words, it nourishes only when the *sentence* or spiritual meaning is considered. When the text itself is a warning against the letter, it is obvious that it should not be taken literally. After what is thus a patently inappropriate quotation, the friar's argument, as Anima parodies it, continues to the effect that one should not give to monks and canons who are not only wealthy but who benefit from well established foundations. Ps. 111.8 is quoted, *Dispersit, dedit pauperibus?* with the explanation:

If any peple perfourme that texte it ar this pore freres!
For that thei beggen abouten in buildynge thei spene,
And on hem-self sum and such as ben her laboreres,
And of hem that habbeth thei taken and ȝyue hem that
            ne habbeth. (321-24)

In other words, the friars give to the poor friars.[24]

The rich, Anima continues in her own person, rob the poor to feed the rich, although to do so is in violation of the principles of charity. Lack of charity makes folk who seem virtuous like coins stamped in base metal. It corrupts learning of all kinds. "This newe clerkes" know their grammar imperfectly, so that none can versify, write formally, or read any language except Latin or English. Doctors and masters of divinity cannot answer an argument or a *quodlibet*. The folk of the church may "ouerhuppe" as their priests do in their offices and hours. If the priests do skip in their services, the belief of the folk is sufficient to make them effective. But the poor example of the clergy misled by the influence of the Friar, may, in other words, corrupt the folk as a whole.[25] Saracens would be saved if it had not been for an evil clerk, Mahomet, who through pride led true folk into heresy. The story of Mahomet is symbolic of the corruption in the clerical orders. The

---

[24] Their extravagance in building was a source of widespread scandal. Cf. Passus III, 48-50. For a similarly ironic handling of the friars' argument, see XII, 146-48.

[25] Cf. XIII, 7-13.

Christian faith is itself in danger because, like Mahomet, clerks have a dove of covetousness with which they may delude the faithful. Such clerks have fallen from apostolic dignity. If they lived as they should,

Grace sholde growe and be grene   thorw her good lyu-
                                                                        ynge,
And folkes sholde fynde   that ben in dyuerse sykenesse,
The better for her byddynges   in body and in soule.

(416-18)

Peace would replace strife in the world, and all who sought spiritual food should receive it in accordance with Matt. 7.7: *Petite et accipietis*.[26] That is, all worthy prayers would be answered.[27] As wives say, "Salt saueth catel"; in the same way the followers of the apostolic tradition are the salt which saves the folk of the church (Matt. 5.13): *Vos estis sal terre, et si sal euanuerit, in quo salietur*. The importance of the apostolic example is emphasized in Bruno's comment:

Vos, inquit, estis sal terrae, vos estis hominum condimentum, vestro exemplo instruit, vestra sapientia doceri, vestra humilitate et patientia componi caeteri debent. Quod si sal evanuerit, si praedicator vires amiserit, si episcopus luxuriae et vanitati se dederit, in quo salietur, in quo populus condietur? *Ad nihilum valet ultra, nisi ut mittatur foras, et conculcetur ab hominibus*. Tale enim sal quia infatuatum est, foras mittitur, quoniam falsus praedicator, ejusque doctrina quae vana sine sapore et inutilis est, ab Ecclesia pellitur. Conculcatur autem ab hominibus, quia dignus est, qui ab omnibus despectui habeatur.[28]

If the eleven faithful disciples could convert the entire world, it should be easier for the many priests and preachers, together with a Pope, to save the people today. At one time England and Wales were heathen countries, but Gregory sent Augustine, who christened the king at Canterbury,

[26] This text represents a conflation of two phrases of the vulgate.
[27] See Bruno's comment, *PL*, 165, 127-28.
[28] *PL*, 165, 101.

And thorw myracles, as men may rede   al that marche
                                                he torned
To Cryst and to Crystendome   and crosse to honoure,
And fulled folke faste   and the faith tauȝte
More thorw miracles   than thorw moche prechynge,
As wel thorw his werkes   as with his holy wordes,
And seyde hem what fullynge   and faith was to mene.

                                                (438-43)

A child who has not been baptised, properly christened, and taught is like those heathen whom Augustine converted; he is like the untilled earth. That is, his heart has not been cultivated by the plow of Piers. He needs to be taught by the example of good priests, as the parable of the wedding feast at the beginning of Matt. 22 shows.[29]

But the parsons and priests of the church militant "that han her wille her" will excuse themselves in spite of the evidence of the gospel and that of Ps. 131: *Ecce audiuimus eam in Effrata.*[30] Popes and prelates today do not regard Christ's instruction: *Ite in vniversum mundum et predicate.* This fact is indicated by the failure to convert the Saracens, although many are supposedly devoted to the task. These prelates of Nazareth, Nineveh, and so on do not follow the direction of John 10.11: *Bonus pastor animam suam ponit,* etc. They do not risk their lives for their flocks and are not true workers in Christ's vineyard. Their task should be easier than that of the apostles, since the Saracens have something of our belief; if they were taught, they would soon turn to the light. The apostles suffered; their only glory was in the cross of the Lord.

[29] The *altilia* of verse 4 are usually taken to mean the apostles. See, for example, Bede, *PL*, 92, 95: "Misit iterum apostolos sub nomine altiliorum notatos." These apostles "folwed his whistellynge"; that is, they lived after the example of Christ. They were also fatted calves, in that they were given spiritual food by Christ. Just as the *altilia* needed example and spiritual nourishment, so do the folk of the church need example and spiritual nourishment. They do not have Christ Himself to lead them but must be dependent on their preachers and teachers.

[30] See above, p. 122, and Lombard, *PL*, 191, 1177.

Now the glory of prelates is the cross on the noble. War and strife have taken the place of the peace of earlier times. Anima warns that covetousness will destroy the wealthy churchmen just as it has destroyed the Templars. "Resoun and riȝtful dome" will judge them at the Last Day. If the lay powers lived loyally, they would deprive bishops of "lordeship of londes," so that they would be forced to live on firstfruits and tithes in accordance with the law. The corruption of the church is indicated by the gift of Constantine, which poisoned the apostolic succession. It might be best if lords were to take this poison from the church. In short, the spiritual welfare of the folk depends on their having leaders who follow the example of Christ. St. Thomas of India should be an example to "suche that of Surrye bereth the name," but they

> hippe aboute in Engelonde   to halwe mennes auteres,
> And crepe amonges curatoures   and confessen ageyne the
>   lawe,
> *Nolite mittere falcem in messem alienam*, etc.[31]

$$(557\text{-}58)$$

Every bishop should make the rounds of his own see, teaching the people, and supplying them with both temporal and spiritual sustenance (Isa. 3.7): *In domo mea non est panis neque vestimentum, et ideo nolite constituere me regem.*[32] The need for such sustenance is especially acute among the unfaithful, in accordance with the words of Matt. 3.10: *Inferte omnes decimas in oreum meum, vt*

---

[31] The text is based on Deut. 23.25. Bruno *PL*, 164,528, takes it as a warning against the hasty and inaccurate reading of Scripture, an interpretation that may be reflected in the phrase "confessen ageyne the lawe." The itinerant bishops not only operate in the jurisdiction of others; they are corrupt teachers. As the poet has shown, their action in itself represents a grave neglect of duties made perfectly clear in Scripture.

[32] See Jerome's comment, *PL*, 24, 66, which reads in part: "Quanti panem non habentes, et vestimentum, cum ipsi esuriant et nudi sunt, nec habeant spirituales cibos, neque Christi tunicam integram reservarint, aliis et alimoniam et vestimenta promittunt, et pleni vulneribus, medicos esse se jactant: nec servant illud Mosaicum: *Provide alium quem mittas. . . .*"

sit cibus in domo mea.[33] We who have the faith have no
need for extraneous bishops. The Jews followed the law,
yet they refused to accept Christ and were lost, as Daniel
prophesied (Dan. 9.24, 26). But the "Pharesewes and
Sarasenes, Scribes and Grekis" are folk of one faith, honor-
ing God. Since they believe the first clause of the Creed,
prelates should teach them, "litlum and lytlum," until
they believe the remainder.

With the aid of all the faculties of the mind together,
or Anima, Will is thus able to see that he cannot learn
Dowel perfectly without the leadership and example of
Piers. When Piers leads the church militant, it is the source
of good in the world, the reasonable guide of the wills of
individual Christians. But when it is led by hypocrites, like
the friars, it is the source of evil. If the leaders of the
church are to promote good, they must practise the charity
of Dobest. That is, they must place their confidence in
spiritual sustenance rather than in *temporalia;* they must
supply spiritual food to the humble, God's prisoners; and
they must wash away the sins of mankind. In short, they
must live well, preach sound doctrine, and administer the
sacraments efficiently. Charity appears among men of all
sorts, since it is something internal, not a matter of clothing
or externals. In so far as externals are concerned, the chari-
table man is not solicitous, and he does not disguise his
cupidity in holy-seeming language as do the friars. In the
church militant there are few charitable leaders. Lack of
charity corrupts learning, which is of no value without
charity. It produces inefficient bishops, typified by the wan-
dering metropolitans of distant foreign dioceses who have

---

[33] The quotation is erroneously attributed to Osee. The "syke" and "fieble"
referred to are those like the Jews addressed in the Bible. The two kinds of
food are indicated in Rupert's comment, *PL*, 168, 833: "non solus cibus
corporalis ex rebus corporalibus, quae debentur vobis, verum etiam quod
melius et quod prius est, cibus spiritualis ex rebus spiritualibus, quas Deo
debetis judicio, misericordia, et fide, et caeteris hujusmodi."

no concern for their flocks. If the leaders of the church practiced charity, the Saracens could be saved without difficulty; but the paganism of Saracen and Greek is a symbol of the failure of the clergy to perform its function anywhere. Foreigners are abandoned completely while those at home are fed only with empty and vain words. We may conclude that since Piers is not visible in the flesh, he may be seen only through the eyes of the contemplative. Anima's teaching thus serves in its implications as a prologue to the life of Dobet, the contemplative search for charity through Piers Plowman.

PASSUS XVI

Will thanks Anima for teaching which is of especial value for the person in the active life. Although her discourse was not specifically concerned with the active life, Anima has shown the widespread corruption of spiritual teachers which is responsible for Hawkin's plight. Without Piers he cannot be saved, but the world's spiritual guides as Anima portrays them are far from representing Piers. However, Will says that he still does not know "what charite is to mene." Indeed, he cannot know, as Anima's teaching has implied, without the guidance of Piers. In speaking of charity, Anima recurs to a figure suggested by Holy Church and used in her own description of inadequate priests (xv, 90-108). Holy Church said:

For trewthe telleth that loue is triacle of heuene. . .
And also the plente of pees moste precious of vertues.
                                    (I, 146, 150)

The tree of charity, the *lignum vitae* of Scripture, represents Christ or the Cross anagogically, the just allegorically, and the individual Christian tropologically. Its leaves are the word of God, and its blossoms are the preliminaries to its fruit of charity. Tropologically, the tree may be either

191

good or evil. That is, it may be bare of the leaves of God's word, like the evil priests whom Anima described, and produce vices. On the other hand, it may be green and produce good works. The good tree is rooted in humility or charity; the evil tree is rooted in cupidity or pride. The tropological values are well illustrated in the accompanying diagrams from the *De fructibus carnis et spiritus*, a treatise printed among the works of Hugh of St. Victor.[34]

Developing the traditional interpretation of the tree, Anima explains that its blossoms are "Boxome-Speche and Benygne-Lokynge," or the preliminary to good works. The tree is called patience and humility, that is, the life of Christ on earth. It produces the fruit of charity through God and through man, since in the imitation of Christ whose new law brought charity to men, the good man may also produce it. Will expresses his eagerness to make a pilgrimage to the tree, and to eat of the fruit of charity.[35] He desires no other fare. That is, Will is preparing for the renunciation and penance necessary to contemplation. But he needs to be directed to the tree. Anima tells him that he must look into his own heart:

'It groweth in a gardyne,' quod he   'that god made hymseluen,

Amyddes mannes body   the more is of that stokke;
Herte hatte the herber   that it in groweth,

[34] *PL*, 176, 107-10. Some commentators use charity and cupidity (or lechery, used symbolically) as roots, with humility and pride as chief fruits. For values of the tree on various levels, and significances for its various parts, see Peter Lombard on Ps. 1.3, *PL*, 191, 63; Bonaventura on Luke 23.31, *Opera*, VII, 474; St. Martin on Apoc. 22.2, *PL*, 209, 413; Gregory, *Moralia*, XIII, LIII, *PL*, 75, 1014; Bruno Astensis, *Sententiae*, *PL*, 165, 878; *Allegoriae in sacram scripturam*, *PL*, 112, 985, 986. And the references above, Chapter 6, note 9. The tree represented by Christ on the Cross beside the Well of God's Mercy was popular in late Medieval art. Cf. D. W. Robertson, Jr. "The Doctrine of Charity in Mediaeval Literary Gardens," *Speculum*, XXVI (1951), pp. 24-49. For the tree see especially pp. 25-27.

[35] Eating the fruit is a symbol of the attainment of salvation. See, for example, Bruno on Apoc. 22, *PL*, 165, 730: "De hoc autem ligno qui manducaverit, mortem non gustabit in aeternum."

| And *Liberum-Arbitrium* | hath the londe to ferme, |
| Vnder Piers the Plowman | to pyken it and to weden it.' |

(13-17)

In other words, charity grows in the heart, where it is a
function of the will. The will must be guided by Piers if
charity is to develop.

At the mention of Piers, Will swoons so that he "laye
longe in a lone dreme." This slumber, which Will enters
"al for pure ioye" should be contrasted sharply with his
spiritual sleep which he began in Passus xi, in "a wynkyng
wratth." The sleep of Passus xi was a sleep of the spirit
as the flesh turned to concupiscence; the sleep of Passus xvi
is the sleep of the contemplative, isolating himself from
the world so that he may enjoy the vision of Christ.[36] In
his dream, Will sees Piers who shows him the tree sup-
ported by the three props of the trinity. Piers explains that
the props are necessary to support the tree against strong
winds, citing Ps. 36.24: *Cum ceciderit iustus, non collid-
etur; quia Dominus supponit manum suam.* That is, God
supports the charitable or just man so that he does not fall.
The winds are the world, the flesh, and the devil, against
which the three members of the Trinity offer protection.[37]
Specifically, the wind of the World produces covetousness
which attacks the leaves of the tree, or the word of God.
Earlier in the poem, we have seen Lady Meed, and later the
covetous friars attacking the leaves in this fashion. The
resulting corruption was described in detail in Passus xv.
The protection against this attack is *potencia-Dei-Patris*
which, by implication, produces the fear of the Lord. As
we have seen, however, fear is not enough. The wind of
the Flesh attacks the blossoms, or the inclinations to char-

[36] Most Scriptural symbols have a dual value. Just as there is a good love
(caritas) and an evil love (cupiditas) there is a good sleep and an evil sleep.
For both sorts, see, for example, *PL*, 112, 913, 1057.

[37] On the winds of temptation, see, for example, Gregory, *PL*, 75, 980.
For the props on the tree, see below, p. 195.

ity, just as Will's inclinations to charity were weakened when he fell into the land of Longing, after his leaves were withered in Scripture's scorn. The blossoms are protected, however, by *sapiencia-Dei-patris*, or the passion of Christ, which induces the prayer, penance, and contemplation to which Will is here being introduced. He has already learned something of the suffering necessary to a true imitator of Christ. The Devil attacks the tree vigorously, but *Liberum-Arbitrium*, acting under Piers' direction, puts him down. When *Liberum-Arbitrium* does not act in obedience to Piers, he sides with the Devil and commits the irremissible sin against the Holy Spirit. As Hugh of St. Victor explains, these three props are necessary to the maintenance of the image of God in man:

Vultus Patris est potentia; Filii, sapientia; Spiritus sancti, benignitas. Lumen vultus est memoria, intellectus, voluntas. De memoria cecidit homo in oblivionem; de intellectu in ignorantium; de voluntate in rectitudinis abusionem. Sed Deus misit Filium suum qui attulit fidem, spem, charitatem. Quibus haec imago, hic vultus signatur super nos, id est rationi imprimitur. Fides pellit oblivionem, memoriam restituendo; spes ignorantiam fugat, intellectum purgando; charitas rectitudinis abusionem, exstinguit, voluntatem relevando. Vultus itaque Trinitatis in charitate, est potentia, sapientia, benignitas. Per potentiam cuncta creavit: per sapientiam cuncta disposuit: per benignitatem cuncta gubernat et fovet. Sed quia ad vultum videndum accedere non possumus, habemus lumen, id est imaginem et similitudinem. Per imaginem ipsum apprehendimus, id est, per memoriam, intellectum, et voluntatem. Per similitudinem eum nobis exprimimus, id est, per fidem, spem, et charitatem.[38]

The association here of *potentia, sapientia,* and *benignitas* with the persons of the Trinity, with the faith, hope, and charity which Christ brought, and with the three parts of the image of God in man is strikingly similar to the development of these themes in this episode.

[38] *Miscellanea*, V, LXVII, *PL*, 177, 794.

THE TREE OF VIRTUES

THE TREE OF VICES

Adolph Katzenellenbogen, *Allegories of the Virtues and Vices in Mediaeval Art*, London, Warburg Institute, 1939.

Piers quotes Matt. 12.32, but verses 30 and 31 are implied:

Qui non est mecum contra me est, et qui non congregat mecum spargit. Ideo dico vobis: Omne peccatum et blasphemia remittetur hominibus; spiritus autem blasphemia non remittetur. . . . qui autem dixerit contra Spiritum sanctum, non remittetur ei neque in hoc saeculo neque in futuro.

Since man must be either with Christ or against him the duty of the will to follow Piers is thus of supreme importance. If it does so it will be free to oppose the Devil with the help of grace and the Holy Spirit:

> Ac whan the Fende and the Flesshe   forth with the
>   Worlde
> Manasen byhynde me   my fruit for to fecche,
> Thanne *Liberum-Arbitrium*   laccheth the thridde plante,
> And palleth adown the pouke   purelich' thorw grace
> And helpe of the holy goste   and thus haue I the may-
>   strie. (48-52)

Only with a good will directed by Piers is man able to obtain grace and to follow the right path.

Will observes that the three props are of equal length; he wonders whether they have come from the same tree. Piers tells him that he is right, that the tree represents the three coeternal members of the Trinity. He then looks on Will "egrelich" in recollection of Will's earlier unguided questioning. But Will shows how much he has learned of patience and loyalty; he spares further question concerning the tree (53-64). He asks instead of the fruits. Allegorically, these are the just men, those who are directed in the way of spiritual perfection with its three inner states of development; the lowest is matrimony, higher is continence (widowhood), the highest is maidenhood. These are conventional symbols for the three states of spiritual perfection, the three fruits which spring from the seed sown in the "grounde of Goodnesse" of Matthew

13.23.[39] The particular symbolic terminology here employed emphasizes the inner quality of the three states, Dowel, Dobet, Dobest, externally manifest as active, contemplative, and prelatical.

Will desires to taste the fruit:

> I prayed Pieres to pulle adown an apple, and he wolde,
> And suffre me to assaye what sauoure it hadde.
>
>   (73-74)

He desires to know charity, the tropological fruit of the tree. Piers knocks down the fruit, all of which are carried off by the Devil until Christ comes to contend for them. That is, he knocks down the allegorical fruits which grew on the tree before Christ brought charity to the world, the just men of the Old Testament, whom Christ wrested from the Devil. The answer to Will's desire to know the savour of the fruit of charity is implicit in the life of Christ, his ministry and passion, the substance, that is, of lines 86-166.[40] The leading image, to be developed at length in XVIII, is that of Christ jousting for the Redemption. The angel announces the Redeemer's mission to Mary:

> And thanne shulde Iesus Iuste there-fore bi Iuggement
>   of armes,
> Whether shulde fonge the fruit the fende or hymselue.
>
>   (95-96)

Christ before his ministry learns from Piers Plowman how to protect himself against evil; that is, Christ learns how to plow the hearts of men and to sow the seed of the word from Piers Plowman who represents, in any age, the ministry of God:

> And Pieres the Plowman parceyued plenere tyme,
> And lered hym lechecrafte his lyf for to saue,

---

[39] Bede describes them as *conjugatos, viduatos, virgines, PL*, 92, 66.

[40] The word *savour* may be a pun: the savor of the fruit (charity) is the *savior* of the fruit (Christ). The pun links the tropological and allegorical meaning of the tree.

That thowgh he were wounded with his enemye   to
                            warisshe hymself. (103-5)

He cures the sick, converts the sinner, raises the dead. Finally he comes to the jousting-day:

On a Thoresday in thesternesse   thus was he taken
Thorw Iudas and Iewes   Iesus was his name;
That on the Fryday folwynge   for mankynde sake
Iusted in Ierusalem   a Ioye to vs alle.
On crosse vpon Caluarye   Cryst toke the bataille,
Aȝeines deth and the deuel   destruyed her botheres
                                  myȝtes,
Deyde, and deth fordid   and daye of nyȝte made.
                                  (160-66)

As the vision of the Redemption ends, Will awakes and goes forth as an idiot,[41] that is, without comprehension, to find Piers Plowman. It is Piers Plowman who must teach him the tropological meaning of his vision of the tree of charity. This search is directly parallel with the allegorical search of the repentant sinners in Passus v: they had been given the elements of Faith by Repentance; Hope had blown the horn which started them on their pilgrimage, but they "blustreden forth as bestes" until they met with Piers, who explained Charity to them and instituted the rule under the New Law. The parallel is continued here in that Will now meets with Faith and then with Hope, preliminary to the meeting with Charity. The equation of Faith with Abraham or the patriarchs, of Hope with Moses (xvii 1-13), or the prophets, and of Charity with the Samaritan, or Christ and his disciples, is suggested by the vision of the tree, the fruits of which (81-85) are in terms of the Old Testament the patriarchs and the prophets, who found their salvation in Jesus. As Faith and Hope are completed in Charity, so the law and the prophets are completed in the apostolic precepts. Augustine makes

---

[41] The word has its original Latin meaning; see *NED*, *s.v.*, *idiot*.

this point in explaining the parable of the Good Samaritan: the priest and the Levite who do not help the wounded man are the priests and ministers of the Old Law, who stand respectively for the law-givers and the prophets; the Samaritan is Christ:

Sacerdos autem et Levita qui eo viso praeterierunt, sacerdotium et ministerium Veteris Testamenti significant, quae non poterant prodesse ad salutem. Samaritanus, Custos interpretatur: et ideo ipse Dominus significatur hoc nomine.[42]

Since the patriarchs, the prophets, and the apostles collectively are represented by Piers Plowman, in meeting with Abraham, Will has begun the process of finding Piers. Faith and Hope have their end and their beginning in Charity.

The remainder of Dobet is clearly developed from Will's vision of the tree of Charity which culminates in the Passion. Faith comes to Will at Mid-Lent. Dobet ends to the sound of Easter bells as Will approaches on his knees the tree of the Cross. The image of Christ as a knight jousting for mankind is fully developed: Faith is a herald, Hope a spy; the Samaritan is going to a joust in Jerusalem. The ensuing action is an explanation of Will's vision. Since it is at the same time an explanation of Charity, it is the culmination of the poem.

Abraham tells Will that he is Faith:

And of Abrahames hous   an heraud of armes.
I seke after a segge   that I seigh ones,
A ful bolde bacheler   I knewe hym by his blasen.

(177-79)

---

[42] Saint Augustine, *Quaestionum Evangeliorum, PL,* 35, 1340. See the *Glossa ordinaria, PL,* 114, 286-87: "Vers. 31.—*Accidit autem,* etc. Sacerdos Dei legem annuntiat: descendit quidem lex per Moysen in mundum, et nullam sanitatem contulit hujusmodi. Descendit Levita, qui typum ostendit prophetarum, sed et hic nullum sanat, quia lex peccata arguit, sed pertransit, quia indulgentiam non largitur. Vers. 33.—*Misericordia motus.* Hoc de sacerdote et Levita non est dictum, quia lex non habet misericordiam, sed judicium et vindictam.

The person whom Abraham saw once was God Himself in the form of three men, Gen. 18.1-2. The *Glossa ordinaria* interprets the passage as heralding Christ's coming, "Tres viri Christi pronuntiant adventum."[43] Abraham the herald is searching for Christ the Saviour, who will make his faith fruitful. Will asks after the knight's arms. Abraham replies that his arms represent the Trinity. The alternate interpretation of the three men of Abraham's vision as found for example in Bede, is that they represent the Trinity: "Quod tres viri ei apparuerunt, mysterium est sanctae Trinitatis."[44] Moreover, Abraham represents Faith, as Peter Lombard explains in commenting on Rom. 4.1-2:

Quod superius dixerat hominem justificari per fidem, ostendit per Abraham, in quo omnes confidunt, qui per fidem adeptus est justitiam et promissionem, et paternitatem.[45]

As Faith he properly expresses his belief in the Trinity; the three men he sees are Christ and at the same time the Trinity. He repeats the fundamental doctrine of the Athanasian Creed:

Fides autem catolica haec est: ut unum Deum in trinitate, et trinitatem in unitate veneremur.

To make clear the Trinity in so far as this is possible through created things, Faith advances two illustrations, both taken from Augustine's *De Trinitate*.[46] The illustra-

---

[43] *PL*, 113, 125. Abraham was the first to whom the incarnation of Christ was manifest, and hence properly symbolic of Faith. See *Glossa ordinaria*, *PL*, 114, 248, on Luke 1.55.

[44] Bede, *PL*, 91, 166.   [45] *PL*, 191, 1366.

[46] For lines 192-201 cf. Augustine as quoted in Lombard, *PL*, 192, 532-33: "Mens enim novit se, et amat se, nec amare se potest, nisi etiam noverit se. Duo quaedam sunt mens et notitia ejus. . . . Item duo quaedam sunt mens et amor ejus. . . . Quia mens vice Patris, notitia Filii, amor Spiritus sancti accipitur. Et est ipsa mens quasi parens, et notitia ejus quasi proles ejus. Mens enim cum se cognoscit, notitiam sui gignit, et est sola parens suae notitiae. Tertius est amor, qui de ipsa mente et notitia procedit." For lines 202-24 see Skeat, II, 239-40. It should be noted that *Deus meus, etc.* (214) is not a reference to Ps. 21.1, as Skeat suggests, but to Matt. 27.47 or Mark 15.34; Christ's exclamation is taken to signify his humanity as distinct from his

tions are related to the fruits of the tree of charity, the first
by the mention of the children of charity, patriarchs, proph-
ets, and apostles, and the second by the use of the symbols
marriage, widowhood, and virginity, which are also fruits
of the tree.

The basis of Faith in the Athanasian creed is belief in
the Trinity. Having established this principle Abraham
now shows through his own life the operation of Faith as
a means of finding grace. He repeats as the basis of this
life of Faith, his encounter with the Trinity (Gen. 18.1-2):

> Thus in a somer I hym seigh   as I satte in my porche;
> I ros vp and reuerenced hym   and riȝt faire hym grette;
> Thre men to my syȝte   I made wel at ese,
> Wesche her feet and wyped hem   and afterward thei eten
> Calues flesshe and cakebrede   and knewe what I thouȝte.
>
>   (225-29)

Abraham's acts of hospitality are symbolic of salvation
through Christ: the washing of the feet represents the
final purification, the flesh and bread both represent the
body of Christ:

Tunc enim mysterium futurum aspexit, unde et pedes illorum lavit,
ut in extremo tempore lavari purificatione monstraret, Pedes enim
extrema significant. . . . Iste autem vitulus saginatus, Domini Jesu
corpus est. Ipse vitulus pro redeunte filio occiditur. . . . Tria autem
sata tres filios Noe significant. Ex quibus hominum genus ortum
est, qui divinae Trinitati credentes, ex aqua baptismatis per Eccle-
siam, cujus imago Sarra fuit, conspergendi essent, et in unum
panem corporis Domini redigendi.[47]

In testimony of his faith a covenant is made between God
and Abraham (Gen. 17.2):

> Ful trewe tokenes bitwene vs is   to telle whan me
>   lyketh. (230)

Godhead: see Bede, *PL*, 92, 290. The reference must be taken with the suc-
ceeding line, "That is creatour wex creature," not with the preceding line
as Skeat's punctuation indicates.

[47] Bede, *PL*, 91, 238.

Foedus meum inter me et te. Legem inter Christum Ecclesiamque demonstrat, quae multiplicatur multitudine populi fidelium; per pactum vero circumcisionis, populi carnales.[48]

> First he fonded me   if I loued bettere
> Hym, or Ysaak myn ayre   the which he hiȝte me kulle.
> (231-32)

Isaac ligatus super struem lignorum ponitur: Christus filius natus est.

> He wiste my wille by hym   he wil me it allowe,
> I am ful syker in soule ther-of   and my sone bothe.
> (233-34)

Quod autem pro Isaac immolatus est aries, significat quod illaesa divinitate manente, secundum carnem crucifixus est, sive quod idem Christus filius natus est.[49]

The second token was the circumcision of himself, his son and his retainers (235-38):

Hoc est pactum quod observabis, id est, lex circumcisionis populo carnali et spirituali, id est, Novum Testamentum populo spirituali. . . . Quid autem significat circumcisio, nisi renovatam naturam per baptismum, post exspoliationem veteris hominis? Et quid octavus dies, nisi Novum Testamentum, in quo per resurrectionem Salvatoris octava die, et post sabbatum factum renovamur, et circumcisi universis vitiis novi homines efficiamur.[50]

In the Redemption is the promise of "londe and lordship' and lyf withouten ende." But even more was granted; "Mercy for owre mysdedes as many tyme as we asken" (240-42):

Cuique omnis terra datur, ut alibi: Postula a me, et dabo tibi gentes haereditatem tuam, et possessionem tuam terminos terrae, usque in sempiternum, id est, pro longitudine temporum. Quae hic sequuntur Christo conveniunt spiritualiter cum Ecclesia sua.[51]

Finally, he is told to do worship to God "with bred and with wyn bothe." (Gen. 14.18):

Revertenti igitur Abraham occurit Melchisedech, proferens panem et vinum: sacerdos Dei summi benedixit Abraham. Hunc Melchisedech Paulus sine patre, sine matre commemorans, figuraliter refert

---

[48] *Ibid.,* 236.   [49] *Ibid.,* 245.   [50] *Ibid.,* 236-37.
[51] *Ibid.,* 233.

ad Christum, qui sine patre in terra, sine matre in coelo erat, et sacerdos in aeternum. . . . Utique per mysterium, ut non pecudum victimas, sed oblationem panis et vini, id est corporis et sanguinis in sacrificio offeramus.[52]

As the "foot" of God's faith, Abraham the patriarch is a representative of Christ's priesthood, Piers Plowman, and thus symbolically learns the Sacrifice of the Mass:

Et si ergo omnes patriarchae et prophetae fuerunt figura Christi, Melchisedech tamen specialius, quia non de genere Judaeorum, ut quidam dicunt, praecessit in typum sacerdotii Christi qui dicitur sacerdos secundum ordinem Melchisedech multis modis, quia solus rex et sacerdos fuit, et ante circumcisionem functus sacerdotio, ut non gentes a Judaeis, sed Judaei a gentibus sacerdotium acciperent. Et non fuit unctus oleo visibili, ut Moyses instituit, sed oleo exsultationis et puritate fidei, nec animalia immolvait, sed pane et vino Christi sacerdotium dedicavit.[53]

Abraham's priesthood was confirmed by Melchisedech, not with oil but in the purity of faith, not in the old sacrifice of animals but in the prophetic sacrifice of bread and wine. As priest in the Faith, he is called by God:

> . . . . . .   his folke forto saue
> And defende hem fro the fende   folke that on me leueden.
> Thus haue I ben his heraude   here and in helle,
> And conforted many a careful   that after his comynge
> wayten. (245-48)

And now, as John the Baptist has declared to those waiting in Hell, the One he seeks is coming: *"ecce agnus Dei."* Will sees Lazarus in the bosom of Abraham; symbolic of Christ's blessed poor:

Sinus Abraham requies est beatorum pauperum, quorum est regnum coelorum, quo post hanc vitam recipiuntur. . . . Quid Abrahae sinus, nisi secretam requiem significat Patris? de qua Veritas. *Multi* (inquit) *venient ab Oriente et Occidente, et recumbent cum Abraham, et Isaac, et Jacob in regno coelorum* . . . fideles

[52] *Ibid.*, 233.
[53] Peter Lombard, *Collectanea in Ep. Ad Hebr.*, PL, 192, 448.

quosque ante diem extremi judicii, super se in requie attendunt, quorum post gaudia contemplari nullatenus possunt.[54]

But until Christ comes, Abraham and those in his bosom are in the power of Hell. Will is grieved that sin should prevent God's mercy. He weeps and Hope appears. Faith, as Hugh of St. Victor says, removes oblivion from the memory. Will's oblivion has been characterized by the foolish questions he has hitherto been guilty of. Through Abraham he learns that belief in the Trinity is the only basis for this search for charity. Will has been reminded of the Trinity and of the true nature of the object of his search, charity as exemplified in the Resurrection. The sequence is identical with that in Passus v where the prayer of Repentance is followed by the sound of the horn of Hope.

PASSUS XVII

Hope too is searching for a knight. This knight has also given him a token: the ten commandments given to Moses by God. By this "maundement" the world should be ruled (3). Will asks whether these letters patent are sealed, that is, whether they have authority. He wonders whether he may see these letters of command. The patent is not sealed, says Hope; that is why he is seeking the knight, the keeper of the great seal of Christendom (6-7). Will asks to see the document. Hope pulls forth a piece of rock on which is written the new law:

Dilige Deum et proximum tuum, etc.

There is a golden gloss:

In hjis duobus mandatis tota lex pendet et propheta.

Hope comes to man through the Resurrection, the promise given Abraham of "londe and lordeship   and lyf

---

[54] Bede, *PL*, 92, 535-37. Matt. 8.11, quoted by Bede, is taken by Bruno to refer to the Harrowing of Hell: "His enim paucis verbis Ecclesiam ex omnibus mundi partibus colligendam, et inferno exspoliato, sanctorum animas ad coelorum regna transferendas," *PL*, 165, 141.

withouten ende." What is a commandment in the Old Law is promise and Hope in the New: when the Law is sealed through Christ's death on the cross, Faith and good works become a pardon, the way to salvation. The Old Law is written on stone; the New in the hearts of men, in charity.[55] Abraham and the good men of the Old Law were doomed to Hell because although they had Faith and Good Works they did not historically have Charity or Christ. The Law sealed by Charity becomes the pardon of Hope. The parallel between this episode and the earlier pardon episode now becomes apparent, and as in that episode, the power of the pardon is questioned because of ignorance. Will is an idiot, it is to be remembered:

'Ben here alle thi lordes lawes?' quod I

To dispel such ignorance is the function of Hope. Again to quote Hugh of St. Victor, "Spes ignorantiam fugat."

Hope declares that in the new law is the way to Salvation. Faith agrees (15-21). But Will remains confused. He does not understand the relationship between the old law and the new, between the law and the prophets, between Faith and Good Works. He wishes to know which is the right way; he feels redundancy in having both necessary to salvation. On the basis of its simplicity and ease he favors Faith: it is hard enough to believe in Abraham, but how much worse to follow the New Law and actually to force oneself to love a shrew, your enemy. Since Faith and Hope are nothing without Charity, they of course cannot resolve Will's doubts. This must wait for Charity itself, who now appears in the guise of the Good Samaritan. The use of the parable is most exact. Faith and Hope have passed by the wounded man, the sinner Will, since they

[55] See Lombard on 2 Cor. 3.3, *PL*, 192, 22: "Hoc digito scripta est lex vetus, sed distat, quia lex illa scripta est in tabulis lapideis; nova autem lex diffusa est in cordibus. [Augustinus] Haec lex est charitas Dei. Illa et lex operum, littera occidens praevaricatorem, ista est lex fidei vivificans dilectorem. Cf. St. Augustine, *De catechisandis rudibus*, 23 (41).

have left him in his state of graceless ignorance; Christ, the Good Samaritan, will heal his wounds. The Parable is of course illustrative of the need to seek Piers Plowman, Dobest; and it is illustrative of the definition of Dowel and Dobet as infinites which seek out Dobest, given by clergy as coming from Piers himself (Passus XIII 127-29).

Faith and Hope having failed to care for the fallen sinner, the Samaritan tends to his wounds:

And to the wye he went   his woundes to biholde,
And parceyued bi his pous   he was in peril to deye,
And but-if he hadde recourere the rather   that rise shulde
       he neure;
And breyde to his boteles   and bothe he atamede;
Wyth wyn and with oyle   his woundes he wasshed,
Enbawmed hym and bonde his hed   and in his lappe hym
       layde,
And ladde hym so forth on lyard   to *lex-christi* a graunge,
Wel six myle or seuene   biside the newe market;
Herberwed hym at an hostrye   and to the hostellere called.

(65-73)

He gives the inn-keeper two pieces of money for the expenses of the wounded man. The series of actions is explained by Bede as follows:

Et approprians alligavit vulnera ejus, infundens oleum et vinum. Peccata, quae in hominibus invenit, redarguendo cohibuit, spem veniae poenitentibus, terrorem poenae peccantibus incutiens. Alligat enim vulnera, dum praecipit: *Poenitentiam agite,* infundit oleum, dum addit: *Appropinquabit enim regnum caelorum* (Matt. III). Infundit et vinum, dum dicit: *Omnis* arbor quae non facit fructum bonum, excidetur, et in ignem mittetur (Ibid.). *Et imponens illum in jumentum suum, duxit in stabulum, et curam ejus egit.* Jumentum ejus est caro, in qua ad nos venire dignatus est. In quo saucium imposuit, quia peccata nostra ipse portavit in corpore suo super lignum. . . . Itaque imponi jumento est, in ipsam Incarnationem Christi credere, ejusque mysteriis initiari, simul et ab hostis incursione tutari. Stabulum autem est Ecclesia praesens, ubi reficiuntur viatores, de peregrinatione hac in aeternam patriam redeuntes. . . . *Et altera die protulit duos denarios, et dedit stabulario, et ait*: *Curam illius habe*. Altera dies est post Domini resurrectionem. . . . Duo denarii sunt duo Testamenta, in quibus aeterni Regis nomen et imago continetur. Finis enim legis Christus (Ro. X).[56]

The episode of the repentant sinners who found their true guide in Piers prefigures the lesson which the Samaritan (Christ) here teaches directly: man must be cleansed of his sins through Confession; then in Faith and Hope, within Holy Church, he may find Charity (Christ, the end of the law) in his own heart. At the same time, the Samaritan's action symbolizes the Redemption through which the sins of mankind are cleansed and the sacraments rendered efficacious. The Samaritan proceeds to explain the relationship between Faith, Hope, and Himself, Christ. He uses the figure of the Christian sacraments, Baptism, Confession, Holy Communion, where the first two are preparations for the grace granted by the Eucharist:

> May no medcyn on molde   the man to hele brynge,
> Neither Feith ne fyn Hope   so festred ben his woundis,
> With-out the blode of a barn   borne of a mayde.
> And be he bathed in that blode   baptised, as it were,
> And thanne plastred with penaunce   and passioun of that babi,
> He shulde stonde and steppe;   ac stalworth worth he neure,
> Tyl he haue eten al the barn   and his blode ydronke.
>
> (91-97)

Historically, the way to Jerusalem was closed through original sin so that no one passed through the world safely except those who lived in Faith or who followed the Law in the will to righteousness. But since Christ has assumed man's flesh, the horse of the parable, and has ridden to Jerusalem and in so doing saved the wayfarer, he has made the celestial pilgrimage safe from the attacks of the devil,

[56] *PL*, 92, 469-70. Cf. Hugh of St. Victor, *Miscellanea*, v, LXXIII, *PL*, 177, 796-97: "Haec sunt opera Samaritani; qui prius vinum, inde oleum fudit. . . . In vino fervor poenitentiae, in oleo lenitas justitiae."

when his road is followed.[57] Faith will point out the way
and Hope will assist the Christian who falls through weak-
ness:

And thanne shal Feith be forester   here and in this fritth
                                                          walke,
And kennen out comune men   that knoweth nouȝte the
                                                     contre,
Which is the weye that ich went   and where forth to
                                                Iherusalem.
And Hope the hostelleres man shal be   there the man lith
                                               an helynge;
And alle that fieble and faynt be   that Faith may nouȝte
                                               teche,
Hope shal lede hem forth with loue   as his lettre telleth,
And hostel hem and hele   thorw holicherche bileue,
Tyl I haue salue for alle syke.... (112-19)

After the Redemption, Faith has the power to teach the
imitation of Christ, not simply to herald his coming. He
can thus direct the pilgrim on the proper road to Jerusalem
since Charity has become manifest. When the pilgrim
strays from the road because he is weak in Faith, he may
be restored through Hope, that is, trust in God's Charity,
which will lead him to works of satisfaction under the new
law. The various symbolic meanings of the parable of the
Samaritan are well summarized in the *Allegoriae in novum
testamentum* attributed to Hugh of St. Victor:

Homo iste, qui de Jerusalem in Jericho descendit et in latrones
incidit, sicut in homiliis legimus, genus designat humanum. Quod
in primis parentibus supernam civitatem deserens, in hujus saeculi
et exsilii miseriam per culpam corruens, per antiqui hostis fraudu-
lentiam veste immortalitatis et innocentiae est spoliatum, et origi-
nalis culpae vitiis graviter vulneratum. *Fecerat Deus,* sicut *alio
loco diximus, hominem ad imaginem et similitudinem suam* (Gen.
I). Ad imaginem, secundum rationem; ad similitudinem secundum
dilectionem, ut per utrumque Deo inhaereret, et inhaerendo beatus
esset. Sed diabolus, humanae beatitudini invidens, contra duo bona

[57] This promise is in general the understanding of *O mors, ero mors tua,*
Hosea 13.14. See Rupert, *PL,* 168, 196.

praedicta duo principalia mala intulit homini in originali culpa. In eo namque quod factus est ad imaginem Dei secundum rationem, vulneravit eum per ignorantium boni. In eo vero quod factus erat ad similitudinem Dei, vulneravit eum per concupiscentiam mali. . . . Sacerdos et levita qui, viso spoliato et vulnerato transierunt, patres antiquos exprimunt, qui vitae praesentis statum tunc sancte vivendo transierunt; sed humanum genus per culpam vulneratum minime sanaverunt. Samaritanus pertransit, dum Christus per humanitatem vitae hujus momenta cucurrit, qui homini vulnerato vinum et oleum infudit, dum per praedicationem suam illi et blandam consolationem et austeram increpationem exhibuit. Alligans vulnera ejus in jumentum suum levavit, dum, per carnem assumptam in cruce suspensus, morte sua culpam illius expiavit. In stabulam duxit, dum intra sanctam Ecclesiam collocavit. Stabulum autem Ecclesiam significat; quia, sicut jumenta in stabulo suas immunditias dimittunt, sic peccatores, qui bestialiter antea vixerunt, per confessionem et satisfactionem in sancta Ecclesia peccata sua deponunt . . . stabulum, Ecclesia; stabularii, praelati; duo denarii, scientia utriusque Testamenti.[58]

The commentary makes clear the general meaning of the parable as it is used in the poem. It indicates precisely why Faith and Hope were unavailing to the extinguishing of unrighteousness which is the work of charity as Hugh of St. Victor says, "charitas rectitudinis abusionem, extinguit, voluntatem relevando." It demonstrates the relevance of charity to the restoration of the image of God: the image is restored through the charity of Christ.

Will still fails to understand; he wishes to know whether he should believe Faith or Hope: in the Trinity or in the New Law. The Samaritan answers directly: you must believe in both against conscience, kind wit, or heretical argument. He gives him certain replies which he may use against the attacks of his own reasoning or that of others. The first of these is the image of the fist. Implicit in the image is the warning against the denial of faith and the loss of hope which leads to despair; that is the sin against the Holy Ghost which is irremissible:

[58] *PL*, 175, 814-15.

So who so synneth in seynt spirit   it semeth that he
greueth
God, that he grypeth with   and wolde his grace quench.

(201-2)

The image of the quenching of grace suggests the next
image of the Trinity, the torch. The point here is that it
is necessary for the individual to have the hot coal of char-
ity in order to ignite the flame of God's mercy:

Namore doth sire ne sone   ne seynt spirit togyderes,
Graunteth no grace   ne forȝifnesse of synnes,
Til the holi goste gynne   to glowe and to blase.
So that the holygoste   gloweth but as a glede,
Tyl that lele loue   ligge on hym and blowe,
And thanne flaumbeth he as fyre   on fader and on *filius*,
And melteth her myȝte in-to mercy. . . .
So grace of the holygoste   the grete myȝte of the Trinite
Melteth in-to mercy   to mercyable, and to non other.

(220-30)

The image of the flint, which follows, shows that to those
who do not practice charity God is the Just God only.
Faith and Good Works are necessary but without Charity
they are of themselves of no avail:

Be vnkynde to thin euene-cristene   and al that thow canst
bidden,
Delen and do penaunce   day and nyȝte euere. . . .
The holy goste hereth the nouȝt   ne helpe may the by
resoun;
For vnkyndenesse quencheth hym   that he can nouȝte
shyne. . . .
*Si linguis hominum loquar (et angelorum, caritatem autem
non habeam, factus sum velut aes sonans, aut cymbalum tin-
niens.)* (250-57)

In the first image the Samaritan has set forth the irremissi-
ble sin against the Holy Spirit. In the second image he has
shown the quickening force of Charity, the Holy Spirit.
In the image of the flint he has shown the result of the
denial of charity, the loss of God. In turning to apostro-

phize those rich in worldly goods, the Samaritan brings
together on the tropological level the meaning of the three
images. The rich man without charity has the "unkindness"
which quenches the grace of the Holy Ghost (269-70).
Cupidity sometimes leads to murder of the body, some-
times to murder of the soul through evil example. Cupidity
in thus destroying man, destroys the image of God and
leads to the sin against the Holy Ghost. Those guilty of
such murderous cupidity dwell with Dives in hell forever:

> For that the holygoste hath to kepe   tho harlotes destroy-
>   eth,
> The which is lyf and loue   the leye of mannes bodye.
> For euery manere good man   may be likned to a torche,
> Or elles to a tapre   to reuerence the trinitee;
> And who morthereth a good man   me thynketh, by myn
>   inwyt,
> He fordoth the leuest lyʒte   that owre lorde loueth.
>   Ac ʒut in many mo maneres   men offenden the holy
>   goste;
> Ac this is the worste wyse   that any wiʒte myʒte
> Synnen aʒein the seynt spirit   assenten to destruye,
> For coueityse of any kynnes thinge   that Cryst dere
>   bouʒte. (274-83)

As we have seen in the *Visio,* the desire for worldly goods
is at the heart of the evils in this world. Charity is the
ultimate source of the good life, and cupidity, the opposite
of charity, is an ultimate explanation for evil. We recall
Holy Church's initial warning about taking reward against
the innocent. It is these innocent whose voices will be raised
in judgment day, crying, "vindica sanguinem iustorum."
They cry out against those who have oppressed them
through cupidity.[59]

Still preoccupied with the easy road to salvation through
Faith, Will enquires if a man may do evil all his life and

[59] See St. Martin, *PL,* 209, 338 on Apoc. 6.10. For the contrast between
charity and cupidity, see Peter Lombard in Ps. 79, *PL,* 191, 765-66.

then repent at the last minute. The Samaritan gives the standard reply to this question: such repentance is possible but not probable. The connection between cupidity and the sin against the Holy Ghost, despair, is real and operative:

Thus it fareth bi suche folke   that falsely al her lyues
Euel lyuen and leten nouȝte   til lyf hem forsake;
Drede of desperacion   dryueth a-weye thanne grace,
That mercy in her mynde   may nauȝt thanne falle.

(305-8)

Man's will, turned from God, becomes so corrupt that it refuses God's mercy even though God's mercy is greater than all man's evil deeds:

Misericordia eius super omnia opera eius. (312)[60]

The Samaritan presents the image of the three evils which beset men: a shrewish wife, the flesh; a leaky roof, earthly suffering; a smoky room, earthly cupidity. The weaknesses of the flesh and the failures due to misfortune man may easily repent; but cupidity which is contrary to all reason quenches charity and God's mercy. With this explanation the Samaritan continues his journey to Jerusalem. Will awakes.

PASSUS XVIII

Through his meeting with Faith and Hope and through his instruction by Charity, Will has ceased to be simply an *idiote*; he is prepared to encounter with something approaching understanding the full contemplation of the Redemption. To put it in another way—a way implicit in the fact that Will is searching for Piers Plowman—Will has been instructed by Abraham, the patriarch, Moses, the prophet, and by Christ, the founder of the apostolic order. All three are represented by the figure of Piers Plowman, historically God's priesthood, the order of Melchisedech, which had its being before the coming of Christ and con-

[60] Ps. 144.9. See Peter Lombard, *PL*, 191, 1265.

tinued after His coming as the Priesthood of Holy Church. On a still further level, Will has come to some understanding of the Word as it appears anagogically (and historically in the order of Melchisedech). The coming vision of the Word incarnate will lead him to a fuller tropological understanding of the imitation of Christ.

Will is now described as "wolleward and wete-shoed." He is no longer dressed as a hypocrite, in shepherd's clothing with the wool outside: the wool is turned toward his skin to indicate that he is truly "reckless" of worldly "woe." He is called lorel, literally a lost one, because he has not yet found Salvation—that is to come in the Redemption. But he has become weary of the world, and in this weariness lends himself to Lent: his vision is now, as it was when he saw the Tree of Charity, the contemplative vision of true forgetfulness of the world. It opens with a reflection of the liturgical services connected with Palm Sunday. The imagery of the Joust, from the vision of the Tree, is once again established, and the two figures, the Samaritan and Piers Plowman are brought together:

> One semblable to the Samaritan   and some-del to Piers
> the Plowman,
> Barfote on an asse bakke   botelees cam prykye,
> Wyth-oute spores other spere   spakliche he loked,
> As is the kynde of a knyʒte   that cometh to be dubbed,
> To geten hem gylte spores   or galoches ycouped. . . .
> Thanne was Faith in a fenestre   and cryde 'a! fili Dauid!'
> As doth an heraude of armes   whan auntrous cometh to
> iustes. (10-15)

Will inquires who is coming to joust. Faith replies that it is Jesus, who will fetch the fruit of Piers the Plowman, again indicating the connection with the vision of the tree. Will, hearing the name of Piers, asks whether he is there. Faith is surprised at the ignorance of Will's question, and informs him that Jesus will joust in the arms of Piers, *humana natura*, to disguise his true "blason," *consummatus deus*. Had he worn this, he would have been invincible *in deitate patris*. There follows a long account of Christ's Passion and of the Harrowing of Hell, elaborated from the prefiguring in the visions of the Tree and of the Samaritan. The ultimate object of contemplation, the absolute revelation of Charity, the matters here unfolded contain the key to Will's entire search. The meaning of the episode is self-explanatory; in splendid, glowing poetry the climax to the poem is achieved. The doctrines set forth have all been explained: here they are synthesized and given concrete vitality.

At the close of the vision the Four Daughters of God are reconciled through the Redemption and dance in harmony.

> Tyl the daye dawed   this damaiseles daunced,
> That men rongen to the resurexioun   and riȝt with that
>   I waked.
> And called Kitte my wyf   and Kalote my douȝter—
> 'Ariseth and reuerenceth   goddes resurrexioun,
> And crepeth to the crosse on knees and kisseth it for a Iuwel!
> For goddes blissed body   it bar for owre bote,
> And it afereth the fende   for suche is the myȝte,
> May no grysly gost   glyde there it shadweth!'
>   (424-31)

This ending may occasion some surprise in view of the sudden introduction of the wife and daughter of Will, hitherto unmentioned. The explanation rests on the fact that the episode has been concerned with the restoration of God's image in man through the Redemption. The will by itself is insufficient to the life of perfection; it must be guided by the intellect under the tutelage of memory. That is, the image of God in man betokens a unity of three faculties all directed toward the love of God. This image is corrupted through sin as is shown, according to Peter Lombard, in the parable of the Samaritan:

Si autem quaeritur in quo possit currumpi anima, in parabola illius qui incidit in latrones qui eum vulnaverunt et spoliaverunt, Luc, 10, clarescit. Indicit enim homo in latrones, quando per peccatum in potestatem diaboli traditur; et tunc per peccatum expoliatur gratuitis bonis, id est virtutibus; et in naturalibus bonis vulneratur; quae sunt ratio, intellectus, memoria, et ingenium et hujusmodi, quae per peccatum obtenebrantur et vitiantur.[61]

The whole sequence beginning with the teaching of Anima, comprising the vision of the Redemption in the tree and the Samaritan episodes, and rising to the great climax of Will's contemplation of the Redemption, essentially signifies the process of restoring the image of God in man, through the love of God. St. Bernard explains this process clearly:

O anima mea, si vis amari a Deo, reforma in te imaginem suuam, et amabit te. . . . Et sicut in Deo tres sunt personae; Pater, et Filius, et Spiritus sanctus: sic et tu habes tres vires; scilicet intellectum memoriam, et voluntatem. Et sicut ex Patre generatur Filius, et ex utroque procedit Spiritus sanctus: ita ex intellectu generatur voluntas, et ex his ambobus procedit memoria. . . . ita anima est intellectus, anima voluntas, anima memoria; non tamen tres animae, sed una anima, et tres vires. . . . Nec solus sufficit de Deo intellectus ad beatitudinem, nisi sit in amore ejus voluntas. Imo haec duo non sufficiunt, nisi memoria addatur, qua semper in mente intelligentis at volentis maneat Deus: ut sicut nullum potest esse momentum, quo homo non utatur vel fruatur Dei bonitate vel misericordia; ita nullum sit momentum, quo eum praesentem non habeat in memoria.[62]

What then can Will's married state imply but that he has ceased, through the love of God and the contemplation of the Redemption to be a hermit? As a fictitious human being, Will is no longer isolated: as a faculty, the will is united with memory and intellect in the image of God. He is truly married; that is, he is at one with memory and intellect in the celebration of the Cross, symbol of the Redemption. From the union of himself and intellect

[61] *PL*, 192, 737.
[62] *Tractatus de interiori domo*, PL, 184, 546-47.

comes the contemplative *memoria*, and all three are as one directed toward charity.[63] Will has been restored to the single unity of the spirit, with memory and intellect to worship God in His own image.

In Dobet the climax of the poem is reached. In the course of his development Will has been shown to be insufficiently guided by the two other primary faculties of the soul: memory and intellect. Only when they are properly operative can the will itself be directed in charity toward God. Faith removes oblivion, the fault of the memory; Hope removes ignorance, the fault of the intellect; charity removes cupidity from the will. At the close of *Visio* when Will could not see the pardon of Piers he was shown to be in oblivion. While he was in this condition, Wit, Study, Clergy, and Scripture could not help him, so that he fell, ungoverned, into the Land of Longing. A recognition of the power of God the Father implicit in the text of Matt. 22.14, awakens him to the fear of God. He cannot yet understand Reason, but Imaginative helps to restore memory and begins the attack on ignorance, the corruption of the intellect. Through Patience, Will's faith is strengthened, but he is still in a state of ignorance when Anima begins her instruction. In the Vision of the Tree of Charity with its development in the episode of Faith, Hope, and the Samaritan, and finally through the instruction of Christ Himself, memory and intellect are restored so that Will may turn altogether toward charity. From the time Holy Church preached to him on the theme *Deus caritas*, Will has been asking, "What is Charity?" In the Redemption he is answered with completeness and finality. Now he shows his comprehension by creeping with memory and intellect to the Cross in celebration of the Easter season within the Church. All the answers he has variously

---

[63] Rabanus Maurus, *PL*, 110, 84: "Toto intellectu, tota voluntate, *et ex omni* memoria Deum esse diligendum."

received are collected in the vision of the Redemption; the Redemption is the ultimate meaning of the Plant of Peace, of the Treasure of Truth, of Sapience, of Patience, of Humility, of the true prelacy of Piers, of Holy Church. In the symbolic act of Creeping to the Cross, Will shows that he has learned humility and patient suffering. In the imitation of Piers he is truly married to the intellect; the will and intellect unite in memory or contemplation. In the *imitatio Christi* Will has restored the *imago Dei*; he has fulfilled the promise of *Faciamus*.

There is more to the discovery of charity than the contemplative vision thereof. Will, intellect, and memory must unite to worship God in His image, but they must perform the worship here on earth. The selection of the homely names Kit and Kalotte, and Will's direction of them in the performance of obligatory Easter duties is a masterly stroke of poetic economy. Not only is the union of man's mind indicated but the need to direct Kit and Kalotte in worship within the church on earth. Will's state of grace must be tested; he must prove his wholeness, his health in leading a just life in faithful loyalty to the Church. Only when he has done this will the cure of his neglect and ignorance be complete. Then he will be prepared for heavenly reward, which as Hugh of St. Victor says, is the purpose of the Samaritan's healing:

Haec sunt opera Samaritani; qui prius vinum, inde oleum fudit, postea ait: *Vade, sanus factus es* (John 5). In vino fervor poenitentiae, in oleo lenitas justitiae; in tertio significatur perfectio.[64]

When Will has lived his time in Faith, Hope, and Charity, he will be rewarded in Charity, God's love, the eternal reward. The direction in which Will must turn is clearly indicated. He must look to the church of the successors of Christ the Redeemer for guidance. Only through Piers Plowman in the status of Dobest can he achieve salvation.

---

[64] *Miscellanea*, V, LXXIII, PL, 177, 796-97.

8. Dobest

PASSUS XIX

WILL, the speaker in the poem, awakes at the beginning of Passus XVI and records his vision. At the beginning of the poem, he was dressed in shepherd's clothing, in habit as a hermit. At the beginning of Passus VIII he was robed in russet, and later we saw him as a mendicant. As a penitent in Passus XVIII, he was "wolleward." At last, in Passus XIX, he dresses himself "derely" in spiritual garments which have been cleansed by the Redemption. The purity of his robe of faith has been restored: he is dressed as a true wedding guest in charity.[1] In this condition he is able to go to church

to here holy the masse   and to be houseled after. (3)

That is, having been penitent for his sins, he is able to receive the eucharist and to benefit by the powers of Dobest.[2]

At the offering, when the priest offers the host to God, the dreamer falls into a contemplative vision of its significance. He sees before him Piers Plowman

. . . paynted al blody,
And come in with a crosse   bifor the comune peple,
And riȝte lyke in alle lymes   to owre lorde Iesu. (6-8)

Will is puzzled by this vision. The figure to whom he turns is Conscience. Conscience becomes once again Will's

---

[1] For the principles underlying this change of clothing, see above, Passus XIV, pp. 168-169.
[2] Cf. Imaginative's defense of Clergy, Passus XII, p. 151.

guide as he was in Passus XIII when he conducted Will into the Church symbolized by the feast at which the false Friar presided. Conscience, with Will and Patience, went forth from the feast to seek Piers Plowman. In a contemplative vision Will found him guarding the Tree of Charity. Now Conscience is again prepared to deal with the actual relationship between Will and the Church on earth: it is the function of the conscience to guide the will syllogistically in action. Will asks Conscience whether the figure he sees is Piers or Christ. Conscience replies:

> . . . 'thise aren Pieres armes,
> His coulures and his cote-armure   ac he that cometh so
> blody
> Is Cryst with his crosse   conqueroure of Crystene.'
>
> (12-14)

The ensuing dialogue between Will and Conscience not only clarifies this seeming paradox, but emphasizes the fundamental nature of Dobest and explains the function of Piers in the church. Meanwhile, Will learns the distinction between the true successors to the Apostolic tradition and their false imitators. Only on the basis of this distinction can he be effectively loyal to Holy Church as distinct from its corrupted counterpart.

Conscience distinguishes for Will Jesus the knight who received baptism, Jesus the King who taught the Jews the Law of Life and defended them against evil, and Christ the conqueror who ravished Hell, releasing Adam and Eve and bringing freedom to all who follow him.[3] By implication, it is Christ the conqueror who, in the supreme

---

[3] Cf. the distinctions in Rabanus, *De universo*, XVI, III, *PL*, 111, 445ff. "Milites autem Christi illi esse dicuntur, qui contra diabolum pugnant, et contra vitia fortiter dimicant. . . ." Kings are those who follow the King of Kings: "Reges enim recte sancti homines dicuntur, qui spiritus auctoritate secundum voluntatem Dei animas suas regunt, et regi regum, Domino videlicet Christo obediendo subjiciunt." Christ is a Prince or conqueror "quia in cruce omnia trahit ad seipsum." The distinctions in the poem seem to be elaborations of ideas similar to these.

act of charity, typifies Dobest. In another way, Christ, whose wisdom, righteousness, and mercy are symbolized in the gifts of the Magi,[4] began to Dowel at the feast in Cana of Galilee. There the transformation of water into wine symbolizes the transformation of the law:

> And lawe lakked tho   for men loued nou3t her enemys.
> And Cryst conseilleth thus   and comaundeth bothe,
> Bothe to lered and to lewed   to louye owre enemys.
> So atte feste firste   as I bifore tolde,
> Bygan god, of his grace   and goodnesse, to Dowel.
>
> (108-12)

As Bede explains, the sense of the law was transformed by Christ's teaching:

> Aqua autem Scripturae sacrae scientiam designat, quae suos audi-tores et a peccatorum sorde abluere, et divinae cognitionis solet fonte portare. . . . Sed quantum inter aquam et vinum, tantum distat inter sensum illum, quo Scripturae ante adventum Salvatoris intelligebantur, et eum quem veniens ipse revelavit apostolis, eorumque discipulis perpetuo sequendum reliquit.[5]

In other words, the wine represents the New Law of Charity. The miracle was made apparent first to Mary

> That she furste and foremest   ferme shulde bilieue,
> That he thorw grace was gete   and of no gome elles.
>
> (116-17)

Or, as Bede puts it,

> *Quid mihi et tibi est, mulier?* significat se divinitatem, quam mira-culum erat patrandum, non temporaliter accepisse de matre, sed

---

[4] The interpretation of the gifts in the poem is a modification of one of the traditional explanations. Whether this modification is due to the poet or some commentator whose work we have not found is uncertain. Cf. Bruno's comment in Matt. 2, *PL*, 165, 81: "Habet enim Ecclesia aurum in sapientia; thus vero in sancta et bene Deo redolente conversatione; myrrham autem in amaritudine poenitentiae et carnis mortificatione." It was in the final morti-fication of the flesh that Christ exhibited His mercy most graphically. In the poem, the gold is covered with incense and the incense is in a gold recep-tacle to show the close connections among reason, loyalty, and justice. It is this fact which gives rise to Skeat's impression, II, 267, that the poet con-tradicts himself.

[5] *PL*, 92, 658.

per aeternitatem semper habuisse de Patre. . . . Qui divinitatem, quam ex Patre semper habui, cum tua carne, ex qua carnem suscepi, non habeo communem, nondum venit hora ut fragilitatem sumptae ex te humanitatis moriendo demonstrem.[6]

Later as a healer and comforter, Christ began to Dobet:

> Thus he conforted carful   and cauȝte a gretter name,
> The whiche was Dobet   where that he went. (124-25)

In His acts of healing and teaching, Jesus becomes "kynge of the kyngedome of Iuda." The bards sing, *Saul interfecit mille, et David decem milia* (131) in token of his universal reign.[7] It is when he is celebrated as a triumphant King that Christ appears as Dobet. As a conqueror in the Resurrection he becomes Dobest so that at the meeting with the disciples, he can teach them Dobest. In other words, Jesus as Dowel is obedient, as Dobet he inspires praise, and as Dobest he brings charity to mankind.

The tradition of Dobest is transmitted through Piers Plowman:

>   Dobest he tauȝte,
> And ȝaf Pieres power   and pardoun he graunted
> To alle manere men   mercy and forȝyfnes,
> Hym myȝte men to assoille   of alle manere synnes,
> In couenant that thei come   and knowleche to paye,
> To Pieres pardon the Plowman   *redde quod debes.*
>   (177-82)

Piers has the power to assoil provided that his subjects do justice (*redde quod debes*) to his pardon, the Redemption.[8] It is thus that Piers has the power of the keys, effective against all sins but one, the Sin against the Holy Spirit, which is essentially a denial of the efficacy of the Redemption. Having brought salvation to mankind and perpetuated his power in Piers, Christ ascends to Heaven, there to

[6] *Loc. cit.,* 657.

[7] Bede's comment, *PL,* 91, 625ff., takes the passage as a prophecy of the Resurrection.

[8] Cf. XIV, 191-94, above p. 174.

await the Day of Judgment when those who have acknowledged His sacrifice will be rewarded and those who have denied it will be condemned. Meanwhile, the Holy Spirit descends upon Piers and his fellows and promises to give them "treasures" to strengthen them against the attacks of Antichrist and his followers. The poet quotes 1 Cor. 12.4, *Divisiones graciarum sunt, etc.* (223). There follows an account of the graces roughly parallel to that given by St. Augustine. In general, they fall under the two headings: gifts of *scientia* and gifts of *sapientia.*[9] The recipients of these gifts are warned to remember that they are given by the Grace of God and that their distribution reflects His will. The powers given by Grace, collectively in a given instance "Crafte," should be subject to Conscience. That is, the "Crafte" of an individual, made up of the graces given him should be subject to his conscience. This warning is specially relevant to spiritual leaders who use their distinctive status merely to set themselves apart from others like the Pharisee in the temple.

The representative of Grace on earth, His procurator, reeve, registrar, purveyor, and plowman is Piers Plowman. It is Piers who will observe and register *redde quod debes,* or observance of the Pardon, on the part of the people. Grace gives Piers a team: the four Evangelists.[10] In addition he is given another team with which to harrow what the first team has plowed: the four great fathers of the Church. The Fathers serve to harrow the hearts of men to receive the Scriptures. For seed, Piers uses the four cardinal virtues:

Thise foure sedes Pieres sewe   and sitthe he did hem
                                                              harwe
Wyth olde lawe and newe lawe   that loue myȝte wexe
Amonge the foure vertues   and vices destroye.

[9] See Peter Lombard's quotation from Augustine, *PL,* 191, 1652-53.
[10] See above, Chapter 2, p. 18.

For comunelich in contrees   kammokes and wedes
Fouleth the fruite in the felde   there thei growe togyderes;
And so don vices   vertues worthy. (306-11)

Piers commands that all who have "kynde witte" should be instructed in accordance with the teachings of the Fathers and that the seeds of the virtues should be sown in their hearts. When Grace suggests that Piers should have a barn in which to keep his harvest, Piers asks for materials to construct it, and Grace gives him the cross, the crown of thorns, and a mortar of Christ's blood and baptism called Mercy. The barn is wattled and walled with His pains and passion and roofed over with Scripture. Grace "called that hous Vnite, holicherche on Englisshe."[11] Finally, Grace gives Piers a cart of "Cristendome" to carry his sheaves, and two horses to pull it, Contrition and Confession. Priesthood is made "Haywarde" while Grace and Piers go through the world to till truth.

The remainder of the passus is devoted to a description of the earthly corruption of the institution which Grace and Piers established. The level of discourse is that of the Prologue, so that in effect the passus describes once more but from a new point of view the manner in which the Field of Folk became corrupted. The emphasis here is on the church as an institution rather than on its individual members in their various states. Although the allegory is obvious, we shall summarize it briefly for the sake of continuity. When Piers is busy with his plowing, Pride, whom Gregory called "exercitus diaboli dux," gathers his host to destroy the fruits of Piers' labors. The work of Pride is essentially the production of a misleading confusion:

Confessioun and Contricioun   and ȝowre carte the Byleue
Shal be coloured so queyntly   and keuered vnder owre
                                     sophistrie,
That Conscience shal nouȝte   knowe by contricioun,

[11] The imagery in this passage is based on the parable in Matt. 13. 24ff. For the barn and its significance, cf. St. Augustine, Sermo LXXIII, *PL*, 38, 471.

Ne by confessioun   who is Cristene or hethen,
Ne no maner marchaunt   that with moneye deleth,
Where he wynne wyth riȝte   with wronge, or with vsure.

(342-47)

The results of Pride's attack have been illustrated in the poem variously. The friars of the Prologue, the friar who declares Lady Meed to be a sister of his order, the priest who quarreled with Piers and the two friars who encounter Will at the beginning of Dowel, and most notably the master Friar have through their falsehood and sophistry obscured true doctrine and violated the sacrament of penance. The result of this falsehood has been made amply clear in the course of Will's painful struggle to find the Treasure of Truth. Hawkin the waferer was lost through false teaching and lack of example. Pride's effort to confuse Conscience concerning earthly treasure was illustrated in the proposed marriage of False and Lady Meed, and the subsequent attempts to win Conscience to an acceptance of Meed. Pride will also confuse Lords through "witte" or *scientia* (348-51), and the results of this confusion have been well illustrated in the wit-counseled realm of the Prologue. Will's problem has been from the beginning to learn to distinguish between those who "putten hem to the plow, pleyed ful selde," and those who "putten hem to pruyde, apparailed hem thereafter." Will is seeking Piers Plowman in the earthly church but finds there only confusion. The present allegory sheds light on the problem by revealing the beginnings of the confusion. Once the confusion is evident, the further problem remains of what to do about it.

Conscience supplies the solution to this problem at once:

Quod Conscience to alle Crystene tho   'my conseille is
    to wende
Hastiliche in-to Vnyte   and holde we vs there,
And preye we that a pees were   in Piers berne the Plow-
    man.' (352-54)

That is, the individual must under the guidance of his own conscience attempt to maintain the unity and integrity of the church in spite of the confusion caused by the friars and their followers. Under the instruction of "Kynde Wytte" individuals are able to dig a protective ditch of true repentance around the church. Only "comune wommen" and others who deliberately maintain sin against the Holy Spirit refuse to assist in the task of digging. Some show their repentance in prayer, some in pilgrimages, and some in other ways, but in any event, the true contrition of the workers in the ditch fills it with tears. The solution to the problem of a corrupt church militant is thus

Clennesse of the comune   and clerkes clene lyuynge.

(377)

When clergy and commons have achieved individual purity, they are in a position to enjoy the Eucharist in the fashion that Conscience dictates, for they have paid justice (*redde quod debes*) to the Pardon of Piers. They have acknowledged the efficacy of the Redemption and have acted accordingly. This theoretical solution to the problem of earthly corruption restates the theme of Passus v, where Reason leads Will to weep for his sins so that confession follows. Just as the pardoner and the common woman of the earlier passus refuse to follow the pilgrimage to Truth, the common woman and her associates here refuse to help in the digging of the moat.

When the people learn that they must acknowledge the Redemption by restitution before taking the Eucharist, a brewer, like the Wasters of Passus vi, objects. His interests are in the food of this world rather than in the food of the spirit:

'ȝe, bawe!' quod a brewere   'I wil nouȝt be reuled,
Bi Iesu! for al ȝowre Ianglynge   with *spiritus iusticie*,
Ne after Conscience, by Cryste   whil I can selle
Bothe dregges and draffe   and drawe it at on hole,

Thikke ale and thinne ale   for that is my kynde,
And nouȝte hakke after holynesse;   holde thi tonge, Con-
                      science!
Of *spiritus iusticie*   thow spekest moche an ydel!'
                      (394-400)

Conscience explains that unless the brewer learns to live
by justice, the virtue symbolized in *redde quod debes*, his
soul will be lost. Moreover, unless Conscience and the
cardinal virtues direct the commons they too are lost,
"bothe lyf and soule." In the actual church, however, there
are many like the brewer who have not learned to follow
the teachings of Conscience. This actual situation, as op-
posed to the ideal situation as described by Conscience,
is described at length by the "lewed" vicar, who is un-
learned in the sophistry of the friars. He has never seen
a man who could tell

                      of cardinale vertues,
Or that acounted Conscience   at a cokkes fether or an
                      hennes! (409-10)

The only cardinals he knows are those avaricious repre-
sentatives of the Pope who scandalize the common people.
In a reasonable world, Conscience should remain at the
King's court to counsel him as he does at the close of Passus
IV, Grace should be the guide of clerks so that they live
in charity, and Piers with the two Testaments should be
emperor of all the world, ruler of king and clerk. The
Pope, unlike Piers, sends his agents to slay his enemies.
Piers follows the example of God himself (Matt. 5.45)
Qui pluit super iustos et iniustos. That is, as Bede explains,
God sends His "doctrinam veritatis, quia bonis et malis
apparuit, et est evangelizatus Christus."[12] The remaining
verses of Matt. 5 are relevant here:

Si enim diligitis eos qui vos diligunt quam mercedem habebetis?
nonne et publicani hoc faciunt? Et si salutaveritis fratres vestros

[12] *PL*, 92, 31.

tantum, quid amplius facitis? nonne et ethnici hoc faciunt? Estote ergo vos perfecti, sicut et Pater vester caelestis perfectus est.

It is in this sense that the Pope is "inparfyt"; not only does he not greet his enemies; he even has them killed.[18] By a direct reference to the episode of the half-acre, his actions are contrasted with those of Piers, who

peyneth hym to tulye

As wel for a wastour   and wenches of the stuwes,
As for hym-self and his seruantz   saue he is firste yserued.

(432-34)

That is, Piers works for all, provided that his beneficiaries serve him in faith and works, and he reserves final judgment on sinners until they have an opportunity to repent. In contrast, the Pope in violation of the Law of God sheds Christian blood so that

It semeth, by so   hym-self hadde his wille,
That he ne reccheth riȝte nouȝte   of al the remenaunte.

(444-45)

Since the Pope is the head of an interdependent hierarchy, the corruption of his will through *amor sui* leads to the corruption of the Christian will in general. Thus the vicar explains that the commons pay little attention to the advice of Conscience or to the cardinal virtues. They have turned the virtues to worldly ends, making them features of *scientia* rather than of *sapientia*, so that

. . . alle tho faire vertues   as vyces thei semeth. (453)

Vices themselves are hidden in hypocritical rationalization. The vicar's observations are interrupted by a lord whose attitude illustrates the corruption that has been described. To him intellect is a means for casting accounts in his own favor, and fortitude is a polite euphemism for exaction. The king who speaks up is clearly not counseled by Con-

---

[18] The *Glossa ordinaria*, PL, 114, 98, explains *perfecti*: "In charitate Dei et proximi. Cumulus perfectionis diligere etiam inimicos, et orare pro illis, sicut et Christus fecit."

science, since he defends the rule of his realm by his own will. To him justice simply means that he is above the law. Conscience admonishes him that he may exercise his will only in reason under law. The vicar takes his leave, for he "hadde fer home."[14] The dreamer awakes, and records his dream. Will has now seen in detail the source of his own corruption, the corruption of the human will.

PASSUS XX

When Will awakes, he is depressed by the Vicar's revelation of the overwhelming corruption of the people through worldly interests. For the cardinal virtues they have substituted a set of worldly virtues. He is concerned about his own relation to the goods of this world:

> Heuy-chered I ȝede   and elynge in herte;
> I ne wiste where to ete   ne at what place. (2-3)

The optimistic mood with which Will as a whole man, healed by his vision of the Redemption, went to church on Easter morning has disappeared. What Will has forgotten under the stress of his discouragement with the erring folk is that temperance as determined by necessity is the guiding principle in the use of *temporalia*. Even though Piers is absent, the principle of temperance should guide Will. As Holy Church expressed it:

> '*Reddite Cesari*,' quod god   'that *Cesari* bifalleth,
> *Et que sunt dei, deo*   or elles ȝe done ille.'
> For riȝtful reson   shulde rewle ȝow alle,
> And kynde witte be wardeyne   ȝowre welthe to kepe,
> And tutour of ȝoure tresore   and take it ȝow at nede.
> (I, 52-56)

Need, the regulating principle of temperance, greets Will foully and calls him "faitour" in much the same way that others had berated him before for his failure to compre-

---

[14] There is a pun here on "fer" and "faire"; in other words, the vicar had a fair home far away, which considering the context, should be taken to represent the New Jerusalem.

hend the basic revealed truths. His present forgetfulness
and concomitantly that of the people as they are described
by the Vicar are especially critical at this point in the poem.
It is nearing "the none" or the Day of Judgment, specifi-
cally for Will since he is growing old, and generally for the
folk since they live in the Last Age.[15] The human will must
learn to scorn Meed and to use moderation as determined
by necessity if it is to render its proper debt to God.

Need asks Will why he did not excuse himself, or ex-
plain his adherence to the principle of temperance. He
shows that temperance is the basic cardinal virtue. A man
in dire need, who represents an extreme case, can do no
wrong so long as he is temperate. On the human level,
fortitude and justice may be carried to extremes, and pru-
dence often fails since the ways of God are inscrutable.
Specifically, it is through a lack of temperance that the folk
described by the Vicar perverted the cardinal virtues in the
interest of the world. Only in a condition of Need can the
bounds of temperance be determined, and only if the goods
of the world are used temperately in true poverty of spirit
can the will focus its attention on spiritual sustenance. For
these reasons wise men have sought to be needy in the
example of Christ:

> That he seyde in his sorwe   on the selue rode,
> 'Bothe fox and foule   may fleighe to hole and crepe,
> And the fisshe hath fyn   to flete with to reste,
> There nede hath ynome me   that I mote nede abyde,
> And suffre sorwes ful sowre   that shal to Ioye tourne.'[16]
> (42-46)

[15] On the symbolism of *noon*, cf. Ps. 54, 19, and Peter Lombard's comment,
PL, 191, 514: "Vespere enim fuit Dominus in cruce; mane, in resurrectione;
meridie, in ascensione . . . in meridie, id est sedens a dexteram Patris, ubi
interpellat pro nobis." Cf. Passus XVIII, 60, 471-72.
[16] The quotation rests on Matt. 8.20; Luke 9.58. The phrase 'on the selue
rode' refers to the figurative cross of bodily abstinence and spiritual com-
passion rather than to the actual cross. See Luke 9.22-23, and Bede's com-
ment, *PL*, 92, 452.

In the Scriptural context, this passage is an answer which Christ gives to one who wishes to follow him for worldly reward. He contrasts his own poverty with the worldly ambition of the false follower. As Bede explains:

Ex Domini verbis ostenditur hunc qui obsequium promittit ob hoc repudiatum, quod signorum videns magnitudinem, sequi voluerit Salvatorem, ut lucra ex operum miraculis quaereret, hoc idem desiderans, quod et Simon Magus a Petro emere voluerat. Talis ergo fides juste sententia Domini condemnatur, et dicitur ei: Quid me propter divitias et saeculi lucra cupis sequi cum tantae sim pauperitatis, ut ne hospitiolum quidem habeam, et non meo utar tecto? Aliter, intelligitur miraculis Domini commotus propter inanem jactantiam eum sequi voluisse, quam significant aves. Finxisse autem discipuli obsequium, quae fictio vulpium nomine significata est. Reclinatione vero capitis humilitatem suam significavit, quae in illo simulatore ac superbo non habebat locum.[17]

In short, Christ through His poverty reveals the danger to the Church from the wolves in sheep's clothing, who, professing Dobest, desire worldly rather than spiritual treasure. In the worldly would-be follower, Christ saw the fox, which is, as the *Glossa ordinaria* explains, a rapacious animal symbolic of those who mislead the faithful, that is, of the Antichrist and his followers:

Vulpes animal fallax, insidiis intentum, rapinas fraudis exercens, etiam inter ipsa hominum hospitia habitans in foveis: ita haereticus domum fidei non habens alios in suam fraudem trahit et a fide seducit.[18]

This conception leads directly into the vision which Will has immediately after Need's speech.

In his dream, Will sees at once Antichrist, not as a fox, but in "mannes forme." The content of what follows has

---

[17] *PL*, 92, 460. Cf. Bruno Astensis, *PL*, 165, 143: "Dicit Scriba: *Magister, sequar te quocunque ieris.* Dicit Jesus: Non est ita; non vis me sequi, non vis mea praecepta servare, non video in te ubi caput meum reclinem. Caput Christi Deus est: Deus autem in humili habitat, et quieto, et tremente sermones ejus."

[18] *PL*, 114, 283.

been foreshadowed both by the reference to "none" and by the quoted remarks of Christ. Antichrist worked to destroy truth and to make the false seem true. He was assisted by the friars, "for he ȝaf hem copes." As we were told in the Prologue, the friars:

> Glosed the gospel   as hem good lyked,
> For coueitise of copis   construed it as thei wolde.
>
> (Prol. 60-61)

The religious ran forth to greet Antichrist "saue onlich folis," or those wise in the ways of God rather than in the ways of the world.[19] Although Antichrist gathered a great following led by Pride, Conscience called the "foles" into Unity or the Church, crying on Nature to defend his followers for the love of Piers Plowman. Nature responded with diseases, Age, and Death with which many were destroyed. But when Conscience relented and bade Nature cease her work of torment, those who were left succumbed to the flattery of Fortune. Lechery armed with idleness like a good courtly lover and a bow with arrows feathered with "faire biheste and many a false truthe" attacked Conscience and his followers among the teachers of the church. He was assisted by Covetousness who led forth Simony to the corruption of justice.

As a result of these attacks, Life laughed

> And armed hym in haste   and leet dagge his clothes,
> And helde Holynesse a Iape   in harlotes wordes,
> And lete Leute a cherle   and Hendenesse a wastour,
> Conscience and conseille   and Lyer a fre man;
>   he counted it a folye. (142-46)

Allied with Pride, Life found Heal or Good Fortune for his mistress. They begot Sloth, which in turn brought on Despair. Attacked by Age, Life tried Physic, but with little success, so that at the last he went forth to drown his cares in Revel, "a ryche place and a merye." In other words, as

[19] For fools of this kind, see 1 Cor. 3.18-19.

we saw in the episode of the half-acre when the folk were attacked by Hunger, the folk of the field refuse to take warning from earthly misfortune; they seek instead to forget their obligations in the pursuit of earthly satisfaction. When their teachers have been corrupted by Lechery and Avarice, they remain oblivious to Nature's warnings.

Will, who has learned now that the picture he saw in the Prologue was essentially a picture of corruption, reacts very differently when Eld attacks him. In the face of the diminution of his physical powers and the approach of Death, Will humbly asks Nature to guide him in his proper task. Nature tells him to learn to love. Will asks the question which occupied him at the beginning of the passus: how then may I sustain life in the body? (208). Nature answers as did Need: God will provide for the man with Faith. Without question then Will dutifully proceeds through Contrition and Confession to go into Unity. What he sees when he arrives is a corrupted church militant which has been destroyed by the friars. The folk represented by Life are misled by earthly love and the treasure of the world. They turn vainly for solace to the physician who cannot heal himself, and finally immerse themselves in earthly joy. Will has learned spiritual love or charity through the Redemption so that he sets his heart on heavenly joy, but like the other folk he does not find a satisfactory physician, for the administration of Penance has been disrupted by the followers of Antichrist. The succeeding exposition (220-377) deals historically with the rise to power and influence of the friars, who wrongfully substitute themselves for Dobest.

When the church is attacked from the outside by Sloth, Avarice, and proud priests, Conscience calls for help. The friars respond, but Conscience forsakes them because "thei couthe nouȝte wel her crafte." Need warns that the friars are, like the foxes, covetous, so that they should be forced to be "beggeres." With this in mind, Conscience welcomes them into Unity, but warns them to maintain their rule after the examples of Francis and Dominic. Quoting Ps. 146.4, he complains that the friars wax "out of noumbre," that is, out of grace, through the desire for earthly reward.[20] Envy sends the friars to school and they become famous for easy penances. When Conscience attempts to send forth a true physician "that coude wel shryue," so that Piers "were payed *redde quod debes*" (302-6), some send protests that the Friar is an easier physician, so that Conscience is itself misled to consent in giving the friars power to hear confessions generally. The friar who gains admission is called *Penetrans domos*, an epithet which implies the full quotation *Penetrant domos et captivas ducunt mulierculas oneratas peccatis* (2 Tim. 3.6).[21] Overcome by Hypocrisy, Contrition is sick. The Friar gains permission to cure him,

> And goth and gropeth Contricioun   and gaf hym a plastre
> Of 'a pryue payement   and I shal praye for ȝow
> For alle that ȝe ben holde to   al my lyf-tyme,
> And make ȝow my lady   in masse and in matynes,
> As freres of owre fraternite   for a litel syluer.'
> Thus he goth and gadereth   and gloseth there he shryueth,
> Tyl Contricioun hadde clene forȝeten   to crye and to wepe,
> And wake for his wykked werkes   as he was wont to done.
> (361-68)

In other words, when the friars have an opportunity to administer penances at large, they corrupt the sacrament for their own selfish interest with the result that Contrition, the basic principle of the sacrament, ceases to operate

[20] Those who are not numbered lose themselves from God's sight by seeking temporal reward for spiritual labor. See St. Augustine, *PL*, 37, 1905.

[21] We may recall that William of Saint-Amour had used the same quotation in his attack on the friars, together with the surrounding verses. See Perrod, *op. cit.*, 157, and above Chapter 2, note 20.

entirely. Without contrition salvation is impossible, but Will finds himself in church where true contrition is unknown. Sloth and Pride attack again and again, but Clergy does not come to the defense of Conscience, and Contrition sleeps at the gate. There is only one way open to Conscience. Since Piers or Dobest has disappeared from the Church, it is the duty of the Conscience of society to seek his return, and it is the duty of the Conscience of the individual to cherish and maintain the ideal which he represents. Conscience must never despair, but must steadfastly cry to God for comfort and grace until he may find Piers Plowman:

'Bi Cryste,' quod Conscience tho   'I wil bicome a pilgryme,
And walken as wyde   as al the worlde lasteth,
To seke Piers the Plowman   that Pryde may destruye,
And that freres hadde a fyndyng   that for nede flateren,
And contrepleteth me, Conscience;   now Kynde me auenge,
And sende me happe and hele   til I haue Piers the Plowman!
And sitthe he gradde after grace   til I gan awake.

Guided by conscience, the human will must search for its true leader in the pilgrimage toward Jerusalem.

9. Some Conclusions

In the preceding exposition we have attempted to describe as exactly as possible the author's purpose in *Piers Plowman*. The result of this exposition may seem to limit the significance of the poem historically. This is far from our intention: to understand *Piers Plowman* we must be prepared not only to see it in terms of the bitter controversy between the friars and the seculars or in the light of the tradition of Biblical commentary; we must understand its full human import, the permanent symbolic value of the search for Piers Plowman. If the thought of *Piers Plowman* is demonstrably clear, if the poem reveals intellectual integrity, and if it reflects a great tradition of Western civilization, it must reveal something of the human heart for all time.

The poem opens with a preliminary vision of the folk of the world, viewed in the perspective of eternity, wandering in the field of the earthly Church between the ditches of Babylon and the hill of Jerusalem. Pitifully few are approaching the tower on the hill. Implicit in the vision is the question of the Psalmist:

> Lord, who shall abide in thy tabernacle? who shall dwell in thy holy hill?

Also implicit in the vision is the answer to this question, Christ's warning: "Few are chosen." The members of the ecclesiastical hierarchy for the most part seek the transitory satisfactions of the flesh, pretending to offices which they make no effort to fulfil. And the laymen have corrupted their institutions in the interests of self love. The words of Christ, "I am that bread of life," are lost in shouts of "Hot pies!"

In this picture of confusion lies the fundamental problem of the poem. When the fourteenth century poet looked around him he saw only the shadow of what once had been. The ideals that had motivated Innocent III in his attempt to bring the new theology of the sacraments to every remote parish, the feeling for a natural hierarchy under Divine Law that had inspired the Magna Charta, the penetrating intellectual elaboration of the doctrine of charity developed in the thirteenth century universities, the operative piety exemplified by such kings as Alfred and St. Louis—all these were now only empty forms. Men walked in the shadows of the great cathedrals, and on some of them work continued, but the spirit which produced them was gone. Structures like the cathedral at Chartres would grow no more in a soil that had become spiritually sterile. The Prologue to *Piers Plowman* gives us a glimpse of this sterility. The poem itself analyzes its causes and describes in detail the ideals which must be reactivated if the Christian world is ever to go again on the greatest of all crusades, the pilgrimage to the heavenly Jerusalem.

To understand the poem in its relevance to ourselves, we must attempt to recapture some of the old enthusiasm for this goal. In many respects, the elaboration of Biblical teaching developed in the thirteenth century schools was history's most significant intellectual achievement. It was the result of centuries of continuous philosophical tradition supported by cumulative pastoral experience. Both the speculative tradition of the schools and the empirical tradition of the parishes were maintained by a single institution so that one could interact freely with and control the other. Philosophers might differ in detail, but in general they agreed on a hierarchy of values the elements of which could be grasped by even the most ignorant and at the same time could win the profound respect of the most cultivated. Medieval thinkers realized to the full that without some concept of value it is impossible to lend the events of everyday existence significance beyond animal satisfaction. To the poet it was of the utmost importance that the system of values which he found symbolized in Jerusalem be maintained, lest the vision fade away entirely from the sight of men. The fears of the poet were justified. What the poet was witnessing and attempting to counteract was the beginning of the great intellectual chaos which produced the Waste Land, a country which has become so much more terrifying than the poet's Field of Folk that the modern reader is apt to overlook as insignificant some of the poem's bitterest portrayals of evil. *Piers Plowman* is the epic of the dying Middle Ages.

The basic structure of *Piers Plowman* rests on contrasts which express in various ways the Medieval ideal and its corruption. The clarity of these contrasts is largely dependent upon an understanding of the application of the traditional levels of meaning. Each level has a symbolic context appropriate to it. The allegorical level, for example, is concerned with the church, and the basic classification of persons in the poem under Dowel, Dobet, and Dobest rests on the traditional division of persons in the church as active, contemplative, and prelatical. More exactly, Dowel, Dobet, and Dobest represent the ideals which persons in these states should follow. Actual persons either exemplify these ideals or their corruption. To illustrate, the chief characters in the Prologue may be classified allegorically or externally as follows:

	GOOD MINSTRELS	JANGLERS
Dowel	The mice who wish to bell the cat	King, council, lawyers, etc.
Dobet	Anchorites and hermits who do not "kairen aboute."	Hermits who wish "her ese to haue," friars, etc.
Dobest	The good plowmen	False plowmen who follow pride, evil priests, bishops, etc.

A similar table may be made for almost any episode in the poem if one remembers that the poet sometimes wishes to stress the absence of one or more of the classifications. The table below presents some of the more striking representatives on the allegorical level of the various classes, active, contemplative, and prelatical, taken from the poem as a whole.

	SEED OF ABEL	SEED OF CAIN
Dowel	The Knight who helps Piers (VI)	The Extortionate Lord (XIX)
Dobet	True Religious "Folis" (XX)	The Friars
Dobest	The Lewd Vicar	The Priest (VII)

One of the principal objects of the poem is to give the various states' inner content. For this reason, the tropological level, which indicates the inner moral qualities of individuals and their moral duties is of especial importance. A general scheme of the tropological level may be represented in terms of the three parts of the image of God in man; the memory, the intellect, and the will. Any individual in any of the three allegorical states ideally preserves the image in terms of faith, hope, and charity.

	THE IMAGE OF GOD	THE CORRUPTED IMAGE
Memory	Faith	Oblivion
Intellect	Hope	Ignorance
Will	Charity	Cupidity

Although each status has as its end charity, the tropological duties of the members of the various external statuses vary. To illustrate the special duties of each status, the poet uses several symbols. For example, the relationship of the various statuses to the world is indicated progressively by the terms *conjugatos, viduatos, virgines.* Again, the person in the active status must learn, the contemplative must teach, and the prelate must practice the highest form of

charity in self-sacrifice for his flock: *disce, doce, diligere.*
The members of all three states must direct themselves
toward charity. Anima explains charity in terms of three
levels which suggest its functions in the three states (xv,
171-78). When it consists simply in desiring and receiving
spiritual food, it symbolizes Dowel. When it includes this
and acts of devotion accompanied by the function of teach-
ing, it is Dobet. Finally, when it includes both of these
and the apostolic act of washing away sin, it symbolizes
Dobest. When they practice charity, the three states are
related to the world in terms of ascending degrees of self
denial; they are related to society in terms of ascending
degrees of service:

	RELATION TO THE WORLD	RELATION TO SOCIETY
Dowel	Conjugatos	Disce
Dobet	Viduatos	Doce
Dobest	Virgines	Diligere

Charity is the basis for perfection in any state, but char-
ity was brought to man by Dobest in its highest form,
Christ. Only through teaching of charity in the apostolic
succession can it be continued on earth, so that the existence
of Dowel and Dobet is dependent on the function of Do-
best. Thus the person in the active state who wishes to attain
the ideal of Dowel must be aided by Dobest. This fact is
illustrated in Conscience's instruction of Hawkin, the active
man who asks how he may cleanse his soiled robes of inno-
cence. The cleansing may be accomplished through penance
in all of its three parts: *contritio, confessio, satisfactio.* But
each of the three parts may be considered a function of
Dobest. Contrition, the waking of the mind from oblivion
in faith, is encouraged by the priest through preaching
and example. The searching of the conscience in oral con-
fession, the casting out of ignorance in hope, is the function
of the priest as teacher. Finally, the setting of penance

and the granting of absolution, the direction of the will away from cupidity toward charity, is a function of the priest exercising his apostolic powers. In Christ all three states find their highest example. Dobest, in the imitation of Christ the Redeemer, teaches the imitation of Christ in the other two states.

When the mind is governed by cupidity rather than by charity, there is a progression of evil beginning with the sin against the Father in oblivion, continuing with the sin against the Son in ignorance, and culminating with the sin against the Holy Spirit and the triumph of cupidity over the will. These conditions may be considered as opposites of the ideals represented by Dowel, Dobet, and Dobest. They reveal increasing degrees of desire for worldly satisfaction and with relation to society increasing degrees of disservice to mankind:

	RELATION TO THE WORLD	RELATION TO SOCIETY
Sin against the Father	Concupiscence of the	False Witness
Sin against the Son	Flesh	Usury
Sin against the Holy Spirit	Concupiscence of the Eyes	Reward against the
	Pride of Life	Innocent

On the anagogical level are revealed the ultimate sources of good and its corruption. The forces of good are symbolized by Holy Church, the bride of Jerusalem; those of evil are symbolized by Lady Meed, the Whore of Babylon:

HOLY CHURCH	LADY MEED
The Father	The World
The Son	The Flesh
The Holy Spirit	The Devil

These levels form the ultimate frame of reference around which the others are constructed. For example, on the tropological level, the memory, the intellect, and the will are governed either by the Father, the Son, and the Holy Spirit respectively, or by the world, the Flesh, and the Devil. The tropological corruption of these levels produces the opposites of Dowel, Dobet, and Dobest. Dowel is characterized by obedience to the Father, Dobet by the removal of the sin against the Son, and Dobest by the maintenance of the Holy Spirit or charity.

The various spiritual levels are exemplified externally and particularly on the historical level with characters from the Bible and the modern Church:

PIERS PLOWMAN	SE IPSOS AMANTES
Patriarchs	Cain
Prophets	Pharisees
Christ and the	Antichrist and the
Apostles	Friars

The basic contrast lies between the true priesthood of God and the ministry of Antichrist. The patriarchs and prophets could not find salvation in the Old Law; only through the New Law of charity were they able to leave Hell. Similarly, Dowel and Dobet cannot be saved without Piers, who bears the tradition of the Redemption. The tragedy of the poem is that the human will seeking salvation cannot find Piers in the Church. The place of Piers has been usurped by the Friars under the guidance of Antichrist.

It is through the character Will that we see these contrasts operating on various levels. Will is many-sided because he has the flexibility of the faculty he represents which moves between the opposites of willfulness and charity. Because the poet has been successful as a poet, he has created in Will so appealingly human a character that through interest in him many have lost sight of the fact that Will is merely a device by means of which the poet may set off the actual against the ideal in the poem and so develop his major theme. For this purpose Will is portrayed at the beginning as one among the wolves in sheep's clothing. His clothes reflect the manner in which he has been misled. They improve as Will, serving as a hypothetical example, is brought nearer his ideal goal. The persons who mislead him typify the misleading forces of the actual world. But the forces which bring about his ultimate rise to a state of grace are not actual forces in the earthly Church; they are the forces which should operate there. Similarly, the pattern of Will's salvation is a pattern of what should be, not of what is. Thus Will is instructed first not by an actual priest but by the anagogical church itself who reveals her own nature to him and the nature and operation of her opposite, the Whore of Babylon. Actually, a successor to Piers Plowman should be the one who explains to the human will the ideal which the heavenly Jerusalem represents and the origin of its corruption on earth; the fact that Holy Church herself instructs Will is a negative intimation of the theme that Piers Plowman is absent from the church militant. Will's Vision of the struggle against Lady Meed carried on by the King who calls Reason and Conscience to his aid is only a vision of the possible, a suggestion as to the means by which the earthly community may be made to resemble its eternal counterpart. Will himself does not take part in the vision, and it is obvious that it is not a picture of anything the poet could see around him or reasonably predict in the near future. As a result of Reason's teaching, Repentance moves the will of the folk to weep, and they confess in a manner which prepares them for the guidance of Piers Plowman. The vision of the Half Acre is an ideal vision of God's ministry, demonstrating the lesson of good works in the earthly church. Even in the episode of the Half Acre, which is an ideal vision, the salvation of the folk of the field is not shown to be assured. Indeed it becomes clear that confession without satisfaction through good works is unavailing. Though the commons assent to the rule of

Reason through their confessions, they must implement their faith and hope through the works of charity. But humans are lazy and are repelled by the need to work; in the face of work many of those who had confessed prefer to sing "Trolli-lolli" in a ditch. Piers attempts to bring them back through spiritual hunger and the threat of eternal punishment, but these threats have only temporary effectiveness. Finally, salvation through pardon is suggested, but the pardon of Piers Plowman is an affirmation that faith, hope, and the labors of charity in the field are necessary, that the way of Piers is the right way. Positively, the pardon shows that only through the fulfilment of the obligation to the redemption is salvation possible. But the position of the earthly church is made apparent at once in the person of the Priest who neither recognizes nor understands his pardon. It is significant that in spite of Will's vision, his position at the end of it is exactly that of the Priest. The human will, although it naturally desires the good, unguided by Piers is incapable of understanding the basic contrast between Jerusalem and Babylon or the means by which the earthly church may be made to resemble its heavenly counterpart.

In the *Vitae*, which are concerned with the way Will may find the truth of Piers Plowman, there is a similar series of contrasts between the actual and the ideal. There is no steady progression toward salvation. Those episodes which are concerned with the exposition of the ideal move to the point at which it becomes clear that what is needed in the church militant is Piers Plowman. Thereupon the poet develops the unhappy conclusion that Piers is not present in the earthly church and the ideal is succeeded by a picture of the corrupt actuality. Although Will has seen Piers in the *Visio*, he does not in Dowel begin his search with instruction by a true priest. Instead he meets two friars. As a result of their ministrations, Will's thought is confused and misled so that he cannot properly act upon the possibilities of both good and evil presented by Wit, the speculative intellect. Although Will still desires the good, he proceeds to corrupt the teaching of the intellect, learns nothing through Study and Clergy, finally corrupts Scripture through his own willfulness, and falls into the sleep of the Land of Longing. Will's progressive descent from being simply misled by the friars to his abandonment of the true good typifies what the human will actually faces in the Church militant. Through God's providence he sees the evils of the friars who have comforted him in his evil life. Through his knowledge of evil he finds loyalty to the true church. With Loyalty, Scripture's teachings become effective and Will is able to profit by the vision of Nature and the teaching of Imagination. But Piers must direct the human will in its study of Scripture and in the understanding of the truth which makes conscience operative, so that the poet is here again concerned with the ideal pattern of the development of the human will. When Conscience comes to guide Will, he must, of course, guide him within the church. Again the poem turns to the actual church from the vision of the ideal to discover that the place of Piers has been usurped by the Master Friar. The result of this usurpation is shown to Will in the figure of Hawkin the active man. Hawkin cannot perform true penance without Piers. Although Conscience teaches him what true penance should be, he makes it clear that true penance without Piers Plowman is impossible. The *Vita de Dowel* ends on the same desperate note as does the *Visio*. Unless the prelatical status reflects Dobest, unless Piers Plowman is in the church, those in the active status face inevitable and tragic doom.

In the *Vita de Dobet* Will does find Piers Plowman, but he does not find him on earth. He learns through Anima what is wrong with the Church militant. When he asks

243

her where he may find Piers, he is told that Piers guards the Tree of Charity. In other words, he may be seen only in a spiritual vision. Will's vision again pictures the ideal. In this episode, the high point in the poem, Will is shown in one supreme figure the ideals of Dowel, Dobet, and Dobest combined. Moreover, Will learns his relation in the image of God to the other faculties of the human mind. He learns that together the three faculties must live in charity. But when he hears the Easter bells tolling, he understands that he must worship God in the Church. Again the poem reaches the place at which it is necessary to look for Piers Plowman in the Church militant: the life of prayer and contemplation also needs Piers Plowman. But in the *Vita de Dobest* it is made perfectly clear that the force which is alone able to bring salvation is absent from the Church militant. Piers has been supplanted by a host of friars under the leadership of Antichrist. The only hope left for the human will is the collective force of the Christian Conscience insisting that in its priests the image of Piers be found. We remember that the evil of the friars had this much of good; it succeeded in awakening Will to Loyalty. The purpose of the poet was not simply to expose the evil of the friars; it was to arouse his readers to a realization of the immediacy of their danger in the hope that they would be stirred to action so that Piers might again walk on earth.

In the figure of Will we have seen one of the chief means by which the poet achieves coherence in *Piers Plowman*. In what Will does and in his reactions are developed the progressive contrasts which contribute materially to the structural integrity of the poem. In the *Visio* these contrasts are based on the most general of possible symbols for good and evil. In the *Vitae* they become particularized and progress in scope and significance until we reach the poet's crowning picture of the Redemption and his description of the historically progressive corruption of the church militant culminating in the vision of the perils in those late days which came through the friars. As the movement of the poem develops naturally from the needs of the human will represented by the dreamer, the structure of the poem may be shown to develop naturally out of the needs of the folk in the field as pictured in the Prologue. The Prologue contains, in fact, all of the major themes of the poem. It sets at once the basic contrast between true and false prelates, and suggests the discrepancy between the ideals of the three states and their actual counterparts. The Babylonian confusion of the Kingdom ruled by self-love implies by contrast the vision of Peace which appears immediately in Passus I in the figure of Holy Church descending from the mountain. It is this same Babylonian kingdom with which is contrasted the Kingdom governed by Reason and Conscience. The members of the Prologue's realm are those who mislead Will in the *Vitae*, and in the closing episode of the poem the poet explains in detail the source of the Babylonian confusion. Meanwhile, the positive ideas developed as ideals or as ideal patterns of conduct stem from the theme of Holy Church's sermon: *Deus caritas*.

There are certain images set in the Prologue, those of food and clothing for example, that are used to give coherence to the poem. The clothing of the plowmen is contrasted with that of the followers of pride as Holy Church's clothing is contrasted with that of Lady Meed. Will's clothing has progressive symbolic value, notably in the change from his early clothing to the "dear robes" of Passus XIX. The clothing of Hawkin is of central importance in Dowel. The clothing image is reflected in the armor of Piers in which Christ fights. Holy Church uses Lot's drunkenness in illustration of the misuse of temporal goods. Piers employs Hunger to frighten the wasters who seek to forget their spiritual hunger in the pleasures of the flesh. The feast placed before Patience and Will is sharply contrasted with the dainty worldly fare of the Master Friar, who must drink before he preaches. In the final passus Will is concerned with the problem of sustenance in the world. There are many other such images repeated and elaborated in Passus xix. The Plant of Peace introduced by Holy Church becomes central in Anima's instruction of Will. The image of the tower set in the Prologue is reflected in Holy Church's sermon, in the instructions of Piers to the pilgrims, in Wit's discussion of the castle of Caro, and finally in the Barn of Christendom. These images and others are used so consistently and repeatedly that it is impossible to do more than supply a few illustrations here. Indeed, we may make the generalization that the structure of the poem is based largely on the repetition and contrast of symbols which are progressively elaborated and developed.

The development by symbolic repetition may sometimes be obscured by the fact that the connection between symbols is often made through an understood Scriptural nexus. Thus Piers' half-acre is closely related to the Barn of Christendom through the parable of the gathering of the harvest (Matt. 13, 24ff.). The tower of Truth, which is the end of man's search, is related to the Castle of Caro through the implied Biblical idea of man made in the image of God. The imagery when taken with the symbolic values it acquires from Biblical contexts serves as a means of poetic condensation in the maintenance of the major themes of the poem. Similarly, the Scriptural quotations when taken on the level of the *sentence* as developed in traditional exegesis furnish a key to wider vistas of meaning which relate the parts of the poem in much the same way that the parts of the Bible were related by the commentators. It would not be surprising if a reader ignorant of the fact that Piers Plowman represents the central tradition of Christ's ministry might be led to suppose that there was a lack of connection between the parts of the poem, each of which is united to the other in an increasing emphasis on the tragic absence of the traditional figure from the Church. If the identification of Holy Church with the heavenly Jerusalem and of Lady Meed with the Whore of Babylon is not kept steadily before the mind's eye, it is possible to fail to see the relationship between the sermon of Holy Church and what follows. Altogether, when the poem is read on the level of the *sentence*, the development of its themes becomes clear and it is seen to progress logically and coherently to its conclusion.

Like any great work of art *Piers Plowman* has a quality which defies critical analysis. It is possible to repeat the testimony of others who have felt the varied powers of the poet from the ecstatic verse with which he describes the Redemption to the realistically powerful picture of Glutton in the tavern. It would be possible to add further testimonial to the way in which in individual passages we have been moved to wonder and delight, to the quietness of spirit which is the particular effect of the greatest poetry. But that has not been the service which we have hoped to render in this book. We have wished first to show that the charge that the poem as a whole is chaotic and formless is false. Then we have wished to show the greatness of the ideal presented in *Piers Plowman* and to demonstrate passage by passage the intellectual grandeur and clarity with which the great ideal is developed. It is true that the architecture of the poem is not so obvious to the modern reader as that of the *Divine Comedy*, but when the principles governing that architecture are known, it becomes clear that the English poem is no less perfect structurally than the Italian. Many of the most startling poetic effects of the poem are achieved through its deliberate Scriptural

247

connotations. The picture of Holy Church descending from the mountain is striking in itself, but its Scriptural connotations make the picture more than merely striking, suggesting as they do the Transfiguration in the Gospel, the Bride of Christ in the Apocalypse, and Sion and Jerusalem throughout the Scriptures. If the *Divine Comedy* is an expression of the ideals of the thirteenth century, *Piers Plowman* is a projection of those ideals against the actuality of fourteenth century life. The English poem is representative of its turbulent and critical age and place, but it is also an expression of some of man's most cherished ideals. Society is still being misled by false leaders. Modern man, like Will, is still searching for leadership which will embody traditional belief with human compassion, which can reformulate and activate the principles of charity and bring the world a little nearer the Vision of Peace. In short, the heirs to the tradition of medieval England may add to the annals of their literature a work of epic scope with only one peer in any other medieval vernacular.

Index

Glossed Texts from Scripture

Gen. *1.24-26*, *Glossa ordinaria*, 109, Rupert, 110; *2.18-25*, Augustine, 114; *3.11*, Bruno, 175; *3.12*, Augustine, 148; *3.19*, Rabanus, 87; *4*, Rupert, 115; *5.3*, Rabanus, 114; *6.4-6*, Rupert, 116; *7.10*, *Glossa ordinaria*, 116; *11.31*, *Glossa ordinaria*, 146; *12.7*, *13.14-16*, *17.4-8*, Bede, 201; *14.18*, Bede, 201-202; *17.2*, Bede, 201; *17.10*, Bede, 201; *18.1-2*, *Glossa ordinaria*, 199, Bede, 199, 201; *22.1-13*, Bede, 201
Lev. *19.17*, Rabanus, 133
Deut. *23.25*, Bruno, 189
1 Sam. *18.7*, Bede, 220
Job *6.5*, Bruno, 185, Gregory, 185
Ps. *1.3*, Lombard, 192; *1.4*, Augustine, 44; *4.3*, Lombard, 179; *4.9-10*, Lombard, 184; *7.6*, Lombard, 181; *7.15*, Lombard, 115; *9.14*, Augustine, 138, 141; *13.3*, Augustine, 68; *14*, Lombard, 36, 53-54, Bede, 53; *22.4*, Lombard, 94; *22.5*, Lombard, 149; *25.10*, Bede, 63, Lombard, 63; *33.11-13*, Lombard, 112; *41.4*, Augustine, 95, Lombard, 95; *42.4-6*, Lombard, 142-143; *50.19*, Lombard, 182; *54.19*, Lombard, 228; *64*, Augustine, 50, 52; *68.29*, Lombard, 81; *68.33*, *Glossa ordinaria*, 84; *70.20*, Lombard, 74; *72.20*, Lombard, 173; *75.5*, Lombard, 172-173; *75.6*, *Glossa ordinaria*, 37, Augustine, 37, 38; *80.13*, Lombard, 111; *80.15*, Lombard, 83; *85.6*, Augustine, 54; *96.7*, Augustine, 179; *99.1*, Lombard, 23; *110.10*, Lombard, 102; *121*, Augustine, 28; *123.2*, Lombard, 83; *127.2*, Lombard, 87-88; *131.6-7*, *Glossa ordinaria*, 122, Lombard, 188; *136.5*, *8*, *Glossa ordinaria*, 50; *142.6*, Lombard, 89; *144.9*, Lombard, 136, 211; *146.4*, Augustine, 232

Prov. *3.12*, Bede, 149; *19.11*, Gregory, 165; *20.4*, Bede, 87; *22.1*, Bede, 64; *22.10*, Bede, 95; *24.27-34*, Bede, 79-80; *25.27*, Rabanus, 178; *31.22*, Bede, 184
Sap. *1.1*, Rabanus, 60; Bonaventura, 60
Ecclus. *1.16*, Rabanus, 112; *4.23-24*, Rabanus, 112; *5.5*, Rabanus, 154; *9.1*, Rupert, 128; *11.9*, Rabanus, 145-146; *38.26*, *Glossa ordinaria*, 18
Is. *1.2*, Jerome, 65; *3.7*, Jerome, 189; *5.22*, Jerome, 161; *55.1*, Jerome, 135; *65.11*, *Glossa ordinaria*, 130
Hos. *13.14*, Rupert, 207
Matt. *2.1*, Bede, 153; *2.11*, Bruno, 219; *2.14*, Augustine, 134-135; *3.10*, Rupert, 190; *5.13*, Bruno, 187; *5.19*, *Glossa ordinaria*, 153; *5.45-48*, Bede, 225, *Glossa ordinaria*, 226; *6.3*, Bede, 60; *6.5*, *Glossa ordinaria*, 63; *6.16*, *Glossa ordinaria*, 183; *6.32*, *Glossa ordinaria*, 40; *7.1*, Bruno, 133-134; *7.6*, Bede, 120-121; *7.7*, Bruno, 187; *7.12-13*, 47; *7.15-17*, *Glossa ordinaria*, 117, Bruno, 180; *7.17*, Bede, 50; *8.11*, Bruno, 203; *8.14-15*, Bruno, 81; *8.20*, Bede, 229, Bruno, 229, *Glossa ordinaria*, 229; *9.36*, Bede, 75; *10.2*, Bede, 76; *10.9*, 25; *13.23*, Bede, 196; *13.24ff.*, Augustine, 222; *15*, Bede, 84, Bonaventura, 84; *15.30*, Bede, 84; *17.14-15*, Bede, 33; *19.23-24*, Bruno, 173; *20.4*, Augustine, 129; *22.1-14*, Bruno, 169-170, Bede, 188; *22.21*, Bede, 41; *23.8-10*, Bruno, 159; *25.1-14*, Pseudo-Jerome, 38; *25.12*, Bede, 110; *25.14ff.*, Bruno, 87; *25.40*, Bruno, 138; *28.19*, *Glossa ordinaria*, 91
Mark *6.34*, Bede, 75; *15.34*, Bede,